BI 3390380 8

D1609717

SOCIETY SERIES

*itors*
*iversity of Edinburgh, U.K.*
*, U.K.*
*Anthropology, University of Delaware, Newark,*

*ersity of Essex, Colchester, U.K.*
*Kent at Canterbury, U.K.*

and A. Hunt
into the Marxist theory of ideology and

Marxism and Law *by* P. Beirne and

*by* P. Fitzpatrick
wards a strategy under late capitalism *by*

rb *by* A. Stewart
*y* M. Brogden
a: legal order or continuing revolution?

f corporate capital *by* K. Jones
f landlords, law and crime *by* D. Nelken

TWO WEEK

LLPAM

# LAW, STATE AN

Edi

Z. BANKOWSKI, *Department of Public Law, Un*
M. CAIN, *Institute of Criminology, Cambridge*
W. CHAMBLISS, *Department of Sociology and*
*U.S.A.*

M. McINTOSH, *Department of Sociology, Univ*
P. FITZPATRICK, *Darwin College, University of*

# The Police:
# Autonomy and Consent

MICHAEL BROGDEN

*Department of Social Studies, Liverpool Polytechnic, U.K.*

1982

## ACADEMIC PRESS

*A Subsidiary of Harcourt Brace Jovanovich, Publishers*

London · New York
Paris · San Diego · San Francisco · São Paulo
Sydney · Tokyo · Toronto

ACADEMIC PRESS INC. (LONDON) LTD.
24-28 Oval Road
London NW1 7DX


*U.S. Edition published by*
ACADEMIC PRESS INC.
111 Fifth Avenue
New York, New York 10003

Copyright © 1982 by
Michael Brogden

British Library Cataloguing in Publication Data

Brogden, M.
   The police. — (Law, state and society series).
   1. Police — England
   I. Title      II. Series
   363.2′0942   HV8195

   ISBN 0-12-135180-7

Phototypeset by
Dobbie Typesetting Service, Plymouth, Devon
Printed in Great Britain by
T. J. Press (Padstow) Ltd., Padstow, Cornwall

# *Preface*

The summer of 1981 represented a major crisis in the history of relations between police and policed in Britain. Civil disturbances in Toxteth, Liverpool, Moss-Side Manchester, and of less seriousness in a dozen other towns and cities, followed a serious riot in the London district of Brixton, at Easter, and a similar conflagration in Bristol the previous year.

The locations of the riots had common elements. Poor housing, high levels of unemployment, and inferior social facilities were the more obvious features. But the primary characteristic of the riots themselves was not an anarchic reaction to that social malaise but virulent hostility to police officers.

For an institution that prides itself (in a myriad of reiterated statements) that it polices by *consent*, the riots were a salutary shock. They signified not so much the breakdown of consent but rather the physical manifestation of a consent that had long since been withdrawn — if, indeed, it had ever existed. The protests were public dramatizations that for certain sections of the population, at least, the core of policing ideology in Britain was rotten. As indigenous and second-generation immigrant youth took to the streets (with the tacit support of their elders) the question of consent and the stratified form of relations between police and civil society were highlighted. The principle of policing by consent was challenged directly and fundamentally.

But the anti-police riots reflected not only the problematic nature of the consent principle. They also, in the event and in the aftermath, spotlighted the contiguous issues of police autonomy and of accountability. Decisions by police commanders in the course of the disturbances, and later reactions to that street-fighting, were for the most part taken without regard to the views of the elected representatives of the notional local communities. The handling of the riots by the police, as the Chairperson of the Merseyside Police Committee succinctly phrased it, raised not the question of the competence or otherwise of the local Chief Constable, but rather, it symbolized the major questions of the extent to which the police institution in Britain is, and should be, accountable to the democratic process. Coinciding as the riots did, with the election to provincial police authorities of uniquely less submissive councillors and governmental attacks on long-standing principles of political autonomy in locally financed matters, the resulting critique of policing policies and operations met with vitriolic denunciation of "political partisanship" from within the police institution. The historically-sanctified police autonomy, it was expostulated, was under grave threat.

These two interdependent issues — *the social relations between police and policed, underlying the consent maxim,* and *the peculiar nature of police autonomy from democratic restraint,* are the subject matter which this text seeks to expose to debate. *Consent,* it is argued, can only be understood by considering the historical relation between the police institution and social classes, and its contemporary product. Similarly, the issue of *police autonomy* must be seen in the context of the development of local and central states, and within the social and political relations of an advanced capitalist society.

In Chapter 1, it is suggested that the police institution in Britain is in a kind of political limbo. There is no clear picture of the political relation between the police, the other machinery of the state, and civil society. In that chapter, various models of the state — managerialist, pluralist, instrumentalist, and structuralist — are outlined and the different assumptions of each about the police institution examined. An orthodox managerialist variant — the polizeistaat — is then considered, and found wanting. The chapter concludes by focussing on the key functionaries in the political relation of the police institution, the 41 provincial Chief Constables of England and Wales, and the two London Commissioners of Police. A much-modified notion of the *urban manager* (which takes account of the underlying class relations of the police institution) is derived, and used as the major heuristic focus of the text.

Chapters 2 and 6 concentrate on the theme of autonomy. That issue has several facets. There is the matter of the relationship between the police and the *local* and *central* states. Autonomy from the political representatives of the social classes is dependent upon a particular *legal relation.* The freedom of the police institution from direct political restraint also depends upon its own *internal cohesion.*

Chapter 2 is devoted to an historical account of the development of early police autonomy through the medium of primary data on the origins and expansion of the first provincial force on the mainland, the Liverpool police. After evaluating conventional assumptions about nineteenth century political relations of the local police, various conclusions are drawn. The formation, policing style, and form of control need to be understood not as so many political footballs booted between local elites but in terms of class relations generated by the local economy. From the outset, policing in Liverpool was relatively free from direct political intervention, and police autonomy was already partially established by the end of that century.

Chapter 3 considers the political relation of the successor force within the local state in the mid-1970s. It is argued that while the latitude from political supervision now enjoyed by the Chief Constable from the local police authority owes something to his managerial skill and material manipulation, the primary source of his freedom lies in changes in the overall economic and political structure. Local elites are no longer of any significance in regard to the police institution.

In Chapter 4, the historical changes in the relationship between the police institution and the central state are considered. Concentrating on the financial connection between Home Office and police forces, it is claimed, that the autonomy of the police institution from local political control has *not* been replaced by directive influence from the centre.

Much of this freedom from political intervention depends upon the *legal relation* of the police institution. Central to policing ideology is an extolling of the claim that police powers derive from traditional common law rather than from statute. Much of the autonomy of the managerial chief officer rests on this correct but ideologically distorted premise. Police autonomy within the state lies within the mandatory permissive and discretionary form of English law. Understanding the class relations of the British police depends primarily upon recognizing the crucial function of *law* in providing the link between police and class society. Of some significance in reinforcing the autonomous practice of police work is the unique prosecutorial prerogative. Chapter 5 therefore locates the core problematic for consideration of police independence within the legal domain.

Chapter 6 documents the role and political orientations of the three intra-police organizations, especially the Association of Chief Police Officers, in buttressing the development of autonomy. Within the managerialist ideology of police professionalism, and shielded by the legal relation, the intra-police associations have spearheaded the drive to near-freedom within the broad boundaries of the underlying economic relations of the society.

The succeeding chapters deal with the reciprocal theme of consent. Chapter 7 demonstrates that different forms of relationship have historically characterized the relations between police institutions and the different social classes. The degree of consent has always been more questionable than as presented in the myths of some conservative historians of police development in Britain.

Chapter 8 presents current evidence on consent. Despite considerable indication of a high level of support for the police institution, there is substantive signification of its tentative and stratified features. In recognition of the fragility of consent, the police institution is forced constantly to re-construct consensual relations with the social classes. Police *service*, in its various manifestations, has recently been given added weight as the major device for consent construction.

Finally, Chapter 9 draws the themes of autonomy and consent together by focussing on the role of the chief police officer, positioned at the nexus between structural demands and organizational restraints, in continually *negotiating* definitions and practices of police work. The autonomy of the police institution, and the level of consent to police work, depends in part, upon the managerialist skill of a chief officer in constructing definitions of policing function and practice, acceptable both to the long-term interests represented through the central state, and to the labyrinthine organization of which he is the key component.

Although a proportion of the evidence accumulated in this text derives from the substance of police-class relations in Liverpool (one aspect of that practice is the focus of a postscript), the argument is not concerned with any peculiarities of that city or of its police force. It is postulated that for the most part, such evidence typifies police-civil society relations generally in mainland Britain. However, although there are considerable similarities between policing in Scotland and policing South of the Border, the Scottish police are excluded from this work given (amongst other things), the different nature of the Scottish police relation to the prosecution process.

*October, 1982*                                            Michael Brogden

# Acknowledgements

Too many librarians, colleagues, and friends have assisted me, in various ways in the preparation of this book, to be mentioned individually. I thank them all. However, it would be unthinkable to leave some out.

There is a tradition in Acknowledgements on books on the police, depending on the political persuasion of the author, to thank either the staff of the National Council of Civil Liberties or the librarians at the Police Staff College (particularly that source of any serious police Bibliography, the Head Librarian, Dennis Brett). Partly to confuse matters, and more seriously because it is their due, I would like to thank both. Jim Ainsworth of the Polytechnic Library Service has assisted assiduously in the search for many an obscure reference. Long may he continue to do so. Janet Smith, the Liverpool City Archivist, her colleagues, and Frank Harris, pointed the way to a treasure-trove of local material.

Some assistance must be acknowledged to sources of material that have been ingested at second-hand. This book would have been impossible without frequent reference to the masterly work of T. A. Critchley. J. J. Tobias first pointed my way to the Liverpool archives and was helpful at the very outset. In a recognizably different way, all critical accounts of policing in Britain depend to some extent on the State Research Group. If it didn't exist, it would have to be invented anew. Somebody, somewhere, ought to recognize the work of the Home Office Research Unit. Particular individuals in that group will note the value of their own contribution here, and its appreciation.

Tony Jefferson provided a detailed and kindly critique of a pretty awful initial manuscript. I trust he finds some reward in the present version for his pains. Maureen Cain's contribution can best be evidenced by the number of references to her research in the Bibliography. Her input into this text ranged from the insistent translation of "gentlemen" into "gentlepeople" to her unerring ability to summarize my own argument better than I could myself. Both as the series editor, and as the doyen(ne) of the sociology of the police in Britain, she deserves the largest measure of thanks.

I give formal acknowledgement of permission to quote from the following sources — from C. Ackroyd *et al.*'s *The Technology of Political Control* (quoted on p.26), from T. Bowden's *Beyond the Limits of the Law* (quoted on p.26 and on p.153), from E. Moir's *The Justice of the Peace in Britain* (quoted on p.174), (all reprinted by permission of Penguin Books Ltd); from E. P. Thompson's *The State of the Nation* articles, which first appeared in *New Society* (quoted on p.147 and on p.177); from S. Hall *et al.*'s *Policing the Crisis* (quoted on p.231) from Macmillan, and from Holmes and Meier; from the article by G. Marshall in D. Butler and A. H. Halsey (eds) *Policy and Politics* (quoted on p.275) from Macmillan, and from Humanities Press; from C. Forman's *Industrial Town* (quoted on p.34-35) from David and Charles; from R. Quinney's *Critique of Legal Order* (quoted on p.229) from Little, Brown and Co.; from J. Alderson's article in J. Brown and G. Howse (eds) *The Police and the Community* (quoted on p.122) from Gower Publishing Company; from I. Oliver's article in *Criminal Law Review, 1975* (quoted on p.128) and from L. Radzinowicz's *A History of English Criminal Law* IV (quoted on p.176), both from Sweet and Maxwell Ltd; from G. Thurston's *The Clerkenwell Riot* (quoted on p.175) from George Allen and Unwin; from P. Cohen's article in B. Fine *et al.* (eds) *Capitalism and the Rule of Law* (quoted on p.223) from Hutchinson; from L. H. Leigh's article in *The Notre Dame Lawyer, 1973* (quoted on p.77); and finally, from I. Fox's article in *The Police Journal 1978* (quoted on pp.25-27).

# *Epigraph*

"The chief speaker was an ex-police sergeant, who, after twenty-four years in the force had brought his men on strike for the recognition of their union. In a few months, he could have retired on a pension of £3.19.0 a week. Though his sacrifice left him in rags, some of the unemployed saw a flaw in it: the man had been a policeman, and no enthusiast could overlook that.

It's a common saying in working-class circles: once a policeman, always a policeman; his previous training makes him; he cannot help but twist. So from the first unemployed meeting, the ex-police sergeant was suspect, particularly in the minds of the younger men who wondered why a cracked voice like that drew the crowds.

. . . here was this shabbily-dressed old fogy, each night on an open-air rostrum, saying he wanted no trouble with the authorities and that violence did not pay. In the opinion of the younger men listeners, he was deliberately keeping the crowds in order, and confirming the suspicion about him; once a policeman, always a policeman.

One Sunday evening, his changed tone made thousands of them stare "The City Council" he declared "won't do anything for any of you unless you go to them in a body to show them how you're fixed . . . I want the unemployed to come here with me. We'll hold a meeting on the Exchange Flags . . . ."

The old police striker asked for other business. Reluctantly he had to listen to most of the committee men expressing their uneasiness over the conduct of the police . . . . They seemed to be acting too quiet; acting as if they were waiting for the first opportunity to run amok and baton down as many unemployed as possible . . . .

The old police striker fidgeted until he lost his temper. He said that all this talk was nonsense. There was no reason why there should be any batoning. The crowd themselves were too orderly.

"I hope you have not forgotten," he went on "that today, twenty thousand of our people paraded past all the big shops without as much as a pane of glass being broken. The police authorities are not blind to that. Lots of the policemen

xi

who walk along are quite decent chaps. I know most of them. They're with us if anything. We don't want to do something that will set them against us . . . ."

To prevent further argument, he again stepped forward to address the crowd, too vast to hear much of what he was saying. "I think we'll go for a walk . . . . It's too late for anything else. We'll all be art critics this afternoon. We'll go across and have a look at the pictures in the Art Gallery. Those places are as much for us as anybody else. They belong to the public."

He moved off down the steps . . . .

Suddenly hundreds of foot police rushed out of the Sessions Court and adjacent building, batoning heads right and left. The frightened confusion of the crowd was worsened as the mounted police galloped and rode full charge into them, trampling and scattering in all directions. Many of the unemployed lay stretched in the roadway.

. . . Inside the Art Gallery, more police caused pandemonium. Men yelled aloud as they were batoned down. Others dashed around panic-striken. A few desperate ones dropped down from an open window into a side street and got away. Those attempting to follow were struck down from behind. The police closed all windows and doors. There were no further escapes. Batons split skull after skull. Men fell where they were hit. The floor streamed with blood. Those lying in it were trampled on by others who were soon flattened out alongside them. Gallery workmen were battered too. The police had gone wild. The old police-striker, appealing to their decency, had his arm broken and his head smashed . . . ."

George Garret—Liverpool 1921-1922

# Contents

## Part Two. Consent

*To Ann, Marcus, and Sasha*

# 1    The Police and the State

When the police apparatus is immune to control by the civil service, the judiciary, and the army, and is an independent leading institution in its own right, a modern police state has been formed. (Chapman, 1970, p.119)

The police institution occupies an amorphous social space in Britain. The 43 separate police forces in England and Wales (themselves the descendants of some 220 small forces of the 1880s), are ideologically and historically rooted in different localities. Yet, despite that separation, they embrace a national identity, and turn a unified face towards civil society. Similarly, drawing nearly half its financial resources from the towns and cities via local rates, and the other half from central government through general taxation, the police institution straddles a financial bifurcation.

Its location is further confused by its legal status. With powers of arrest and prosecution derived initially from the traditional common law of pre-industrial society, and drawing upon the original rights and obligations of local citizenry, police officers operate and are organized according to Parliamentary statute. Nowhere, however, is the confusion over the deposition of the police institution more opaque than in its political relation. The complexity of the connection of the police institution with the legitimate political authorities prevents any easy unravelling. Accommodating, on one hand, a formal subservience (for provincial forces) to the local Police Committee, and, on the other hand, some obeisance to the institutional arm of the central state, the Home Office, the police apparatus has constructed for itself, and has in turn been thrust, into a political void. The precise nature of the relation between the police institution—individual officers, local forces, and the intra-police organizations—and the local police authority (that peculiar composite of municipal representatives and non-elected magistrates), the Home Office, and ultimately Parliament, is ambiguous and subject to quite different interpretations. Similarly, the class relations of the police apparatus and its degree of subordination to economic and political interests, is far from clear.

The key concern of this text is with the relationship between the police institution in Britain, other apparatus of the central and local states, and civil society. What is the formal relation as embedded in constitutional practices, and to what extent do they differ from the material structures underlying those formulae? In particular, interest lies in the consequence for policing practices of changes in those relations.

Crucial to these considerations is an analysis of the web of political relations within which the police institution is entangled. The connection of the police to the central and local states, and the extent to which in that relation, particular interests are embodied, provides a central problematic.

In this introductory chapter, various approaches to the analysis of the police-state-civil society relation are outlined and their relevance for the study of policing in an advanced capitalist society evaluated. In the first section, four prominent models of the state — *managerialist, pluralist, instrumentalist,* and *structuralist* — are outlined. The merits and defects of each perspective are considered, and the central issues of the political relation of the police institution spotlighted.

The second section deals with the application of a particular managerialist model — the absolutist polizeistaat — to advanced capitalism. Though its contemporary relevance is currently popularized within the police institution, the model is summarily rejected, primarily because of its failure to make problematic the form of state itself.

Finally, in this chapter, a discrete sociological treatment of managerialism and the local state — the concept of the urban manager — is considered and (with substantial caveats, drawn from instrumentalist and structuralist perspectives) utilized as the heuristic basis for the development of guiding propositions on the position of the police institution in Britain. The succeeding chapters follow directly from this adaption of the urban managerialist model to the position of chief police officers, in an attempt to delineate the construction of *police practice.*

## Models of the State

The lack of any precise statement of the nature and form of the state under advanced capitalism has handicapped not only studies of policing. The variety of conceptions of the composition, functions, and origins of the state provides for any predisposition but, nevertheless, confuses rather than advances any substantive analysis. More often than not, however, the position of the state apparatuses, and their wider social relations, are constructed through the medium of frenetic empiricism and offer little more than an intellectual legitimization of the established social order.

To avoid this confusion and commitment, several major contemporary accounts of the state will be outlined in order to lay bare the police-state problematic from opposing perspectives.

Four major representations of the state are commonly distinguished: managerialist accounts, encompassing the work of Max Weber and his successors; pluralist conceptions, best formulated in the work of Robert Dahl; the instrumentalist contribution of Ralph Miliband; and the structuralist conception, of which the foremost exponent was Nicos Poulantzas.

The early managerialist conception of the state emerges in the work of Thorstein Veblen. Writing in the early 1920s, Veblen argued that capitalist society could not last, because of its inherent inefficiency in supporting a non-productive or leisured class. But the authority of the capitalist class would not disintegrate through the power of working-class action but rather as a consequence of the functions of the new class of technological specialists —the "engineers" (Veblen, 1921). To modern industry, the latter were indispensable, and that indispensability made them most fit and competent to take over the reins of authority. Through their function as the key directors of the industrial system, the engineers, by the same move became the arbiters of the community's material welfare. Unlike the capitalist however, these new controllers were no longer driven by commercial interests. Indispensability and technical expertise together provide the basis for the formation of a new type of state.

This theme is reflected in Weber's essay "Parliament and Government", when Weber argues that the state bureaucracy would rule alone if private capitalism were eliminated (1917). The expert administrators of the rational-legal society would assume supreme disinterested power.

Adopted within quite different frames of reference (over the issue of the degree of self-interest of the managerial state) by Burnham (1962) and Berle and Means (1932), the technical/administrative/managerial state theme was revitalized in the work of the French Marxists, Mallet (1969) and Touraine (1966) in the early sixties (combining notion of indispensability with that of a capital-labour relation, in the class struggle). More recently, much of the work in the U.K. on the local state, particularly with regard to housing allocations and to planning decisions, has been influenced by managerialist themes. Notions of the local state bureaucrats as the managers of resource allocation, with their own unique professional perspective on the appropriate guidelines in decision-making, emerges particularly in the work of Pahl (1975, 1977). A similar figure, the corporate manager, (with substantially less autonomy and less disinterest) appears in the work of Cockburn (1977). These various images of the manager-ialist state with their different nuances (some more influenced than others by concern with political economy, and with the degree of economic restraint on the autonomy of the managers), have considerable attraction as a framework for the analysis of the police institution, in relation to central and to local decision-making.

The apparatus of the advanced industrial state consists of serried ranks of impartial bureaucratic experts, in police work, as elsewhere, operating according to established rules. These experts who conduct police decision-making have no economic or political allegiance. Expertise in the construction of the social good via crime prevention, is at odds with the apparent naked self-interest of the politicians on the various police authorities, and in Parliament. The introduction of management techniques into police organization, the enhancement of specialized police departments, the development of technical expertise in an array of policing functions, all reinforce the superficial view of a society in which the police authority members make politics, but the police/managers enforce the law and impartially determine the social good.

At the level of the central state, experts in the police executive — the officers seconded to the Home Office Police Division, and the members of the specialist sub-committees of the Association of Chief Police Officers (A.C.P.O.) are consulted (and effectively determine), the priority of resource allocation in the maintenance of social order. At the local level, the chief officer of police as an urban or corporate manager, the major gatekeeper in the allocation chain, determines the rationing of resources to specific tasks and duties, weighing-up the requests for police action, and evaluating their relative importance. The police managers, centrally and locally, are independent of economic and political interests, if inevitably constrained by finite resources. Professionalism and technical expertise determine the outcome of the decision-making process. In return, all that the police authorities require of the managers is that they explain — account for — their decisions. Autonomy of the police institution is guaranteed as long as the factors affecting its dispositions can be seen to stem from rational consideration and impartial, expert, evaluation.

Freedom from partisanship is at the centre of this construction. Action on behalf of one group, against a second, infringes the spirit of law from which police authority derives. Police management decisions are only legitimate in so far as they uphold the rule of a law and the maxim of equality of subject before it.

Within the managerialist conception, the police apparatus as a branch of the state, consists of an institution with central and local arms, devoted to the specific, unarguable, function of order maintenance within the law. Like other state apparatuses, the police are accountable by way of explanation, for their enforcement or non-enforcement policies to the various components of civil society — to politicians, to pressure groups, and to local communities. The latter have no legitimate right to interfere with the decisions of the police managers. Indeed, the safety and well-being of the non-experts, the sanctity of the rule of law, depends upon the lack of violation of the authority of the experts.

But, limited though this summary of the managerialist concept of the relation between the police and the state is, the flaws at the general level are evidential.

The managerialist approach has only a limited power of explanation of policing within advanced capitalism.

Critically, application of the managerialist credo to the activities of the police institution, ignores the discretionary nature of police action under English law. By certain statutes, and by judicial decision, the law requires that police officers themselves select and determine which enforcement decisions to take, and which prosecutions to conduct (Chapter 5). Apart from the general guidelines of experience, the early police chiefs' requirement for "sober judgement" (Chapter 2), and "rules of thumb" (Wilcox, 1972), the majority of incidents occurring within the police orbit, are subject to a variety of occasionally crude factors (Powis, 1980). The principle of discretion does not necessarily embody a similar principle of expertise in its application.

Secondly, the managerialist model only latterly takes account of the extent to which decisions about the form of police response, necessarily reflect the location of the institution within a stratified society. The early managerialist notions, especially, whilst having the particular virtue of concentrating upon the work of the administrators themselves — on police officers and on the police institution — fail to take account of the objective context of the decision-making process. The police institution, as a branch of the state, is embedded in a complex of social and legal relations, incorporating essential inequalities of position, and deriving from the primacy of the economic problematic of the capitalist mode of production, (C.M.P.). The manager's discretion to make decisions is structured by constraints which inevitably reflect those inequalities.

At national level, policing priorities, the expert decision-making processes, rarely differ from the long-term commitment of the dominant economic class to social and political stability. Groups that threaten social order are dealt with, expertly, within the law, according to the discretionary values that are congruent with those of the dominant class. Similarly, locally, different social groups and class fractions are variously susceptible to police management, as a branch of the local state. Police experts may efficiently clamp down, within the law, on street traders rather than on shopkeepers.

Nevertheless, the focus of the latter-day managerialist on the actions, beliefs, and functions of the managers gives this perspective a significant advantage over the major alternative, consensual, conception of the state in industrial society. Pluralism pays primary attention to the social context, largely ignored by the managerialist perspective, but neglects the question of the personnel. To the pluralist, the state is a set of institutions residing outside civil society, neutral in its functions, and independent of any partisan or class interest. The state, above and beyond society, functions to regulate and mediate amongst the various social groups and political interests. It intervenes to ensure the pacific conduct of social affairs.

To the extent that it possesses the above characteristics, the pluralist model is similar to the managerialist. But then the differences surface. Whereas, the managerialists saw the state apparatus, that combination of impersonal bureaucrats, as untarnished by the proclivities of self-motivated politicians, pluralists view the state as being susceptible to external pressure. The state is a citadel to be captured, or at least held and persuaded to favour sectional interests. Its power to make decisions is a prize to be striven for.

However, the seizure of the state citadel is rare. More often than not, as one pressure group develops and demands state action, another, countervailing, group arises to balance out that invocation. The state is not liable to effective and permanent capture by one party because of the natural equilibrating dynamic of power relations in society. As the proponents of a cause organize to bring pressure to bear upon the state, its opponents similarly mobilize.

Indeed, the organization of individuals in a political lobby is unusual. Normally the lobbies remain dormant because of the threat of the development of counter-pressure.

Serious demands of partisanship by the state and its officials are further thwarted by the composition of the pressure group. Most requirements for action by the state are expressed in the form of single issues. Many campaigns for police action, for example, are framed as demands for clamp-downs on "muggers", homosexuals, prostitutes, street-traders and so on, but rarely for action on several fronts simultaneously. Because these demands cross-cut class and economic boundaries, there is no potential for a significant, lasting, schism, in attitudes to the state, or within civil society itself. Moreover, the alliances between and within pressure groups continually fluctuate. Feminists and fundamentalists may combine against pornography but oppose one another on the question of the legalization of abortion. There are few long-standing and multi-issue alliances.

In other words, underlying these surface conflicts is an essential consensus. Pressure groups, and individual citizens, may challenge the state bureaucrats, the police, on occasional issues, but they agree ultimately with other citizens, on the need to support the state, and its police apparatus. In practice, this consent is based not so much on active support for the institutions of the state but instead, on passive acquiescence. In Dahl's New Haven ". . . high confidence in all-round justice, legitimacy, and stability, and fairness of decisions in one's political system may make one's own participation seem unnecessary" (Dahl, 1963, p.63).

At both national and local levels, the neutrality of the state and its legitimacy is continually acknowledged, paradoxically, pluralists argue, by minimal political participation. This neutrality is reinforced by the mechanism of the electoral process, which institutionalizes dissent into approved channels.

As in the managerialist model, state agents are continually required to explain the basis for their actions. Their mandate is only renewed so long as these explanations are deemed satisfactory by the elected democratic authorities. But whereas in the managerialist perspective, chief officers exercising discretion, would justify their actions in terms of their professional expertise and impartial judgement, the accountability of the chief officer, in the pluralist state, lies, in the maxim that the decision was made according to the "balance of interest" — or in the "public interest".

However, the defects in the pluralist model, with regard to its potential to explain the political location of the police within the advanced capitalist state, are more serious than in the managerialist case. Indeed, there are only two redeeming features. The model correctly draws attention to cross-pressures upon the state apparatus[1]. Secondly, it focuses upon the question of consent, justifying the actions of the state in terms of the general cross-class agreement to the majority of the actions of the state agents. Whereas the managerialists ignored the composition of the pressures on, and attitudes to the state, and its institutions, pluralism gives them some primacy.

There are critical problems however. Pluralism equates lack of dissent with consent when, in fact, the former may relate more to the way certain issues have been deleted from the political agenda. Within the local state, for example, the question of housing may be relegated to the province of the state agents, and one not to be raised critically by the representatives of the political parties (Hindess, 1971). Lack of protest about specific police activities may have more to do with the way such issues are not deemed relevant for the consultations of the local police authority (Brogden, 1977).

Secondly, while it is correct that many issues posed before the police institution are one-dimensional, more often than not, there remain multiple considerations. Prostitution, vice, street trading, thefts from cars, handbag snatching, and so on, may all, separately, precipitate moral panics or crusades for police action. But their progenitors can nearly all be located within the same structurally-formed residuum, in the city. The targets of pressure group activity are often closely connected by economic and social factors as, indeed, may be their critics. More importantly, the cause of the panic or agitation may have an underlying economic imperative at the societal level (Hall *et al.*, 1978). Finally, the neutrality of the state agents — or rather the way they construct a notional public interest which guides their activities, in the exercise of discretion — can be questioned in a different way. As in the managerial model, the police may impartially apply the law but that of itself does not guarantee the neutrality of the law itself. The impartiality of one institution of the state, given the interdependence between the state apparatuses, is no guarantor of the disinterest of other components. Legislation, constructed through class pressures on the state, may be enforced equally by the police institution. Chief officers, balancing up the various pressures on them in the enforcement of the law, necessarily ignore the extent to which the law itself may be skewed.

Instrumentalist accounts of the state, whether they reflect non-Marxist elite theories of power (Wright Mills, 1956) or other materialist considerations, suggest a more instructive relation between the state and civil society. Essentially, the state is conceived as the instrument by which elite or ruling-class, achieves domination over a second group or class. To Miliband, for example, "The intervention of the state is always and necessarily partisan: as a class state, it always intervenes for the purpose of maintaining the existing system of domination" (Miliband, 1977, p.91). Within the materialist conception, the state itself consists of ". . . institutions — the government, the administration, the military, and the police, the judicial branch, sub-central government, and parliamentary assemblies . . ." (Miliband, 1969, p.54). As in the managerial and pluralist perspectives, the state stands outside civil society. Crucially, it acts on behalf of the ruling class but not necessarily at the direction of that class.

For example, where the ruling-class (or fractions of it) is not conscious of the "real" parameters of an issue, it may attempt to achieve short-term gains at the cost of the lower classes. In that situation, the state may resist those immediate pressures in order to safeguard the fundamental structure of the capital-labour relation. The state is able to take a loftier, more detached view, being partly removed from the daily conflictual relations between social classes. Police officers may prosecute all cases of local business corruption that they can prove. What counts ultimately is not whether or not a single capitalist is penalized by a legal agent but rather the long-term legitimization of the enforcement agency and the rule of law, in contributing to the stability of the capitalist order. The class bias of the state, in Miliband's account,[2] is maintained in three ways — through the character of the leading personnel of the state, through the economic constraints that the capitalist class can exert over its activities, and through the "structural" determinants of the capitalist mode of production. In the first place, the state is controlled through:

> . . . the personnel of the state system . . . the people who are located in the
> commanding heights of the state, in the executive, administrative, judicial,
> repressive, and legislative branches, have tended to belong to the same class
> or classes which have dominated other strategic heights in society . . .
> (Miliband, 1977, p.68)

Senior police officers, from the inception of the various forces (Liverpool Mercury 5th February 1836) to the immediate pre-World War II period, were largely recruited from the lower ranges of the middle-class or from ex-military officers, and consequently shared common bourgeois values. Latterly, while police officers may, as Reiner (1979) argues, be in a "contradictory class position", the dominance of occupational socialization, and training programmes, ensures an affinity between policing values and the values of the dominant class.

Even when the personnel come from a different class, they still rule on behalf of the capitalist class:

> As the recruits rise in the state hierarchy, so do they become part, in every significant sense of the social class to which their position, income and status gives them access. (Miliband, 1969, p.64)

Secondly, the dominant class wields influence over the state through various economic decision-making powers, ranging from its influence over resource allocation to the state institution to the more general powers of investment and production dispositions. As a class fraction, employers, through investment programmes, decisions over employment and unemployment, wield considerable influence over the activities of the state apparatus. The intention by a multi-national conglomerate to close an industrial plant, and consequently to ignite a conflict with organized labour, may create a "policing problem" where none previously existed. Decisions taken in the economic sphere, by groups within the dominant class of capitalists, constrain and structure the form of state response.

In Miliband's later work, a third factor is developed. The state and the state agents are compelled to work on behalf of the dominant class by structural factors:

> the state is the instrument of the ruling-class because, given its insertion in the capitalist mode of production, it cannot be anything else . . . A capitalist economy has its own "rationality" to which any government must sooner or later submit . . . (Miliband, 1977, p.72)

The raison d'etre of capitalism, profit maximization, is the core problematic to be solved by the state. Where the rate of profit is constantly in decline, all the agencies of the state, in the last instance, are structurally committed to maintain the conditions conducive to a diminution in that decrease. The police apparatus, as part of the state, irrespective of occasional truces with labour, with the disavowals of the personnel, and despite occasional actions against the immediate interests of members of the capitalist class, is in the final analysis, concerned with the implementation of legislation which will maximize the social reproduction of appropriate labour, repress the "social dynamite" of threatening and costly marginal groups (Spitzer, 1975), and combat the power of organized labour. In Hirst's words, " . . . the policeman, a state functionary, is necessary for the reproduction of capitalist social relations. He protects the property of the capitalist . . . and secures certain of the conditions of labour discipline" (Hirst, 1975, p.58).

To this outline of the factors affecting the autonomy of the state, Miliband adds the question of "legitimization". With the pluralists, he notes the importance of ideology, of the central belief system, in ratifying the actions of the state amongst the different social classes. Whilst the primary responsibility for mobilizing support for the social order, and consent to the various agencies of the state, is through class-mediated organizations in civil society—that is, through organizations sponsored directly by the capitalist class, the state itself has become increasingly concerned with the problem of consent. It is no longer committed to a simple repressive role, as in the earlier stages of the C.M.P., but has taken on a major role in ". . . engineering consent" (Miliband, 1969, p.183). The various state agents assume both coercive and consensual functions. Police officers appear not only as agents of state repression but also as educators, concerned with emphasizing the rule of the law and the centrality of the police institution to the subvention of social order (Chapter 8).

To the instrumentalist, then, the state and its constituent parts, the various state apparatuses, are tools of the dominant economic class. Under the capitalist mode of production, the functions of the police institution as part of the state, are necessarily and inextricably bound-up with the needs of the capitalists. The state, therefore, is a means of class domination. The police institution has the fundamental function of aiding that domination but there is no direct link between the ruling class and the institution.

This account has the particular merit, as in the case of the managerialist model, of focusing upon the state agents themselves. It makes problematic the form and features of the state institutions, in requiring an analysis of their elements. It brings to the forefront of academic enquiry the composition of the state. Secondly, the instrumentalist model demonstrates the importance of the complementarity of the state institutions with the institutions of civil society, such as the schools and the media, in mobilizing support for the social order. Finally, and critically, in locating the core of the state in the economic realm, it gives recognition to the key factor of determination in the capitalist state. The mode of production and the state apparatus are linked.

But there are problems. Namely, while the economic question is raised, it is not explored. The concentration, especially in Miliband's earlier work, on institutional analysis; focusing almost exclusively, at the inter-personal level on relations between state and class, fails to give sufficient attention to the inter-dependence between the two concepts at the economic level. The problems of personnel, and for that matter, of ideological and political factors, predominate. The forms of the state apparatuses must be explained on economic terrain, as well as with regard to political and social factors (Jessop, 1977).

Furthermore, the crucial question remains unanswered—the degree of autonomy of the state from the dominant capitalist class (Saunders, 1980, p.162). Given that the state enjoys some autonomy—state agents such as chief police officers enjoy substantial discretion—there is no attempt to explain or theorize the limits to that discretion. In the absence of a delineation of those parameters, it may be either that chief officers enjoy substantial, indeed, overwhelming, discretion in formulating the nature of police work and police targets. Or, as the factors of socialization, of the economic power of the dominant class, and of the structural constraints of the mode of production, take effect, their discretion may be minute. This problem—the autonomy of the state from the dominant class or classes—is not significantly clarified in the structuralist model.

The structuralist account of the state largely denies the utility of the form of institutional analysis to which this text is directed. A primary contention of Poulantzas (1976) is that classes, not individuals or institutions, are the primary units of analysis. While the latter may be utilized as units of observation, structuralists are committed to an analysis of the state which views it as the site of class struggle. The managerialist and instrumentalist models of the state, which require accounts of the pursuits and inter-personal relations of the state officials, are largely excluded from discussion, except in so far as the latter merge directly with class relations.

As the major terrain of the conflict between social classes, the state can be neither a direct instrument of class domination, nor can it be a set of apparatuses independent of social classes. It is "relatively autonomous"—somewhere in the limbo between the two positions. Its defining feature lies in its essential fluidity. The state represents the balance of class forces, at a particular point in time. Different stages in the development of the mode of production will give rise to different forms of state. At the present stage of advanced capitalism, the era of monopoly control of production and distribution, the state necessarily ultimately represents the interests of monopoly capital since in the current social formation this gives rise to the major political class, and the dominant political force.

As the changes in the mode of production constantly engender new conflicts in civil society (the problems of production, distribution, and consumption)

> The state increasingly intervenes . . . . but as an expression of class society, the state, in practice, acts according to the relations of force between classes and social groups, generally in favour of a hegemonic fraction of the dominant class (Castells, 1978, p.3)

The form of this intervention, its special characteristics, and its intentions, are determined according to the form of conjunction between economic forces. Different economic stages give rise to distinctive forms of conjunction, which result in varied reactions by the state agencies. That intervention occurs through either the Ideological State Apparatuses (the educational, religious, and welfare bodies) or through the Repressive State Apparatuses (the police and the military). Repressive police action in necessary at some conjunctions, while the function of the welfare agencies in mobilizing consent is more relevant to other periods (Althusser, 1971). In practice, the state apparatuses, Repressive and Ideological, may reflect in their actions the conflict between classes within the state:

> The state is a complex institutional ensemble in whose institutions and interstices is reproduced the contradictory, conflicting inter-play of political forces and its policies necessarily reflect the constantly shifting equilibria of compromise that emerge from the political struggles within and among departments and branches of the state apparatus. (Jessop, 1980, p.57)

Welfare agencies, the judiciary, and the police may provide competing definitions of the proper object of control, and competing solutions. But, in the last instance,

> . . . . all the state preserves a basic unity. All the parts work fundamentally as one . . . . in Lambeth, the homeless are finding . . . . that the police, the electricity board, the social security, and the local council reveal a practical unity, in their efforts to end squatting. (Cockburn, 1977, p.48)

In the local state, as in the central state, the various apparatuses act with an ultimate cohesion to maintain the interests of monopoly capital.

On occasion, interventions by the state apparatuses may favour the working-class at the expense of the dominant class. But in the long-run, the objective relationship between monopoly capital and the state ensures that the latter serves the central purpose of capital accumulation.

In those interventions, the ideological apparatuses play a key role. Control through ideological domination is a key feature of the monopoly capitalism stage. They promote support for the social order through the manipulation of ideology. On one hand, for example, the state agencies may seek to interpret aspects of the lower class culture and to insert these interpretations within the culture of the dominant class. Notions of working-class status may be re-cast and inserted into bourgeois images (Hall *et al.*, 1978). The life experiences of the working-class are re-shaped and given a modified and adapted meaning within the dominant culture. The life-space of the lower strata, is, as it were, "captured".

On the other hand, the state apparatuses assist in the construction of an ideology which serves to fragment working-class unity and thereby to diminish its potential for opposition, and to replace it with a constructed "national unity". For example, in conferring the status of citizens upon members of that class, and in guaranteeing them equal rights under the law, their essential class unity is atomized, and these artificials constructs, the citizens, are united with members drawn from other classes into a fictitious unity—the nation (Balbus, 1978). Class interests disappear and popular or national interests emerge. Cockburn continues

This detached integrity (of the state) is important at an ideological level too because it helps to perpetuate the idea that the state does not represent the particular interest of capital but the general interest, the general will, the political unity of "the people and nation", bosses and workers alike (p.48)

The merits of the structuralist model lie in its dynamic and cohesive conception of the state. The actions of the state apparatus alter according to the particular economic conjuncture but retain an essential unity. Secondly, the structuralist model re-emphasizes the centrality of the capital accumulation problematic to that unity and to the ultimate rationale for state actions. Finally, it reiterates and develops the role of ideology in the maintenance of class rule. But conversely, there are major problems in applying the model to an examination of the relationship between the police apparatus, other branches of the state, and social classes.

Despite disavowals, the structuralist model largely denies the possibility of empirical examination. "It is impossible to envisage any conceivable test of its key assumptions . . . the Althusserian epistemology from which it derives, rules out any resort to empirical disconfirmation as 'empiricist'" (Saunders, 1980, p.184). It follows that if the general propositions on the state are not open to empirical examination, then the lower level propositions regarding the particular relations are necessarily based upon intuition rather than upon observable manifestations. Secondly, Poulantzas mystifies the nature of the state and of its apparatus. ". . . the 'state' is not an institution with power at all: it is a relation. The 'state' is generalised to become everything that constitutes the cohesion of a social formation, including the family, religion, and so on" (Gough, 1979, p.156). Institutions cannot be conceptually separated from the state or, for that matter, from civil society, for examination. Thirdly, the structuralists seem to oscillate between two extreme positions — in reductionist fashion, arguing that the effects of state power are necessarily circumscribed by the economic relation, so that in the long run, its exercise can only correspond to the interests of monopoly capital. But simultaneously, they suggest that the state and the state apparatus, may be an instrument of a power bloc, independently of monopoly capital (Jessop, 1977, p. 358). The problem of the autonomy of the state from the ruling class is no more resolved in the structuralist model than in the instrumentalist.

In consequence, none of the major contemporary models of state-civil society relations seems readily available for the consideration of the particular position of policing under advanced capitalism. Nevertheless, certain factors do emerge as critical from this discussion — the significance of the societal problematic — capital accumulation — for the ultimate determination of the role of the state apparatuses; the function of ideology in legitimizing the class structure (and, in this context, police authority); the historical specificity of particular forms of state and police power — the extent to which police actions alter according to the conjunction of class forces; and the utility of an institutional analysis, in distinguishing the form and practice of the discretion and decision-making latitude of the state personnel.

But before returning to elaborate these themes in the following chapters some attention must be paid to an orthodox analysis of the police-state relation, and one currently espoused within the police institution itself. Conceptions of the relation between the police and political authority must necessarily take account of the ideological construction put on that relation by the chief actors themselves, in so far as, it is contended (and opposed to the structuralist interpretation) that perception contributes to the objectification of the relation. The state agents have their own, varying conceptions of the problematic, and the older model of the polizeistaat is currently assuming some significance.

## The Perspective of the State Agents

Primary concern within the institutional literature, with the problem of the police and the state, has centred around the question of the directive relation between the police institution, and the central and local states (or rather the police authorities embedded within those structures). But more recently, a version of managerialist theory has been incorporated within policing ideology in Britain, and a new perspective on the relationship between the institution and the state constructed.

### *The old orthodoxy—the national–local debate*

The traditional debate in police circles has centred around the structure of the police institution—whether or not the benefits from the local structure of the separate forces outweight the assumed benefits from possible re-structuring on a national basis. Specifically, the argument has been concerned with the change in political direction that a new national force might experience. The debate has spasmodically been vented both within the police service, and academically, since the formation of the first provincial forces. Recently, the dialogue has been given new impetus. For example, on one side authorities such as the former Chief Inspector of Constabulary, Eric St. Johnston have argued vehemently for a new national structure to police organization. ". . . . the time has come for us to have a national police force . . . . most thinking policemen have come to the conclusion that it is desirable and, indeed, inevitable" (*The Sunday Times*, 25th July, 1976). In an echo of the early attempt by the Benthamite Edwin Chadwick, in the Constabulary Report of 1839, to organize the New Police within the central state, a corps of senior police officers have argued for a final resolution of the amalgamation process of the last forty years (during which period the existing

180 forces in England and Wales were reduced to a rump of 43). This view was given its most strident exposition in the Minority report by Goodhart, to the 1962-63 Willink Commission (which preceded the major 1964 Police Act).

Equally there has been continuing, and successful, opposition based primarily on the reiterated fear of political intervention from outside the police institution. For example, Sir Frank Newsham, the civil servant primarily responsible for police re-organization in the post-war period:

> There will never be nationalization or regionalization of the police. If we want to succumb to all the perils that have brought about the downfall of all other empires, the quickest way is to allow for the machinery for the enforcement of law and order to become a mere instrument of the state. It is the duty of the police in this country to enforce the law, according to the law, and not according to political influence . . . . If ever any attempt were made by a politician to bring about the State control of the police, he would be thrown out . . . . (A.C.P.O. Conference 6th June, 1949)

Notions of centralization are bound up with an image of the police institution being reduced to a tool of the ruling political party. The movement towards a unified national police force is identified with a diminution in the autonomy of the police institution.

This confusion and over-simplification comes out vividly in a speech by the former Metropolitan Commissioner, Sir Robert Mark. According to *The Times*, he

> . . . spoke of his opposition to the suggestion that a national police force be formed in Britain, 'There are those who would like to see a national police force controlled by a Minister. It would be a sorry day for the police, local authorities, and the public alike, were that to happen.' (23rd June, 1977)

Traditionally, harangues against the centralization argument are accompanied by graphic references to Continental practices (again echoing the rhetoric of anti-police sentiment of the early years, from the urban elites). But what those references have largely ignored have been the examples, from Continental policing, where the police institution has been part of the central state, but not inextricably linked with the dominant party or class. For example, the police system created by Joseph Fouché in Revolutionary France (historically, the normal reference for propagandists wishing to demonstrate the superiority of the English system of policing), survived intact the transition to the Napoleonic period, while carrying out an identical function for each regime (Fowler, 1979). Central direction from the Ministry of Police did not embroil the state apparatus directly with the intentions (nor the fate) of the dominant political class. Political masters changed but the police system maintained sufficient autonomy and distance from that class to guarantee its own future. It was for the political class but not directly of or subservient to it. External political direction is not a necessary consequence of organizational centralization. Indeed, those contemporary writers on the police institution (Critchley, 1979, pp.297-9; Bowden, 1978, p.213), who have documented the increased centralization of the police institution in Britain, have made the major mistake of equating changes in organizational structure and practice with a movement towards external political direction.

The development of centralized services, of Regional Crime Squads, of police national computer banks, and the regionalization of some local police forces, are all aspects of organizational uniformity and standardization. Political direction by the dominant class in not necessarily a corollary of that organizational process. Even where there exists an identity of practice between class and police —for example, over the prosecution of the Shrewsbury pickets[3]—this does not provide evidence of external intervention. On the contrary, centralization of policing may occur concurrently with a diminution in formal political intervention in the decision-making process of policing (Chapter 6).

What is peculiar about the debate over centralization within the police institution is the conception of the state. That construct is conceived not as an autonomous complex of apparatuses but as the equivalent of the political dominant class.

The political apparatus of the State—the Home Office and its officials—are confused with the personnel of the social classes. However, the superficiality of this debate over centralization and political control has been exposed by a developing second debate, over the nature of the police-state relation. The concept of the police state, which has always been in the background of serious discussion of the police institution in Britain, since the early defence by Sir Robert Peel of the new Metropolitan police in the 1820's, has been restored to new prominence.

### The New Orthodoxy — the Polizeistaat

The notion of the police state, popularized in academic literature by Chapman (1970), contains a re-working of the managerialist model, making it more directly applicable to the relationship between the police institution and the modern state. The term has been used conventionally, until recently, in pejorative sense, by police officers (Alderson, 1980, p.14) and by politicians (Fowler, 1979, Chapter 2) as a straw person to demonstrate the defects of other national forms of policing, and the comparative merits of the British. These contrasts have been based upon two separate propositions.

The police-state is assumed to be a society in which the source of police powers lies in legislative statute, unlike in Britain where the powers of arrest and prosecution are original and derive from traditional common law. Where original powers do not exist but instead, are conferred by decree of the dominant political class or party, police work will vary according to the particular demands framed by that class or party through legislation. Conversely, (Chapter 5) where original powers legitimize police authority, no political intervention from the centre can affect police decisions and law enforcement.

Secondly, it is assumed that in the police-state (as in the centralization debate) police organizations are centralized and subject to political decree by a Minister of Police, nominated from the ruling political party or class. Fortunately, it is argued, the community origins, and the continuing decentralized structure of British policing (discretely overlooking the history of Ulster and the colonies) enable the strength of the local community to be mobilized to resist the demands from the central political authority. Community power balances out the interventionist power of the central government.

But this contrast with a notional Continental police-state has been overtaken by recent arguments that have cast the concept of the police-state in a new mould. The older, vaguer, model is juxtaposed with an interpretation of police work that draws heavily upon the managerialist model of the state. Two key principles of Weber's political sociology are expressed within the new construct. There is no necessary relationship between economic class, and political control, and direction. The mode of political domination in industrial society is increasingly bureaucratic.

The clearest outline of this new model was provided by Albert Laugharne, Chief Constable of Lancashire, in 1979 who reflected on the virtues of the traditional polizeistaat. The concept he argued:

> . . . . had always been used in English as a term of political abuse but, in Europe, the term was a technical one with no pejorative connotations. A police-state or polizeistaate was regarded simply as one form of administrative and judicial organisation. Many E.E.C. countries (had) an administrative and judicial structure which was similar to the *traditional*—as opposed to the pejorative use of the term. In such "traditional police-states" police power, though exercised nationally, was benign and subservient to the will of the majority—just as benign and subservient, some said as it was here. (joint A.C.P.O./A.M.A. Annual Conference 1979)

The fear of enhanced police powers, and especially the opposition to a national British police force, reflected an image of the police-state drawn from the Third Reich, rather than the more direct and neutral model derived from eighteenth century Prussia and Austria.

While Laugharne's paper, of itself, provides no more than a provocative outline of the argument, the fact of the introduction and defence of the police-state model to an assembly of fellow chief officers and local Police Authority members, significantly legitimizes it, and reflects a concrete change in the way senior police officers view their role vis à vis the state. Acceptance of the managerialist police model provides the rationale, the legitimation, for an extension of police powers and for a wider definition of police work, in the service of an apparently neutral expert bureaucracy—an institution of police managers. Through the mechanism of expert practice, the pervasion of the police institution throughout civil society, and the acquisition by the institution of wider decision making powers, are legitimized. Impartial police administrators take-up the strain which the partisan members of the different classes are, by definition, unable to handle in disinterested fashion.

Accountability to the political organs of civil society is necessary, in the new police-state model, only in so far as the political representatives would merit an explanation of the parameters of policing policies. Police officers, like other expert state functionaries would exert unquestioned authority over those specialist, operational, matters within their technical domain.

But Laugharne advances the argument one major step beyond this managerialist position. With a revival of the sentiments of the doyen of conservative police historians, Charles Reith (1940; 1956; Chapter 7), the police as the sole legitimate, expert purveyors of force in civil society, are portrayed as the cornerstone and bastion of the social democratic state.

This schematic model of the police-state relation is in one sense a step forward. It challenges the assumption, held by some police pundits, that centralization of police organization is the inevitable precursor of political direction. Police managerial proponents deny any necessary subordination of the police institution to the class interests represented through the various police authorities.

However, this loosely formulated conception of the police state provides in itself, little guide to the definitive form of the police relation to the state, and to civil society, in the contemporary industrial state. Only by returning to Chapman's original model, can some headway be made.

That sketch of the traditional police-state allows some preliminary observations on the substance of Laugharne's managerial model. Chapman does not pretend —was not concerned with the question of—who benefited from the rule of the police autocrats of eighteenth century Prussia and Austria. Patently, however, those states conferred more benefits on the rulers than on the ruled. Moreover, the model espoused by the Lancashire chief officer, and supported in practice, if not by name, within the ethos of professionalism within the police institution, appears on certain dimensions to approximate more to the contemporary, rather than to the traditional conception of the police-state relation. A pre-industrial society and its state apparatus is hardly comparable with the role of the state under advanced capitalism.

In fact, Chapman provides a number of criteria by which applicability of the traditional police-state model may be tested. These indicators are at the core of the polizeistaat model.

## Applying the police-state model

Five dimensions of the police-state relation according to this conception can be identified: *centralization, politicization, penetration, determination,* and *militarization.* Each of these yardsticks will be assessed briefly in the light of the preliminary evidence on the police institution in mainland Britain. More detailed discussion will be reserved, where appropriate for later in this text. However, at the outset the criticism of this formulation can be made that while the indicators vary in quality and in appositeness, they do not allow the form of state itself to be made problematic.

### Centralization

This indicator encompasses two discrete elements—organizational unification and central direction. The former relates to technological and structural changes that have been a feature of police organizations in Britain since their inception; the latter, to the cohesion of police command within one body.

'In part, organizational centralization has been a result of the tendency, accelerated since World War II, for changes in the concentration of state power, relating to the ". . . growing socialisation of production and the increasing inter-dependence of social relations" (Jessop, 1980, p.63). The development of monopoly capital has required more definitive state intervention by the repressive apparatus. The transition from the highly decentralized Victoria forces, with their local peculiarities, has correlated with changes in the economy of the central and local states. The movement from mercantile capital to local industrial capital (Chapter 3) to the national co-ordination of production to the present monopoly capital stage, has been accompanied by changes in the state's responsiveness. Secondly, centralization has been given an occasional boost by social industrial and political strife. The co-ordinating office set up in 1973 at Scotland Yard to pre-empt activities of "flying pickets", the development of central networks to organize activities against drugs and illegal immigrants, (Ackroyd *et al.*, 1977; Bunyan, 1976) are all examples of the tendency of the state to respond to particular crises by developing centralized planning and control capabilities. Added to those factors were the inexorable organizational changes relating to economies of scale and to specialization. Police force amalgamations enabled some savings on common services and on the cost of the specialists necessary for the new police technologies.

But this organizational centralization has not always flowed smoothly. St. Johnston (1978) notes the fratricidal strife between the heads of large and small forces over the proposed disappearance of the latter, in the name of efficiency. Senior police officers, like other corporate managers, favour centralization not merely when it enhances efficiency but also when it has minimal effect upon their own individual authority and autonomy.

Secondly, organizational changes have involved not just the formal structure of police organization but also that of intra-police arrangements (Chapter 6). The structure of Victorian policing, with its multiple focii, precluded any substantial intra-police relations across force boundaries. But as forces amalgamated, internal relations became easier, and communications between officers less dependent upon the goodwill of their local masters. Eventually, such intra-police organizations—of chief officers, of superintendents, and of the rank-and-file— became substantially more centralized (partly through the influence of the Desborough Committee)[4] than allowed for by the formal organizational structures.

This centralization, and acquisition of influence, was partly a consequence of the battle between police authorities and Home Office for control. Each side could effectively undermine the power of the other while not necessarily boosting its control over the police. In earlier days, Watch Committees denied the Home Office the right of intervention. Latterly, since the 1919 Commission, various Home Office procedures, as well as legal decisions have, contributed to the downfall of the local police committees. Each institution, in turn, negated the power of the other while failing to reinforce its own.[5]

That denial of external political intervention gave rise to a "cuckoo-in-the-nest" syndrome, with the development of the Association of Chief Police Officers (A.C.P.O.) and to a much less significant extent, of the two junior intra-police organizations in England and Wales. Watching from the sidelines at first, and playing only an occasionally overt part in the conflict between the two erstwhile masters, chief police officers have emerged largely victorious as the official combatants retreated or failed to make progress (Chapter 6). Centralization of policing in Britain has developed through two organizational structures —the amalgamation of local forces and the construction of intra-police associations. The latter development has been more extensive but has been given less attention.

As Goodhart pointed out in a minority report of the Willink Commission, the debate between national and local politicians and civil servants over the control of the police neglected the extent to which the increasing complexity of policework gave more power to the administrative manager and diminished that of the paymaster. To that Minority Report writer, the chief constable's power was becoming the ". . . most important, because the power of the two governments is primarily financial, while his is the power of administration" (1963, p.163). Ensconce the chief constables and the two Commissioners, the police managers and the administrators, together in one highly centralized organization, the Association of Chief Police Officers, and the result is centralization and a significant degree of power independent of political party.

The centralization criterion of the modern police-state is fulfilled in terms of the organizational centralization factor, but modified by the peculiar nature of the form in which police managerial power has been combined.

*Politicization*

Police officers in the advanced industrial state are necessarily concerned in "political" decisions. "The enforcement of laws and maintenance of order involve the exercise of constraint, and are thus broadly political" (Reiner, 1980a, p.1). Decisions about the sustenance of public order deriving directly from the legal structure, which requires police intervention in particular contexts in civil society, are invariable manifestations of state practice. The state requires political adjudication by the police apparatus.

Secondly, the discretionary form in which police powers arise, both compel (in the sense that the discretion is required) and allow some degree of voluntarism in the form of that intervention. But apart from the broader powers explicit in the 1936 Public Order Act, (which gives chief officers considerable authority over public processions and demonstrations), the political decision-making process has traditionally followed from the legislative determination of official discretion. Whilst the prosecution of minor public order offences may ultimately be related to wider political ideologies, they do not constitute other than situationally required political interventions. The discretionary enforcement of laws in a partisan manner is within the permissive structure of law (McBarnet, 1978a). The politicization of police-work relates to the attempt to change the governing rules—to amend the structure of law defining police practice.

The development of a police-state depends not upon intervention within the established rules but upon extending the rules and a simultaneous re-ordering of the priorities of police work.

But in the British state, the police institution has always attempted to influence the laws guiding police-work. The successful legal entrepreneurship by the first Metropolitan Commissioners, Rowan and Mayne over street offences legislation in 1839; the critique by the Liverpool Head Constable in 1910 (H.C. Report, 1910, p.22) of new powers taking responsibility for probation work with young offenders out of the hands of the police; and the more recent success of the police institution in restricting the purposes of the Royal Commission enquiring into police procedures; are examples of the continuing political interventions by the police institution. But what is new is the self-confidence with which these interventions are expressed. In 1910, the Liverpool Head Constable contritely apologized for his intercession. In 1980, Goodson, the then, A.C.P.O. President claimed: "It is only right that the police should shape public opinion on important questions . . . they are the professionals and have first-hand experience . . ." (*The Times*, 23rd April, 1980). Managerial expertise requires the expansion of political influence. This modification in police style represents a movement away from "low" policing—the policing of the "les filles,

les boues, and les reverbères". Police work is directed away from the practice of order maintenance within the law to a more general concern with re-structuring societal rules about the nature of the social order.

As Stead says of Minister of Police, Fouché, "His business was primarily with the equilibrium of the state . . . now he saw himself as the apostle of a new and orderly scheme of things" (1977, p.72). The police institution has gradually moved away from the mundane administration of street patrolling to concern with the practices of the "high police" ("the regulating power which is felt everywhere, without ever being seen and which, at the centre of the State, holds . . . the place, which the power which sustains the harmony of the celestial bodies holds in the universe" (Chapman, 1970, pp.29–30)). Increasingly, the police institution makes forays into ". . . the public political arena in order to change the content of the rules both within police organization and at the societal level" (Reiner, 1979, p.2). The re-focusing of the primary concern of the police/managers has developed smoothly without any visible impact on the consciousness of the groups and classes in civil society. Hall notes the value of the managerialist model for that police offensive:

> . . . a source of serious concern is the manner in which the technical factors associated with the problems of policing an increasingly restless society, have become a legitimate basis for far-reaching administrative re-structuring of the police function — virtually without reference to the public and certainly without legislative debate . . . this profound change in the character and exercise of the policing function has been accomplished . . . under the apparently neutral banner of technical rationalization and modernization. (*Guardian*, 5th January 1980)

This alteration in function, in scope, and in style, is one of degree rather than absolute. No contemporary chief police officer matches the skill and contrived institutional power of that paragon of police managers, Joseph Fouché. But within the confines of Chapman's model of the modern police-state, the police institution has climbed several steps.

With the change in the substance of the economic and political problems facing the advanced capitalist state; the economic and ethnic crises of the Bristol, Brixton, and the Liverpool riots; the industrial foci of Saltley Coke Depot and secondary picketing; and the political re-emergence of the I.R.A. — have succeeded the "low policing" of the 1960's epiphenomena (Harry Roberts, the Kray brothers, and the gang-busting of the mythical "Fabian of the Yard").

*Penetration*
For Chapman, the third criterion through which to assess the development of a modern police-state is the ". . . encroachment of the police apparat, under one pretext or another, on the general police powers of other institutions — licensing,

social security, the professions, education, the media . . ." (1970, p.118)—the
degree of colonization and penetration of other state apparatuses. Any outline of
the penetration by the police institution is faced with an immediate dilemma.
The historical evidence is that, in many cases, the functions conducted by the
other apparatuses were originally part of the work of the police institution. The
Victorian police in Liverpool inspected lodging-houses, clothed and licensed
juvenile street traders, arranged for the demolition of slum properties, conducted
truancy patrols, dealt (in one manner or another) with the city's inebriated, and
generally conducted an array of functions that have since devolved to other
agencies of the local and central states. Police officers, as managers, managed the
basic elements in the social life of the city. In considering police penetration of
other institutions, some acknowledgement must be made of the wider prior
police role in the general organization of city life.

In the present day, the police institution both generally, and in times of crisis,
provides the coercive power and the information resources to support the activity
of other state agents. It provides a clearing-house for authority, and for resources.
Police work may involve physical assistance to Housing Departments and Court
Bailiffs in the eviction of tenants, and information to Social Security investi-
gators on claimants (see, for example, Campbell, 1980).

Activities such as these flow from the conjunction of the police institution
within the other state apparatus and are contiguous rather than competitive or
pervasive. Any increase in those roles is only part of a general expansion of state
intervention in civil society.

Where police work usurps—as opposed to complements—other state
apparatuses and the institutions of civil society, is in the invasion of the media,
and of the educational and the recreational realms. As Chapter 8 documents, the
involvement of the police institution in the latter two areas, has been substantially expanded in recent years. It represents an attempt to re-structure—
and thereby modify and control—a particular potential problem population.
Police incursions into the media (by way of example) are spasmodic and
unsystematic rather than representing a sustained offensive. Most local forces
attempt to modify the "police news" in order to construct a more "positive"
image. Amongst other forces, the North Yorkshire, the Derbyshire, the South
Yorkshire, the Lancashire and the Avon Police, all maintain special Press
Bureaux to ". . . ensure that a true account of police work and problems is
presented to the public" (N. Yorks Annual Report, 1978, p.25). Police officers
may recall the injunction of John Alderson (formerly the Chief Constable of the
Devon and Cornwall force, and the primary exponent of "soft" police intervention in civil society) in a major Police Staff College speech to "Remember
you can reach more people in five minutes of television than in a life-time of
public speaking in halls and class-rooms (Alderson, 1976, p.89).

Chibnall (1977) has documented the way local forces may structure and control police news. The police institution supports with resources those media accounts which present the "positive image" (Hurd, 1979), including initiating partisan fictional accounts of police work.[6] A string of recent incidents reflects some of the ways in which the police institution has attempted to use the media for its own ends—'vetting' agreement between the BBC and the Metropolitan Police on media representation of police work (State Research Bulletin 9), the issue of special police press passes only to journalists approved by that force, and the use of the Merseyside Police of a major television documentary series (much criticized by minority groups and others) for image-building—". . . a true portrayal of policing on Merseyside and the everyday problems faced by members of the force . . ." (*The Listener*, 2nd November 1978). But the media involvement by the police institution in Britain is low-key. Police managerialism, in its attempts to penetrate the media in particular, has collided with the self-interests of other apparatus.

Its effects are confined to image-building and in no way measure-up to Chapman's penetration criterion for the development of a modern police-state. Conflicts between apparatuses, and indeed the hesitation of the police institution itself, have severely limited police penetration.

### Determination—the judicial function

Despite its formal executive, structure—the implementation of state practice—the police institution has always embraced judicial and quasi-judicial functions (Chapter 5). The judicial apparatus, in practice, if not in form, has been success-fully subverted by the police institution. More decisions of a judicial type, in interpreting and determining the rule of law, are made by the police executive than by the judiciary and by the courts.

Police judicial power is employed in three forms. Law enforcement action is discretionary. Police officers exercise quasi-judicial functions under certain statutes. The police institution may exert open pressure on the judiciary and on the production of judicial decisions.

Decisions to enforce and not to enforce particular laws are, in effect, judicial decisions. Police powers contains mandatory discretion in enforcement practice. Similarly, the enforcement choice—by caution or by prosecution—does not fall within the traditional conception of the "separation of powers" and of the autonomy of the judicial function. The *selection of charge*[7] is also a form of judicial decision and one that in most other advanced industrial states falls outside the powers of the police institution.

Secondly, contravening the spirit of traditional Anglo-Saxon common law, particular statutes (Section 4 of the 1824 Vagrancy Act (repealed in 1981), and the "stop-and-search powers" enshrined in certain Local Corporation Acts), reverse the traditional assumption of innocence on the part of the accused. In a peculiar form of judicial action, police officers determine the guilt of the suspect under these statutes (the onus being on the latter to prove his or her innocence). Many of the encounters between patrolling police officers and "residents of the street" are structured by stop-and-search legislation, and are not bureaucratically regulated nor statistically recorded, granting the police institution considerable quasi-judicial autonomy. Comparatively few decisions about guilt or innocence, in the vast range of assumed misdemeanours, are constructed through due process.

Finally, the police institution may exert more open pressure upon the judiciary and on the production of judicial decisions. Sir Robert Mark's long-drawn out and ultimately successful campaign to achieve majority verdicts by juries; the black-listing by the Metropolitan police of a list of criminal or "bent" lawyers (Baldwin and McConville, 1979), the practice of jury-vetting (Thompson, 1979a, p.501; *Guardian*, 15th March 1980); and the routine condemnation by bodies such as the Police Superintendents Association (P.S.A.) (Chapter 6) of magistrates and judges for "over-lenient" sentences are all attempts to assume a judicial function.

However, the degree of usurpation of the judicial function by the police institution bears little comparison with police-rule in the absolutist traditional police-state of Prussia or in the near-contemporary Third Reich. In the traditional (as well as in the modern) police-state, police power was at the centre of state-power, and the judiciary were the servants of the police apparatus. The police-state model, with regard to the judicial function, does not allow for the complexities of the relationship between the apparatuses.

*Militarization*

The final criterion devised by Chapman to measure the development of the modern-police state, lies in the degree of military capacity of the police institution. Despite two mutations—in weaponry and in unit specialization— and despite the views of some commentators, the British police have not developed a "third-force" capacity. There is no force in mainland Britain comparable to the Italian *Carabenerie*, the Dutch *Marèchaussees*, the Japanese Kidotei, the French *C.R.S.*, or even to the North American *National Guard*. A Police Journal article lists the arguments in favour of the development of military capability by the police institution:

> . . . by being relieved of normal police duties, they are in a position to mobilise speedily and concentrate quickly at crucial areas, possible resolving a public order problem by sheer "saturation" policing; secondly . . . they can apply all their energies to becoming a specialised force, acquiring skills in tactics and weaponry that will allow them to deal more effectively with a problem than either the police or the army; thirdly, they would reduce the need to call out the army in support of the civil power; . . . fourthly, they can serve as a "shock-troop", the mere appearance of which would help to break the resolve and morale of the mob; and fifthly, by relieving

the regular force police of a distasteful and overt, hostile duty, they would indirectly help to preserve the reputation of the police. (Fox, 1978, p.33)

The police institution in Britain has moved part of the way on that path in recent years, in terms of weaponry (although it should be noted that early police forces always had stocks of weapons at their disposal. Inspectors in the early Liverpool police carried cutlasses, and supplies of pistols were retained at the central police stations). In the last decade, there has been a substantial increase in police access to weaponry in mainland Britain. "It is hard to remember the shock which greeted the bringing-out of riot shields at Lewisham and Notting Hill in 1970 . . . but shields, strengthened helmets, and other protective equipment, are now regular sights" (Reiner, 1980b, p.54). Similarly:

It is a common boast of the British that in contrast with less law-abiding nations, they do not require an armed police. The reality is fast becoming far removed from this conventional truth. Some police officers including the members of the Special Branch and other specialist squads . . . are permanently armed. It has been estimated that at least 200 policemen in London carry guns all the time. In all, an estimated 10,000 policemen—a tenth of the regular force—are qualified to shoot. (Ackroyd et al., 1977, p.139)

Bowden comments on forces other than the Metropolitan (whose tasks uniquely include Diplomatic Protection, where the risk of armed civilians is presumably greater than in other parts of civil society):

As early as 1967, Bristol Constabulary formed a special armed unit of 40 men, it soon became the prototype for other forces. The Leeds, Essex, Southend, Thames, City of London, West Midlands, Lincolnshire, North-umberland and Lancashire forces all followed suit, and today all forces have similar squads . . . (Bowden, 1976a, p.14)

But the digression into weaponry has met strong, and effective resistance from the state agents themselves. An ideological relation contradicts the push for police armaments. As Sir Robert Mark says in the Hunt Report on Northern Ireland, (1969, p.21) ". . . policing in a free society depends upon a real measure of public approval and consent. This has never been obtained by military or para-military means". The major barrier to police weaponry in mainland Britain has been the nature of public consent to the police institution—the form of legitimization on which police authority rests in civil society. Inspector Fox continues:

The sympathetic regard of the public is probably the greatest weapon in the police armoury. This has long been recognised by extremists and is precisely why they would be delighted to see squads of visored helmeted, club-wielding riot police used against strikers or demonstrators, so long as any Third Force was looked upon as being a wing of the police . . . the public would identify its members with the regular police—the effect on the police image would be disastrous. (Fox, ibid)

Although Hall qualifies the importance of the consensual relation:

The fact that the accessibility to arms and similar equipment is still limited does not undermine the substantive fact that . . . in all those cases where it matters, the British Police are now an armed and full-equipped technical force. (Hall, *Guardian*, 5th January, 1980)

and it remains true that the acquisition by the police institution of the equipment necessary for a Third Force role, would be a crucial denial of the consensual source of police authority.

However, the last 20 years have witnessed the construction of certain specialized units within the British police. As early as 1962, Birmingham had a "commando" unit (Cain, 1973). In 1965 the Metropolitan Special Patrol Group was formed upon which provincial counterparts were later modelled. There followed the organization of local Police Suport Units after the industrial crisis of the early 1970s (Fox, ibid), new Task Forces, and mutual aid agreements, which reached their zenith in the Toxteth districts of Liverpool in July 1981, when units from 39 different forces patrolled the streets of inner Liverpool. Nonetheless, these units do not provide a direct parallel with the Continental para-military units. Although several forces now have ". . . officers permanently engaged in Task Forces, such as the "Commandos" of Sussex, the Special Squad in Lancashire, the Tactical Aid Group in Manchester, the Special Services Squad in Bristol, and the Special Patrol Groups of Birmingham and the . . . Metropolitan Police . . ." (Hall, 1980), they are, as Bowden suggests, more akin to "crisis response" units than to the foundation of a permanent para-military Third Force.[8] Given a significant development of industrial and political strife, and the general breakdown of public consent, those units *could* be used as the core for the construction of Third Force capacity. However, outside periods of crisis, tactical factors—in the handling of demonstrations to prevent escalation—and strategic considerations—the problem of long-term consent, hinder the promotion of a para-military role for elements of the police institution.

### The aridity of the police-state approach

The application of the five police-state criteria to the position of the British police institution establishes not so much the lack of relation between policing in the United Kingdom, and the polizeistaat, traditional or modern, but rather the failings of the managerialist perspective on the state, from which the model is developed. Within the limits of the model itself, the position is confused. On each of the criteria—centralization, politicization, penetration, determination, and militarization—no definite conclusion can be adduced. The police institution in mainland Britain self-evidently does not fit into either a traditional or modern police-state mould. Nor, however, does this preliminary evidence do much to support a democratic notion of policing within the state. At best descriptive in Chapman's model, and prescriptive in Laugharne's outline, the police-state model is deficient on a number of counts.

It does not detail other relationships within civil society or even within the state itself. The police institution does not operate within a social and economic void. The police apparatus as an agency of the state, polices a society characterized by differences in economic class, in social status, in ethnicity, in age, and in gender. The conflictual relation arising from these primary features results in differences in interest, of which the primary is the capital/labour dichotomy. The police apparatus would be remarkable if its functionaries as individuals, and the police institution as a corporate body, did not reflect these distinctive interests and levels of power in practice.

Secondly, the concept of the polizeistaat, apart from the distinction between the traditional and the modern models, says nothing about the particular form of state. States with absolutist, mercantile, and capitalist modes of production are subsumed under the general heading of police-state without any consideration of the effect of the different modes of production on the relationship between classes, and with the state apparatus. Effective analysis of the connection between the police apparatus and the composition and form of state must take account of the influence of the economic level.

Finally, while the discussion of the police-state model has a particular value in that it exposes the ideological rationale of the state agents themselves, it suffers a major limitation. It does not make the concept of the state itself problematic. Espousal of this mangerialist model takes as given, the disinterested actions, and the technical expertise of the police/managers and the neutrality of the state. An essential ingredient of the pluralist, the instrumentalist, and the structuralist models, outlined earlier, was their challenge to that construction. Although pluralism, in particular, did not offer any substantive analysis of the nature of the state's role, all three models denied that there was any inevitable impartiality in the action of the state agents—whether it was the contrived balance of interests in pluralism, the class role of the state in the instrumentalist approach, or the state as a servant of monopoly capital as in the structuralist perspective. The police-state approach begs the question of partisanship.

## The Chiefs and the Local State—Towards an Alternative Theorization of Urban Managers

This elaboration of the police-state model has allowed us to focus firmly on the managerialist typification of the relationship between the police apparatus, the state, and civil society. The earlier outline of managerialism was reoriented by concentrating on the political relation of the police institution through the evocation of the polizeistaat.

But while the utility of both models was largely denied, one major component of the managerialist perspective can be restored to the developing analysis. Drawing on the work of urban sociologists, a managerialist variant can be related more directly to the central state—local state split of the police institution. The contribution of British sociologists, such as Pahl (1975, 1977) and Rex and Moore (1967) working within the Weberian tradition, focuses attention on the urban manager—the gatekeeper in the allocation of scarce resources at the local level.

Given the peculiar location of the police apparatus, bestriding the financial, the legal, the ideological, the historical, and the political schism between central and local states, its functions at that nexus are analogous to that of urban management. Chief police officers—the 41 provincial Chief Constables, and the Commissioners of the City of London, and of the Metropolitan Police—are situated at that bridge between the twin structures of political power, and between the state, in general, and civil society. The chiefs, while ultimately answerable to the state (or rather to its legal form for their allocation decisions) exercise substantive power and influence in their separate bailiwicks.

Moreover, by virtue of their formal command office, the chiefs guard the pass between civil society, and the dispensation of police favours, as a form of state action. They act as a conduit through which flow the external demands and pressures from social classes, and from the pluralistic interest groups, which impinge upon the internal predispositions and constraints of local police organizations.

More publicly visible, and legally accountable, than their juniors, chief officers negotiate a *modus vivendi* between the contrary demands on the police institution, weighing alternative enforcement and prosecution policies, whether through the sieve of managerial expertise, or through the mesh of the pluralist construction of the balance of interest, and hemmed in by a variety of restraints, from material class relations to occupational ideologies and prejudices. The chiefs determine the general nature of police work. Neither cardboard figures nor free agents, absorbing the tension between stratified society and police force, they assign categories of legitimacy and illegitimacy to the diverse calls on the police institution, and to the definition of police function. In reacting to outside pressure, whether from the political arm of the local state, through the medium of the police authority, or via the political machinery of the dominant class as vested in the central legislature, and its Home Office organ, or through the variety of appeals that are articulated to the police institution, within civil society, they interpret, mediate, and legitimize. By decisions over deployment, over training, over resource allocation, and withn the organizational reward structure, they determine the form of police work within local society. They delineate the parameters of the organizational responses, and influence but do not determine law enforcement outcomes. They are the vanguard functionaries for the distribution of legal resources within the local state. In short, chief police officers can be conceived of as similar in function, and in practice, to the conception of urban managers.

To Pahl, in 1975 local officials both public and private—from housing managers to building society managers and estate agents—were gatekeepers of the urban system. With the rise of corporate planning (Cockburn, 1977)[9] in the local state, succeeding the immediate post-war hiving-off of some state functions to central control (in the supply of gas, of electricity, and of health care); and the extension of local state intervention in the remaining services (in education, in social services, in planning, and, above all, in housing provision), the relevant officials charged with the supply of the commodities, accrued new powers. As disinterested bureaucrats, it was argued, officials in the state sector, interposed impartial expertise between the political dogmas and injunctions from central government on one hand, and from local pressure groups and social classes, on the other. Chief police officers as a form of urban manager, control resources and determine the allocation of a particular commodity—policing resources—in a way analogous to that of Pahl's housing managers.

Not, as Pahl points out in later work (1977), that the urban managers enjoy unrestricted autonomy. Three sets of relation constrain the gatekeeper—the ecological, the political, and the economic forces of the market. Different geographical distributions of the local population, from inner city to suburbia to rural village, structure the distribution of the supply of both housing and police service. In the same way that housing is less expensive to construct in some areas than in others (perhaps a more pertinent example is in the supply of fire services), police resources are easiest to supply when distances are short, and the human terrain favourable.

Secondly, a political relation qualifies the autonomy of the urban managers. The freedom of housing managers to determine allocation policy is a relative freedom—they cannot contravene too markedly the claims of the constituents of the political authority. Chief police officers who deny all duties of policy explanation to their Police Committees, may temporarily frustrate the local political relation but, in the long-term, merely consolidate the political restraints on their activities. Similarly, in both the housing market, and in police service, high economic costs at a time of low public return, make them susceptible to increased political intervention from central government. The urban managers are subject, within parameters of varying gauge, to the general interposition potential within the political structure.

Finally, there are major economic restrictions on the urban managers. The revenue base from which local services are funded, contracts concurrently with an expansion in the costs of intervention (O'Conner, 1971). Other priorities of capital and service accumulation take priority. The commitment to direct capital accumulation is a primary imposition upon the state as compared with housing and police service. City centre shops may have first claim upon resources in the form of municipal car-parks, as compared with the provisions of patrolling police officers or of council housing. The economic laws of capital ultimately restrain the intentions and the goals of the resource allocators.

However, within these boundaries, Pahl argues, managerial ideology (in the sense of the system of ideas through which the urban managers determine priorities, and organize decisions) decides resource provision. A degree of disinterested, technically-informed autonomy and responsibility rests on the shoulders of the local managers. They, like the chief police officers, in judgements over the appropriation and allocation of law enforcement resources, are an independent variable and a legitimate focus of independent research.

But even this managerialistic profile (with its overtones of pluralism, in the acknowledgement of the heterogeneous pressures on the urban manager, from local sources) is only of limited value, in relation to the chief police officers. It understates the significance of capital accumulation to the practices of the state apparatus. It uses the notion of ideology in too narrow a sense. The organizational complexity of the apparatus is obscured. And, the managerial concept lacks an historical connection.

In the first place, irrespective of the short-range decision-making power of the chief, the police apparatus is committed not to a temporary, limited, or localized involvement with capital accumulation but to a primary, if indirect, one. As Chapter 2 demonstrates, the police institution in Britain developed as the major device by which a locally dominant class sought to diminish the dysfunctional effects of the contradictions inherent in a particular mode of production. The police institution is inextricably bound-up with the form of state, and however obliquely, serves to support the kind of social relations conducive to the social order within which it emerged. Any analysis of the political relation of the urban manager/chief police officer to the other parts of the state apparatus and to civil society must take account of the underlying objective economic relations.

Further, the managerialist approach in this, its latest manifestation, treats the notion of ideology in a highly restrictive sense—simply as the co-ordinating system within which organizational decisions are constructed. Managerial ideology is presented as neutral, dispassionate, and clear-cut, in its essence. Alternatively, in Miliband's instrumentalist use of the concept, managerial ideology may be perceived as a masking stratagem which serves to occlude reality. Representations of bureaucratic expertise secure legitimacy for potentially controversial political decisions. Chief police officers, like housing managers undertake decision-making in key areas of civil society, while simultaneously demarcating those interventions as non-political.

A further nuance is possible in the critique of the managerialist construction of ideology. In the structuralist account of the state, ideology is a central pivot of the social order, and crucial to the mobilization of consent, to domination by capital interests. Chief police officers, as impartial experts in law enforcement, are able to relate working-class anxieties over crime to bourgeois concerns of social order. The working-class problematic becomes incorporated, through the mediation of the state functionaries, within the problematic of the dominant class, rendered harmless and a unity knot tied between the classes. Through the agency of ideology, working-class interests are linked with both social stability, and with the formulation of the problem by the institution. Thirdly, as Ginsburg points out (1979, p.167) in a critique of the gatekeeper concept, the urban manager is merely the front-man for a complex organization, and system of decision-making, over which he, in his person, may have little concrete control. Police organizations are labyrinthine structures consisting not just of formal ranks, in the bureaucratic tradition, but also of specific legal relations (which may conflict with the formal chain of command), and with its own occupational ideology and traditions. The chief cannot be divorced from the organizational complexities of which he is part.

Finally, the managerialist construction lacks a historical specificity. As it stands, the urban manager model, the gatekeeper, the commissary and allocator of local resources, is a creature in a vacuum. The institution personified by the managerialist chief police officer has no history, no traditions, and only static ideological relations with the central and the local states, and with the social classes.

However, there is one major factor that paradoxically reinforces the view of the chief officer as an autonomous urban manager. The chief police officer, unlike the housing manager, acquires his authority (so far they have all been male) not just from his mode of expertise but also from a legal relation. The legal structure from which the powers of the chief police officer derive, is permissive in form, and discretion is mandatory in its exercise. While the chief police officer, in the original application of the urban manager model, may be conceived of as restrained by the ecological factors, by the political relation, and by the fundamental economic problematic of the state, he has in his legal relation a degree of autonomy which restores some credibility to the conception of him as a gatekeeper in the allocation of law enforcement resources.

All these issues are explored in the following chapters, in a qualified application of the urban managerial model to the police institution in Britain. This revised conception overcomes the difficulties identified in the preceeding pages, and both specifies the relations between the police institution and the central and local states, and also situates historically the changes in these relations which are constantly occurring. Thus Chapter 2 locates the historical development of the function of the chief officer, exploring the particular attributes of the office, in the context of the local state. In Chapter 3, the contemporary local relation is examined. Having specified those local relations, the fourth chapter seeks to clarify the connection between the police institution and its major incumbents, and the central state. The following chapter details the form of the legal relation, which provides the chief officer with his unique authority as an urban or corporate manager. The *associational* links which contribute significant extra power to the chiefs are outlined in Chapter 6. The final chapters, 7, 8 and 9 are directed at an analysis of the role of ideology in the support of the autonomy both of the chief officer and of the police institution as a whole.

The *historical* sources and interpretations of that *consent* are discussed in Chapter 7. Chapter 8 details some of the contradictions underlying that consent, and demonstrates the importance of police service work in its mobilization. In conclusion, Chapter 9 draws these strands together, illustrating the way that the chiefs, as the brokers of law enforcement resources, systematize the pressures on their office to produce specific forms and definitions of police work.

# Notes

1. Historical documentation on the Liverpool Victoria Police provides several illustrations of chief police officers attempting to strike a balance between the various cross-pressures on their office. For example, Head Constable Greig:

> Without doubt, the duty of the police is to enforce the law. At the same time, it is most undesirable that they should be used as an instrument by one class of trades-men against the interests of another class, however, poor, and the Head Constable need not remind the Committee of the persons complained of (street traders) by the Shopkeepers Organisation . . . are held in great respect by a numerous section of the community. (H.C. Report 26th April, 1881)

2. See Quinney (1974) for the most explicit view of the police role from this perspective.
3. The conviction and imprisonment of three building workers, in Shrewsbury, after a controversial case involving the use of mobile pickets during the course of an industrial dispute.
4. The Desborough Committee was set up by the Government in 1919 in the aftermath of World War I. According to Critchley (1979), it had three major effects on policing in Britain — inducing a degree of centralization through the creation of the Police Council, as a central negotiating body; provided the basis for the formation of the Police Federation (Chapter 6); and ensured that half the total costs of local forces were borne by central government.
5. One of the informants in Charles Forman's study of the town of St. Helen's in the 1920s, provides an account of what became a classic case in police-civil society relations, and one from which a different lesson than the following is conventionally drawn:

> The Chief Constable was a real vicious type — he was the one the Watch Committee sacked (in 1926) . . . . They got rid of him for a few months, then had to re-instate him. In theory, police were controlled by the Watch Committee, which was a sub-committee of the Town Council. But the government paid half the cost. It was done through the Inspector of Constabulary, who was usually a retired general or something like that. When he came round, they showed him the officers, the force paraded for him and he went off to sign the Certificate of Proficiency.
>  When they sacked the Chief Constable, the government demanded a court of enquiry. Though the Watch Committee refused to attend the enquiry, it was held just the same. During this time, the Inspector of Constabulary refused to sign the Certificate of Proficiency — he'd obviously been told not to. That meant that the Town Council would have to pay the whole cost of the upkeep of the police force. After a little while, they met the government again and decided on another enquiry. This time the council were represented and brought witnesses to prove their case. He was a bully and tried to browbeat everybody. The decision of the enquiry was that he should be re-instated, and he was, as the council couldn't afford to pay the whole cost of keeping up the police force. (Forman, 1978, pp.169-170)

6. St. Johnston (1978), for example, claims the credit for the long-running and soporific B.B.C. "Z-car" television series, filmed initially (and somewhat incredibly) in the economically-shattered Liverpool over-spill area of Kirkby.
7. The unique prosecution power of the police in England, Wales and Northern Ireland (not Scotland) is discussed in Chapter 5. This form of judicial power represents an extraordinary extension of police authority.

8. There are clearly different perspectives on the Third Force readiness of the British
   police. For a viewpoint that differs markedly from the stance of this text see
   Bunyan and Kettle (1980) but the shambles of the initial police reaction to the
   urban riots of 1981 suggests a lack of both commitment and preparation for that
   alternative role.
9. For a detailed discussion of the principles of corporate management, see Dearlove
   (1979, pp.132-144).

*Part One*
*Autonomy*

# 2 The Chiefs and the Local State: I. The Development of Managerial Autonomy

It will be a curious remark in the annals of Liverpool, and future generations may perhaps mistake a mere coincidence for a matter of fact, as they read that "about the beginning of 1836, Thieves and Tories were put down about the same time" . . . (letter in *Liverpool Chronicle*, 6th August, 1836)

## Introduction — the Political Relation

Provincial police forces in Britain stem from the joint parentage of central and local state. Conceived by statute under the permissive provisions of the Municipal Corporations Act, 1835, the County Police Act, 1839 and the County and Boroughs Act, 1856, they were, however, incubated, hatched, and reared as creatures within the local state. While in a minority of cases (usually rural forces) in England and Wales, the Home Office Inspectorate was the mid-wife who supervized the gestation, the provincial police were structured and policing polices formulated, according to local designs. Although three major forces (Manchester, Birmingham, and Bolton) were initially planned as Ministerial-directed organizations (the only political legacy of Edmund Chadwick's designs in the Constabulary Report of 1839), these interventions from the central state were soon negated by the strength of the local bourgeoisie, which consolidated its own authority over the new instrument of social engineering and control.

The significance of the political relation of the police apparatus is epitomized by this early conflict between local and central elites.

Debates over the degree of subservience to the urban middle-classes of the nineteenth century, and over the connection between contemporary police forces and local political fractions and interest groups, are central to the interpretation of police practice. But conventionally, accounts of police relations with the dominant groups in civil society have made twin assumptions. In the first place, it is claimed in the older orthodox histories, that some Victorian police forces were little more than hatchet-men for sections of the manufacturing class. Secondly, it is contended in the new orthodoxy, by both commentators on present-day policing and by spokespeople for the police institution, that certain local police authorities attempt to subvert the urban managerial role of the chief police officer, by challenging on *political grounds*, his (it is always a man) policies and, occasionally, the operations of the force under his command. The evidence in support of these twin propositions (which have achieved the status of truisms within the police institution itself, and, by extension within dominant ideological accounts of policing) are here through the medium of documents on the first provincial police force in England and Wales, the Liverpool City Police, and its successor forces in the 1970s. Using material from police, Watch Committee, and local government records, from secondary accounts and from interview data on the Liverpool and Bootle Police Authority (from the early 1970s), it will be argued here and in the next chapter that a more complex relation exists. There is a political relation between the police apparatus and the local political elites but the relation has little to do with *directive* intervention.

This chapter is devoted to the historical context of local policing and is divided into seven sections. The first section illustrates the conventional claims about political intervention in the last century. Secondly, the importance of economic factors for the genesis and operation of the Liverpool Police is outlined. The third section consists of an examination of the origin of the city police, and is followed by a description of the pre-professional police situation. Fifthly, the political relation is linked with the economic structure of the city through an explanation of the peculiar domination of the mercantile class in the city, and the implications of that hegemony for policing practice. The nature of the political relation in the nineteenth century is then outlined, culminating in a detailed examination through one major incident, recounted superficially in the orthodox histories, of the way in which police autonomy developed after the force inception. Police urban managerialism is already evident in the last part of the nineteenth century.

# The Historical Relation between Police and Local State

## *The orthodox view — the police as subordinate to the city elite*

The various studies that directly and indirectly document police history contain numerous (if, in practice, similar) references to the relationship between the first chief police officers and local Watch Committees. Together, they produce an accepted account of self-interested Watch Committee members, occasionally and arbitrarily utilizing the New Police for their own economic or moral ends. According to Hart, for example, one of several police historians in the conservative tradition:

> Some Watch Committees interfered with the work of the police, particularly with proceedings against publicans and brewers. As the liquor interest was often represented on the Committee, this had a most deleterious effect. (1955, p.424)

Mather (1959, p.117) in an account of the Chartist movement in the middle of the last century, similarly noted cases of political direction of the Victorian police, drawing examples from Norwich and from Liverpool. Critchley, (1979, p.131) in the major source text on police development in Britain, contents himself with referring to clashes between Chief Officer and Watch Committees because of the lack of statutory demarcation of their relative powers. The general picture to emerge from these and from the more partisan accounts of some retired police officers (see, for example, Nott Bower, 1926), is that while Watch Committees in the nineteenth century were content to leave the *minutiae* of patrolling to the discretion of chief police officers, they were always ready to intervene over issues which affected their personal interests.

The accusation of direct political interference in police work, is one commonly levelled at the Liverpool Watch. For example, Cockroft in an institutional account of Liverpool police development (based almost entirely upon the Watch Committee Minutes) says

> Early Tory-dominated city councils favoured the brewing interests, and often forced the head constable — vis the Watch Committee — to safeguard public house licenses. The Liberals . . . . were often bigoted, and in their zeal for temperance took little heed of police experience. (Cockroft, 1974, p.155)

and, for example

> . . . . a publican, who had had an information laid against him by one of the
> Liverpool constables, came to the local police station with a member of the
> Watch Committee. The publican who had been chairman of the member's
> election committee, threatened to "take the policeman's coat off his back" if
> he dared proceed . . . . (Cockroft, 1969, p.173)

Similarly, in a well-known early Anglo-American primer for police officers,
Fosdick claims that, as late as 1890

> . . . . the Chairman of the Watch Committee was the attorney for large liquor
> interests in the city, while another member was the physician for most of the
> brothels. Needless to say, the activities of the police in respect of liquor and
> prostitution were negligible. (1914, p.56)

In cooler fashion, Marshall (1978, p.59) uses the 1890 situation to illustrate a
point on changes in police accountability!

> A good example is the action of the Liverpool Watch Committee . . . which
> issued orders to the Head Constable . . . . "to proceed against all brothels
> without any undue delay and such proceedings shall be by way of prosecution

Midwinter in a useful account of the early police in North West England,
illustrates the early exertion of influence by the Watch over the Liverpool police,
by reference to the dismissal of chief officers, and to the Watch's recurring
investigations into the force:

> The force had its troubles. Four chief constables were in office over those
> first twenty years, and several committees of enquiry were appointed to
> examine various aspects of police work. (1971, p.65)

This high turnover of chief officers related in part to clashes over their degree of
autonomy. In 1844, for example, Head Constable (the Liverpool title for the
chief officer until it was discarded in 1921) Miller was required to resign for
taking fifty officers of the Liverpool force to the assistance of the Birkenhead
Watch Commissioners, across the River Mersey, without first requesting
permission from the Liverpool Watch Committee. The *Liverpool Mercury* says
of this resignation:

> . . . this unexpected step has been taken by Mr. Miller owing to the inter-
> ference of the Watch Committee in matters which he thought should have
> been left entirely to his management

A second Head Constable was not given the resignation option. He was dismissed

. . . for having cut out of a police book, called the North Division Report Book, a report by Sergeant Tomlinson impugning the conduct of the police, with intent to suppress the same. (L. W.C.M., 6th March, 1852)

But these accounts, while accurate in detail (apart from Fosdick) are episodic and fail to contextualize the events within the wider political and economic relations of the city. Only on a larger canvas, constructed on principles of *political economy*, can a more substantive interpretation of the police–civil society relation be developed. In order to explain how the Victorian police apparatus, in Liverpool, came to express specific class interests and yet was only rarely, and with great difficulty, subjected to directive control from the dominant class, it is necessary to focus the debate away from the inter-personal relationship between Watch Committee and chief officers, towards a structural account of the development of the police institution within the local state.

## The Political Economy of the City at the Time of Police Reform

Central to the appreciation of police development within English cities at the outset of the Industrial Revolution is an understanding of their core problematic, as local states. While the driving force for all cities at that period—or rather the momentum for their ruling classes—was that of profit accumulation, through appropriate investment and industry, the form of profit accumulation differed markedly between the major seaport of the country, Liverpool, and the rising towns and cities of Northern England. Secondly, in so far as the form of accumulation varied, so did the structure of social relations and of stratification. Contemporaries in the Victorian era talked of the "merchant princes of Liverpool, the cotton lords of Manchester, the textile kings of Leeds, or the metal magnates of Birmingham" (Fraser, 1976, p.15). Capital production in Liverpool (which at the time of the New Police, handled roughly half of all imports and exports for the whole country) and marginally less so, in London, and in Bristol, was substantially different from the rest of the United Kingdom. Its dependence on foreign trade was the predominant feature of the city. Consequently, the source of accumulation lay in the exploitation of two forms of exchange relationships in the accretion of profit directly from trading trans-actions and in the acquisition of surplus value from the input of particular types of labour.

The primary source of profit was from overseas trade. For the Liverpool merchants, that profit had derived in the eighteenth century from the triangular run of the slave trade (the West Africa, West Indies, Great Britain circuit). With the formal abolition of the slave trade in 1807, slavery as a source of profit was replaced with transactions in material commodities—post 1813, a new Far East market was being opened up; North America had become almost an exclusive market; and South American countries, newly independent from Spain, had become a major focus for Liverpool trade. Manufactured goods from the Lancashire and West Yorkshire hinterland furnished the manufactured goods for exchange for raw materials from the new markets in the Colonies.

In other words, the source of profit for the merchants, was both quite distinct in its mode of production, compared to that of the manufacturers of industrial England, and also at some considerable geographical distance from the city. Primary exchange relations were separated by the merchant fleet and canal barge from the physical location of the mercantile and banking decisions. Consequently, the merchants, by far the dominant class in the city, were distanced from the class of whom they were the primary exploiters. The merchants were cushioned from direct contact with productive labour.

Secondly, essential to this form of economic activity were two similar types of labour—the seamen who manned the ships of the merchant fleet, and the casual labourers who were engaged in the onshore transit of goods. Both categories of labour were characterized by episodic and low paid employment. For sailors, work periods depended on variations in the wind (one Liverpool Head Constable attributed fluctuations in the crime rate to the effect of the wind on shipping in the harbour!), on trade conditions, and on the pool of surplus labour. For the shore labourers—from dock workers to the "badge-porters", there were similar variations. In the latter case, the period of employment tended to be shorter perhaps more intensive, and without any pretensions at skill.

The labour pool from which the merchants drew was structured by irregularity of employment, by low income, and by lack of internal cohesion. It was necessarily domiciled in the cheapest shelters, adjacent to the docks and warehouses.

In turn, this form of labour, seamen and casual shore labourers, had a particular effect on the economic life, and on urban recreation.

A *secondary economy* of the street, encompassing the provision of services and the sale of goods, co-existed with the primary economy that serviced the respectable classes—the merchants, the new professional, the tradesman, the expanding strata of clerks[1] to the merchant houses and the relative minority of artisans (especially building workers) and manufacturing workers. The secondary economy that served the lower classes featured low costs, low overheads, and irregular hours of provision. It was the domain of the street hawker, the street market, the pawnshop, the fence,[2] and included betting shops, beer houses, common lodging houses and brothels. The secondary economy ensured the maintenance of services for the major form of labour in the city—the docks-related activity. Inevitably, the provision of commodities on this market did not coincide neatly with the new ideas of Benthamite legal regulation, and the new emphasis upon crime-prevention, in the post-Napoleonic period. Two factors added to the complexity of the political economy of the city — the relative decline of the city's early manufacturing industry, and Irish immigration.

Stedman Jones (1971) in his important study of the construction of the residual economic strata, in London, dates their development from the last half of the nineteenth century, with the gradual disappearance of those industries suitable for factory production. In Liverpool, that decline, and its substitution by casual labour production, dated from an earlier period.

As trade boomed in the period after the Napoleonic War, there was a concurrent erosion in the existing industrial base of the city, and of those forms of industrial concentration necessary for the development of a conscious proletariat. Where iron-ships, were replacing timber-built vessels, Liverpool foundries could not compete with iron-foundries adjacent to the coal-fields of East and West Lancashire (White, 1951; Muir, 1907). Small concerns, such as the Liverpool potteries, which had been established for some hundred years, retreated to the Black Country for similar reasons.

The only forms of industrial production to survive the early years of police reform were those industries directly inter-related with the port (such as rope-making), some newer industries which were directly dependent on the import of goods with a finite life (cereals and sugar later became important), and, as in London, employers of small numbers of highly-skilled workers (watchmaking), and labour related to the physical fabric of the city (builders, joiners, and stone-masons). According to one estimate (Baines, 1859) by 1850, the proportion of the population engaged in direct manufacture did not exceed five per cent. If, in the capital in the 1870s, a sizeable minority of the population was concentrated into marginal production, in Liverpool already at the time of police reform, in the 1830s, the majority of the work force was thus engaged. One further factor complicates the social structure of the city — immigration. Although Irish immigration into, and through Liverpool, did not reach its peak until the mid 1840s [some 300,000 Irish arrived at the city's docks in 1845 (White, 1951)], the city port acted as a transit area for migration for a considerable period prior to the potato famines of those years. In addition, the city had been a recipient (if only temporarily in some cases), of the rural-urban migration within mainland Britain itself.

The effects of the continuing and increasing influx, on the economy and on the political relations of the city were several. The Irish, in particular, settling in cellars and cheap lodging houses in the Vauxhall area of the city (Tobias, 1974) in close proximity to the major city docks and warehouses, provided a ready pool of unskilled labour, available as Engels had noted in Manchester, to undercut wage claims by the indigenous labour force and to ensure low costs of production for the merchants.[3]

Secondly, the formation of Welsh as well as Irish enclaves, in addition to the religious divisions among the Irish themselves, reinforced a divide between the residual classes that was both cultural and linguistic. Outside the casual employment market, there were few opportunities for the development of solidarity class consciousness. Lower class groups were divided from one another by work opportunities, by culture and by race.

Immigration in itself boosted the secondary economy—both in the provision of clients and of participants. Various indigenous occupations within the secondary economy—lodging house-keeping and baggage handling especially were parasitically attached to the immigration phenomenon and to the temporary residents. Finally, immigration accentuated the demand for essential services, particularly over accommodation. In 1810, it was estimated (Muir, 1907) that one in ten of the population lived in cellars, a situation which worsened with the growth of immigration. This competition for scarce resources provided the key dynamic within the secondary economy. (The expansion of housing and the enclosure of outlying townships was a major feature of the Head Constables' demands for enhanced establishments over the succeeding century.)

Together, immigration, the lack of a manufacturing base, and the dominance of the port in the economy of the city combined to produce a peculiar problem of control for the merchant class. The gap between the resultant secondary economy and the new legal order was mirrored in the social chasm between the merchants and the majority of the city inhabitants. Uniquely, it was not a gap that was bridged in continuing confrontations in the work-place. For the merchant class, the problems of maintaining their rule in the city were complex but not those of a ruling-class (as elsewhere in Northern England) faced with a nascent industrial proletariat. It was the social milieu of the streets and the street economy—the "proletarian public realm" (Cohen, 1979, p.119), that provided the context of the spasmodic conflict between the classes.

The contradictions between the political economy and the new legal order are apparent. The old order featured arbitrary and exemplary punishments, with twin powers of mercy and patronage regularizing the subordination of the lower classes (Hay, 1975; Phillips, 1980, p.158). The new developing legal order combined principles of individuality, of legal codification, and rigid application. The application of the latter to the apparently disorganized and chaotic "criminal areas" of Liverpool (as seen by the Benthamite Liverpool police entrepreneur Walmsley) necessarily led to compromise.

The secondary economy was indirectly essential for the sustenance of the merchant class. Yet its character clashed with changes in the conception of law, promulgated through the political apparatus of the central state, and by the missionaries of the new ascendant political class, the industrial bourgeoisie. The intolerance of social deviance noted in the "Report of the State of Crime" by the first Chairman of the Liverpool Watch Committee, in 1835 (Walmsley, 1879, p.82) was at odds with the interdependence of the economy of the city with quite different manifestations of economic and social life. The contradictions at the heart of the economy created a double bind. The secondary economy (and its social attributes) was an inevitable consequence of the dominant mercantile relations of production and distribution, but its particular form could also handicap that primary economy. Note, for example, the contribution of a later Liverpool legal entrepreneur and city merchant in an assault on police practices over public house inspection:

> Round the Liverpool sailors' home, where my own men are paid their wages, within 150 years, the magistrates have licensed forty-six public houses!!! As a Shipowner, I feel bound to say to the magistrates in licensing such an undue number of Public Houses, and the Watch Committee in leaving these Public Houses and Music Saloons partically uncontrolled, have betrayed the interest of my men . . . we, as a firm, suffer grievous prejudice through these manifold temptations, as our men instead of getting to their families with the money in their pockets, are entrapped in the Public Houses where they, too often, spend all their hard won earnings, and do not have a penny left for the purchase of their outfit for a new voyage . . . (Memorandum to the Watch Committee, 1875 on 'Drunkenness and Crime' from Alexander Balfour)

The merchant class and the dockside and lower class communities were enmeshed in a dialectical relation, which gave neither strata particular unity nor satisfaction. The connection between this complex economic structure of the city and the political relation of the new police institution can be most effectively analysed by focusing on four separable issues—the immediate cause of police reform; the pre-1836 police apparatus; the conflict within the merchant class over police reform; the *general* form of the political relation of the police with the local ruling class throughout the nineteenth century. The discussion is concluded through an analysis of the major example of direct political intervention; and the implications of that incident for the development of police managerial autonomy.

## The Origins of the Liverpool Police

There is little disagreement between the major authorities on police history on the reasons for the development of the professional police apparatus in the 1830's.

The differences (despite a recent critique by Hart, 1978) between conservative and radical historians of police reform, are not that great (see Manning, 1977 for the best recent account). The explanatory factors lie in the conjunction of demography with the processes of urbanization and industrialization, and both are tinted with a particular ideological conception of law.

While in Liverpool, the over-riding cause of police reform lies in the relation between the primary economy of the city (developing at rapid pace in the first quarter of the nineteenth century) and the secondary economy of the urban poor, the precipitating factor lies in the consequence of the increasing population for interaction between the classes.

Demography was of primary importance in the search for new means of social control in the city. Landless peasants, dispossessed by the new capitalist-based agriculture of Cheshire and Lancashire, as well as Welsh and Irish immigrants, were flooding into the economic centres of the North-West throughout the last part of the eighteenth century and the first part of the nineteenth. Together with high birth-rates and better medical facilities,[4] the population was on the move into the city. While elsewhere, the post-Napoleonic depression resulted in a flooded labour market, in Liverpool, there was relative opportunity for new settlers (due partly to the effects of the peace in restoring freedom of navigation).

Population density in the city doubled and doubled again. Between 1792 and 1831, the population is estimated to have increased (within the existing boundaries of the city) from 60,000 to 200,000 with another 40,000 incomers in the new townships surrounding the town (Muir, 1907) and with a further 80,000 settling in the town itself between 1831 and 1841 (White, 1951). According to

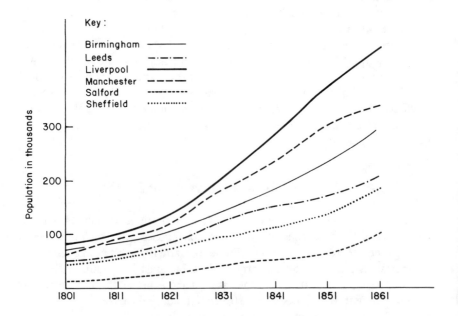

Fig. 1. Population growth of major English cities, 1801-1861.

the Liverpool Medical Officer's 1841 estimate, the average density was 100,000 per square mile (Muir, 1907). Liverpool grew faster than any other city in this period (see Fig. 1).

As long as the participants in the secondary economy restricted their activities to existing areas of lower class settlements, then the problem of social order was ecologically manageable. Social behaviour, deviant according to the mores of the merchant class, was tolerable, as long as it did not intrude. But population pressure—and the richer pickings—pushed deviance (and the concomitant disease from overcrowding and lack of sanitation) over the established boundaries into the business and trading thoroughfares, and perhaps more importantly, into the areas of bourgeois residence.

While a subsidiary rationale for police reform was the complaint by tradesmen against the competing elements of the street economy—hawkers and pedlars (a form of pressure on policing policy institutionalized over the next century), what seems to have been most important was the spill-over effect from slum to the area of merchant residence. In Liverpool, some of the housing zones were only narrowly divided. In South Toxteth, for example, were the mansions of the major merchants. Next door, in North Toxteth, there were compressed (according to the Municipal Inquiry into the Corporation of Liverpool) in 1831, some 24 000 people ". . . of a class most degrading to human nature". The services of the inhabitants of North Toxteth were interdependent with the provision of casual labour to the city economy, but inconvenient when they spread over the boundary.

Hence a letter from a Toxteth Park resident three weeks after the formation of the New Police:

> Already the environs of Town begin to find the benefits of the New Police, in the diminution of the number of vagrants. Previous to the establishment of the force, Toxteth Park . . . . was visited with herds of beggars and other disorderly characters who together with the licensed hawkers, disturbed the domestics, and all respectable houses to a great extent; in many houses, a servant will have to open the door 70 to 100 times during the day, which made it impossible that they could attend to other domestic organisation . . . they were frequently subjected to insolence and the greatest abuse . . . When the (old) constables were appealed to, they invariably said they could not relieve the nuisances; if they took them up, the magistrates would not convict any one . . . . the (new) policemen . . . . would protect the public from the insolence and brutality they have been subjected to by those ruffians . . . .
> (*Liverpool Mercury*, 11th March 1836)

In effect, a major catalyst for police reform was the requirement by the merchant class for control of the boundaries between their areas of residence and the location of the lower classes.[5] As Scott says (in a short account of police reform in Liverpool,

> ... there was increasing concern throughout the twenties and early thirties
> by the merchant classes of the ease ... and frequency with which the thieves
> carried out their work ... the close proximity of the criminal classes caused
> the wealthier inhabitants to pay volunteer contributions to maintain a patrol.
> (1968, pp.2-45)

But a secondary problem for the merchant class, in addition to the normal depredations that spread from the secondary economy, (whether in its begging, peddling, thieving,[6] or disease form), was the occasional, and episodic event when the lower classes, seamen or labourers, burst-out en masse.

Parris, in an older study of police reform in Britain notes:

> .... there seems to have come a point .... (such as the Bristol Reform Riots
> of 1832) .... when a riot let the authorities conclude that an efficient police
> was a lesser evil than periodical anarchy. (1961, p.267)

The violence of "King Mob" was a threat not just to the physical well-being of the respectable classes but to the economy of a city whose life-blood was dependent upon safe passage through the streets. Occasionally, the disturbances contained a more directly political challenge, from lower classes not incorporated within the political institutional structure.

Lyman, for example, gives a graphic interpretation of the conditions under which the original Metropolitan legislation had been passed in 1829, and the effect of the troubles on uniting the dominant classes in favour of police reform:

> London had been the scene of riots almost since 1815. Poor economic
> conditions and the unemployment and striking Spitalfield weavers, aroused
> the fears of the middle-class, the manufacturers, and the upper classes.
> During the debates on Peel's Bill, there were outbursts of rioting and frame-
> breaking. The Times daily carried reports of violence ... It had become
> obvious that any attempt by the Government to enforce the law would
> necessitate both the immediate availability of troops and the willingness to
> risk mob violence. When a weaver was sentenced to be whipped for the
> distance of one hundred yards, Peel told the House that "all the civil forces
> that could be spared" were at the scene. If these proved insufficient, he had
> authorised the Magistrates to call "the military arm of the state to their
> assistance" ... the trend of events seemed to indicate approaching crisis.
> The Monarchy was unpopular, republican sentiment was being heard
> openly, there was fear of revolution, fear of mob, and apprehension for the
> security of property. The demand for protection became widespread as
> business and industrial interests exerted a pressure which transcended party
> lines, a pressure which Parliament dare not ignore. The Metropolitan Police
> Act was passed ... (1964, pp.151-152)

In Lancashire, throughout the 1830s and 1840s, similar disturbances are said to have precipitated reform of the policing apparatus of the local states. But Midwinter, while illustrating this argument by reference to disturbances in the new manufacturing towns (for example, in the arson by Bolton unemployed workers of the local Town Hall), claims that the major reason for police reform in Liverpool was the more mundane fact of everyday crime ". . . the large scale public disorder which is frequently used to explain police reform was rarely found in Liverpool" 1971, p.571.

In fact however, riots were an important Liverpool phenomenon. At the time of the inauguration of the New Police in the city in 1836, the major labour conflict of 1775 was still part of the background repertoire of city history. In that year (Brooke, 1853, pp.326-344) the town was effectively taken over for seven days by sailors as the outcome of a labour dispute.[7] Muir claims "this episode was an alarming proof of the dangers that might accrue from the turbulent character of the Liverpool populace and the ineffective policing of the town" (1957, p.268). Two years later, the city council appointed a temporary police committee to deal with a similar dispute, and in 1779, the Yorkshire militia, then on garrison duty in Liverpool, were stationed throughout the town to maintain social order.

But more significantly for the cause of police reform, although several lesser disturbances occurred intermittently over the next fifty years, in the months during which proposals for the new provincial police were being debated, in Parliament, and in the city, Liverpool experienced several riots of varying seriousness. For example, on 6th February, 1835, the Watch had been unable to cope with what appears from the numbers arrested to have been only a minor affair. But a much more tumultuous conflict occurred after a Boyne day celebration by Irish Protestants.

The event and the ineffectiveness of the available police apparatus is described graphically by the *Liverpool Mercury*:

> . . . a violent commotion in Ben Johnston Street called for the interference of the Watchmen, who though they were strongly opposed in the execution of their duty, succeeded in capturing one ringleader. This was the signal for a general assault. The mob set upon the Watchmen, rescued the prisoner, and assaulted the officers so hotly that they were driven from the street. At the same time, a great tumult arose in Great Cross-Hall Street. The officers of the nightly Watch from the adjacent district were quickly summoned in, and ran to quell the disturbance. The mob instantly turned on them with the greatest fury, and as they were 50 to one in strength in numerical strength against the guardians of the peace, the latter were driven before them. The fury of the mob seemed to increase as they proceeded and their conduct became so outrageous that the watchmen were compelled to take refuge in the Vauxhall Road lock-up to save their lives . . . (17th July, 1835)

After several days of tumult, including the capture of the outer Bridewell by the rioters, social order was restored with the aid of four hundred special constables and two hundred regular soldiers.

But the occasional riot, the level of crime, and annoyance to the respectable classes from beggars, pedlars and the like were not themselves the *cause* of police reform.

The development of a new control system to divide off, to map-out, the lower class areas, was the inevitable consequence of the antithetic features of the economy of the city.

Although the form of development of the new Police relates to the particular conjunction of Benthamite ideals, the precedent of the Metropolitan example, and the nature of the conflict between fractions of the merchant class; police origins in Liverpool lie in the contradictions at the centre of the local economy. Given the requirement for a unique form of labour power to deal with the transhipment of goods, and the derivative secondary economy, the related forms of habitation, and street recreation, social deviance was an inevitable expense. Although factors only indirectly related to the local economy contributed to the social disorder as perceived by the merchant class, the central problematic at the heart of the demand for a new policing system lay in the mode of production. The specific requirement by the dominant class in Liverpool in the 1830s, was for a force that could control the streets, not a police that was primarily directed to suppress the manifestations of direct economic conflict (Chapter 7).

## The Old Police

In part, the reform of the Liverpool police related to the ineffectiveness, or rather the inappropriateness, of the existing forms of social control in the city. The styles of policing existing prior to 1836 were self-evidently unfit for flourishing mercantile order. But what was curious about those styles was not so much their quality but rather the underpinning economic rationales in their changing status, that prepared the way for the policing of an industrial capitalist order.

Certainly, the evidence from contemporary critics supports the conclusion by present-day police historians. Critchley's general comment that the constables prior to police reform ". . . were at best illiterate fools, and worse, as corrupt as the criminal classes from which not a few sprang" (1979, p.19) reflects the Liverpool situation. The chairman of the first Watch Committee, described the "Old Charlies" as ". . . so aged and feeble that the inhabitants could only account for their filling the post by supposing that when men were considered to decrepit for other employment, they were elected guards of public safety" (Walmsley, 1879, p.17). The *Liverpool Mercury* gives two apparently typical examples of the inefficiency and callousness of the Night Watch:

. . . the Watchmen were discharged for inhumanity in leaving a drunken man, Benjamin Carzeau who had broken his leg, lying in the street for several hours on Sunday morning. When taken to the infirmary, Carzeau was quite delirious and died a few days afterwards. Two other watchmen were discharged for indulging in a treat of beef-steak and ale provided by some disorderly female. (1835, p.70)

Even the Superintendent of the Day-Police had been moved to complain:

I cannot miss the opportunity . . . of stating that in some of the instances of inefficiency than procuring recommendations for situations from persons of respectability, many of whom I have found consider a man fit for a constable when he is not fit for anything else. (Common Council Proceedings, 5th February, 1829)

Although there is some reason to suspect the tenor of these comments[8] the available evidence suggests that by any reasonable criteria, and for whatever reason, the pre-1836 police in Liverpool were ineffective in their several functions (Brooke, 1853, p.288).

One reason for this deficiency lay in the tripartite organization of policing in the city. There were obvious complications for a merchant class that depended on three distinct forces—the *Day Police*, the *Night Watch*, and the *Dock Police* (each with own separate economic relation to the social order) for its support.

The Day Police (or Borough Police) were the inheritors of the mediaeval rank of constable. Vested with traditional common law powers of arrest and prosecution, they signified through their Staffs, the symbolic juxtaposition of local and central authority. In Liverpool the first constables were elected from the Freemen, the wealthy non-tax-paying merchants of the city, in 1721. It was ". . . ordered that six proper and fit persons, freemen and inhabitant be yearly elected as deputy constables . . ." (Brewer, 1968, p.2). They were not so much a crime-control agency, as a body delegated to react to emergencies, or simply required to serve warrants. A mere fifty or so in number, by the 1800s they were mainly posted to guard the Cotton Exchange, (the centre of the local economy); to lubricate the practice of exchange, by serving distress warrants; and, occasionally, to arrest "known felons".

Although the original designation of them in 1721, had been akin to Colquhoun's (1799, p.198) description of the functions of the pre-industrial constable in London ". . . so that suspicious night-walkers are ordered to be arrested and detained", their activities were soon restricted to day-time work while patrol duties were assumed (in the middle of the eighteenth century) by the Night Watch.

As their role was gradually restricted to a primarily commercial function, so did their status change. The merchant Freemen, preoccupied with the acquisition of commercial assets, soon found the occasional duty as constable, both demanding and demeaning. There was little profit or prestige to be gained, in the early years from disciplining the city poor, or later, from conducting the more mundane sections of commercial life. Substitutes were employed. In a period of developing capitalism, ". . . anyone capable of making money preferred to pay someone else a small fee for taking the post, rather than interrupt his own enterprise" (Robinson, 1978, p.133). The first paid police are recorded in 1784, and a hierarchical rank structure imposed in 1811 (Brewer, 1963).

As their status diminished, the constables were increasingly recruited from the same class that they were to police. But with the diminution in the social rank of their office, the limits on their actions were tightened. Central to the establishment of the professional police within the new capitalist order was this transposition of *office of constable* with rights and duties derived from traditional common law, to a new status as the *paid agent of a particular class.*

Traditional common law assumed the treatment of subjects according to principle of equality of rank. However, through its discretionary component, it permitted selectivity of law enforcement. For the new paid constable, although his power remained *original* and derived from common law, his discretion was circumscribed by his employment status. As a cost from the surplus revenue of the class of merchant Freemen, his value was now assessed according to specifically economic criteria. What had been convention — the use of the constable to control one class on behalf of another, as one aspect of his general order-maintenance function — was converted into the driving imperative. In Liverpool, the new employee status of the constable signified the transition in the form of police apparatus to a new relation with the developing capitalist order. The policing function was ranked with that of other employees of the merchant class, as a necessary cost in the production of profit.

As the duties of the constables were compressed to day-time forays and to guarding the centre of commercial exploitation, the lack of night-time protection for premises, for goods, and for persons became apparent. Consequently, powers were obtained by the Corporation (the ruling body of Freemen) under an Act of George II, 1748 to set up a new police force ". . . for enlightening and cleansing the streets of the said town and maintaining a Nightly Watch there" (Peet, 1915, p.377). In a foreshadow of Colquhoun's later description of the function of constables:

> . . . a watchman is to examine night-walkers, that is persons strolling about at unseasonable hours, and to bring such persons as behave either in a disorderly manner, or refuse to give a good account of themselves to the Watch House . . . The Watchmen have the power to apprehend all night-walkers and all disorderly persons or suspected persons, and must deliver them up to the Sub-Bailiffs or Assistant Constables. (ibid)

Although the Night-Watch was intertwined with the Day-Police, in the juris-diction over suspects, the Watch had its own peculiar relation with the stratified social order and with the focii of power within the city.

Because the Corporation's right to collect taxes was limited by statute, any new cost-incurring function required a separate institution with new powers over taxation. Consequently, the 1748 Improvement Act, which established the Watch, simultaneously give birth to a new controlling body, the *Commissioners of the Watch*. That latter institution was elected from a franchise substantially wider than that of the Corporation (with its electorate drawn from the Freemen minority of the merchant class). As a result of this development, this new source of police powers, the Commissioners of the Watch (in the 1820s and early 1830s) became a forum for fractional opposition by the non-Freemen merchants. It provided a political vehicle by which the hegemony of the Freemen could be challenged.

Secondly, the functions of the Watch were not limited to the control of the night-time streets but included the all-embracing tasks of cleansing the thorough-fares.

This inclusion of this latter function, had, in turn, two separate effects. It reduced the cost of the Watch—profits from the collection and sale of night-soil was shared amongst the Watchmen. The scavenging tasks subsidized the direct policing duties. Finally, in so far as the Act defined the task of the Watchmen in this all-embracing form, it reinforced the conception of the control instrument as a "social police" (Donajgrodzki, 1977)—police functions were institutionalized as any duty in relation to the social order and social engineering of the city. The Night-Watch was reformed on Metropolitan Police lines, in 1830, by an officer newly-recruited from that force (Cockroft, 1974).

In addition, to the Day-Police and to the Night-Watch, at the beginning of the nineteenth century, the Corporation (or rather its dock sub-committees) set up a third force. The expansion of trade had resulted in new, more specialized policing duties. The dock area had grown from eight acres in 1760 to 72 acres in 1835 (Muir, 1907). Police protection on the docks was a necessary cost of the direct loading and unloading of goods.

The new Docks Police were especially important as the forerunners of the New Police. The formation of the River Thames police, in 1789, by Colquhoun and his compatriots was the first police force formed in Britain with the direct aim of minimizing the loss of revenue through depredations (I. Macdonald, 1973). That police organization was the instrument by which the London merchants sought to prevent the expropriation of their goods by the river ". . . lumpers, glutmen, scufflehunters and mudlarks . . .". The London example had been copied by Bristol merchants in 1806, and in 1811, the newly founded Liverpool Docks Police were given similar wide-ranging powers to ". . . detain suspected persons and seize goods supposed to be stolen" (Scott, 1968, p.21).

In establishing the pattern for later professional developments in Liverpool, the Docks police were important not just because of the method by which their costs were raised (by direct levy on the goods passing through the port) but principally in organizational form. Re-modelled in 1829 and in 1833, they were the basic model for the New Police of the city (with whom they were amalgamated in 1837). In uniform, in access to weaponry, and in rank structure, they were the nearest equivalent in the city to a para-military force. The office of Superintendent, at the head of the force, was the prototype from which the later urban managerial role was to be contrived.

These three policing institutions, Day-Police, Night-Watch, and Docks Police, in their practices, in the object of their actions (the "suspected persons"), and in their focus of control, illustrate the complexity of control structures prior to 1836, the relation between the policing functions and the economy of the city and the potential for conflicts between merchant fractions, with the different forces representing symbolic and commercial weapons in the struggle for political dominance in the city. Control of a unified police force, it was argued, would give particular parties, Tories or Liberals, or class fractions, Freeman merchants or non-Freeman merchants, the power to intervene in a variety of aspects of civil society. Increasingly, in the period immediately prior to 1836, control of a unified police became a prize.

## Fractional Conflicts over the New Police

The struggles between class fractions, and between the old ruling class and the new urban bourgeois, documented in the major accounts of police reform (for example Hart, 1978, pp.182–185; Phillips, 1980, p.172), materialized in Liverpool as elsewhere. But this local conflict, with its national connotations, must be set within the peculiar economic context of the city, of the development of the local state. While these fratricidal disputes are important in respect of the nature of the eventual *political direction* of the Liverpool Police, they were subsidiary to the general unity of the dominant merchant class over *policing function*.

The early differences over the establishment of professional policing in the city were *within* the merchant class. The two elites, Freemen and non-Freemen, Tories and Whigs (or Liberals) managed successfully, if temporarily, to incorporate trading and working-class groups in their own interpretation of the nature of the conflict, which reached its peak over police reform.[9] As a class, and as political elites of that class, the merchants themselves were quite distinct from the industrial elites developing in the manufacturing towns and cities of the period. (Liverpool was the last major stronghold of the eighteenth century upper class.)

Their general concern was the preservation of the existing social order *not* with the inculcation of the new mores of work discipline and of the Protestant Ethic, as in the manufacturing towns. The trade of the merchant class and the organization of their labour, differed only in volume from that of a century earlier. The interest in police reform was not to combat the nascent power of an arising working class but rather to maintain traditional forms of social relations and deference, within the pressure-cooker of the expanding seaport. The conflict between the elites arose from the monopoly of economic (control over the port) and political (control over the Corporation) authority by the city freemen. The latter ". . . were not only a self-elected body but a family party . . . the immense patronage at their disposal was too often considered as the heirloom of the Corporate family" (Fraser, 1976, p.117). "Before the Municipal Reform Act, the Council . . . had looked on itself as the trustee for the small privileged body of Freemen" (Muir, 1907, p.309).

Freemen paid lower Dock dues than non-Freemen, controlled the allocation of warehouses and port facilities, were exempt from town rates, and were solely responsible (until the 1835 Act) for the election of the Parliamentary representative. The conflict between the Freemen and non-Freemen merchants was institutionalized through political party, through local newspapers, and through struggles for control of the focusses of power, other than that of the Corporation the Commissioners of the Watch, and the Select Vestry.

The latter, set up under the Select Vestries Act, 1819, was an agent of political and social reform in its own right. As the apparatus statutorily obliged to enforce the Poor Law, in that context, it set the standard for police reform. It was already in the 1820s attempting to distinguish between the deserving and undeserving poor.[10] Expenditure on poor relief was reduced despite the population growth, by screening all applicants (Muir, 1907). When a decade later, the plans for New Police were being debated, this principle of the efficient application of resources was uppermost.

It was the Select Vestry which, in 1835, first mooted in detail the construction of a New Police in the city, pre-empting the Municipal Corporation Act. Through a fluctuation of merchant politics, the Vestry at the time was under the control of the Freemen elite, while the Commissioners of the Watch were controlled by the Dissenting Whig merchants. In other words, the original plan for police reform came not from the reforming Whigs and Liberal, but from within the established elite. The conflict that ensued over what became popularly known (in the Liberal Press, at least) as the "Parson-Police Bill" was *not* over the desirability of police reform but rather over the question of *control* (and financing) of the proposed force.

The Select Vestry's Police Bill proposed the establishment of a new force of day constables, financed largely by the Corporation (which was soon to have a much larger electorate) but controlled jointly by three Commissioners—the

Mayor and two churchwardens. The Commissioners were to possess sole rights of appointment and dismissal of constables, could arm the force as they thought fit, and were to be empowered to levy whatever rate was required to finance the force (*Liverpool Mercury*, 27th February, 1835). The opposition emphasized the issues of control, of finance, of alleged subsidy to the clergy resulting from the Bill, and the failure to consolidate the Day and Night police into one body (*Liverpool Albion*, 9th March, 1835).

However, the rival merchants were hindered in their resistance to the proposed force by two factors. The Tories had captured the remaining oppositional citadel of the Commissioners of the Watch, and that body, reversing its previous position, had voted in favour of the Day Police Bill. Secondly, according to the *Liverpool Mercury* (5th June, 1835), petitioners against the Bill were denigrated (the *Liverpool Standard*, a Tory newspaper, described them as "Irish Paupers" and "pig-drivers") and a substantial number of the petition signatures were stolen from the Mercury Office.

But this antagonism from within the merchant class, was not against the *intention* of a new reformed police. When the Day Police Bill was defeated in the House of Lords, there was continuing pressure from both merchant elites, Whig and Tory, for police reform. For example, the *Liverpool Albion*, which had been violently opposed to the "Parson-Police Bill", urged

> . . . the necessity of the establishment of a Day Police. The want of such a force is universally admitted. But why do the Magistrates not establish an efficient police? The money they now spend on inefficient force would, if properly applied maintain an efficient body. (20th April, 1835)

Immediately after the implementation of the extended franchise, as required by the Municipal Corporations Act, the Liberal elite captured the new Liverpool Council, formed a new Watch Committee from its own nominees, and constructed a force that replaced both Day constables and Night Watch with a united force. Within six months, this New Police was being assailed from the ranks of the protagonists of the previous proposal.

The *Liverpool Mail* used a number of cases of police violence to sharpen its attack, commenting sarcastically on the ". . . outrage committed on the person of Mr. Marky by a policeman . . . Under the new system of our patriot council, an Englishman may not indulge himself in a hearty laugh (without being assaulted)" (20th September, 1836). A High Tory newspaper, it followed up these allegations the following month with some powerful polemic. The New Police are charged with being:

> venal and inquisitorial . . . acting under instruction that would have disgraced Venice in the most despotic and corrupt period of its history . . .

constables are directed to consider every man (not a member of the Council) to be a rogue and every woman to be an accomplice sharing in the rogue's spoils . . . the system of the New Police, as it prevails in this town under the exclusive direction of the Corporation would not be tolerated in Venice or Algiers. It is domiciliary visitation in its worst form, it is local tyranny in its most frightful state . . . under the pretext of discouraging vice, it gains a knowledge of every person's character and occupation, in order that a influence might be exerted over him by the Police . . . instructions . . . given by certain members of the Council to the petty officers and constables have been of such a nature to make the police the masters of their employees and that some of the men obtained by these a hold over the Council, that the latter dare not dismiss them in any circumstance . . . (16th October, 1836).

An earlier reply to a similar invective sums up the Liberal view of these attacks by the usurped old Freemen elite:

It has afforded us great satisfaction to read the presentiment of the Grand Jury expressing their high opinion of our New Police, who have been so foully and scandalously libelled by the tools of Tory freedom . . . All the rogues and vagabonds raised an outcry against these invaders 'of their sacred rights' as all our vested right men in Liverpool, happened to be Tories. (*Liverpool Chronicle*, 8th July, 1836)

But, significantly, the most vehement and detailed replies to the Tory criticisms, and particularly to attacks on the police by the Licensed Victuallers (concerned about the new practice of police inspection of public houses), came from the first Head Constable, James Whitty (*Liverpool Chronicle*, 16th October, 1836). Although humbly phrased, and innocuously ignoring his practical discretionary powers, the office of Head Constable was of sufficient status for him to engage in public debate to defend his force. There was no question of Whitty, the former head of the Night Watch[11] displaying the reticence of later officials of the local state; from the outset the role of the Liverpool chief police officer was plainly not one of servitude.

Despite the early invective between the old and new elites, the differences in relation to the new police apparatus remained at the level of rhetoric. In 1841, after an interregnum of five years' Liberal rule, the Tories re-captured the Council, and with it the majority of seats on the Watch Committee. Examination of the records of the Watch Committee[12] and of the contemporary Press, provides *no evidence of any perceptible change in the relationship to Whitty, the Head Constable, and to the force and its operations generally, from that of the previous Liberal administration.* Indeed, criticism of the New Police had largely disappeared from the local press two years earlier.

Brewer notes the essential similarity of objectives and of intentions with regard to all the apparatus of the developing local state, by both class fractions. *Once the distinction between the rights of Freemen and non-Freemen had disappeared, they were indistinguishable in their view of the police function in sanitising and containing the lower classes.* Whilst elsewhere, power in the cities had been transferred to men with different backgrounds and economic interests to that of the old governing classes, "this was not so in Liverpool . . ." (1968, p.9). Thompson has claimed that as a rule, police reform represented a victory for the local middle classes of shopkeepers and of new manufacturers ". . . the local bourgeoisie triumphed absolutely" (1978, p.52). In Liverpool the old regime, and a modernized version of the old policing system, designed to separate the secondary economy and habitations of the labouring poor, from the commerce and residences of the wealthy, remained in post.

## The Political Relation 1836–1910

Mercantile hegemony over the city remained intact throughout the nineteenth century. Consequently, the primary functions of police work, and the most visible representation of police activities, continued to be those of urban social engineering and hygiene. Policing was a prophylactic against contagion from the urban mass. The social structure of the city changed little until the end of the century, when industrial concentration began to emerge, and changes in police form in imitation of the forces of manufacturing towns began to develop.[13] As the century progressed, there was a decline in the *general* direction of the force by the dominant city class of merchants, through the Watch Committee. Although the potential for intervention remained (and surfaced occasionally), by the beginning of the twentieth century, the chief officer had obtained a high degree of autonomy. Through a variety of stratagems—taking advantage of conflicts between class fractions to establish an independent position; exercising professional knowledge to demonstrate the fallibility of political intent; practising legal discretion to avoid clear directives; and falling back on the organizational opposition at patrol level to duties that were inimical to occupational life; the independence of the prospective urban police manager grew gradually. But it was an autonomy structured on one hand, by routinized organizational practices, evolved early in the life of the force, and on the other, by the constraints of the dominant problematic of the merchant class (the requirements of confinement and control) on police function.

The continuing authority of the merchant class in the city is demonstrated in Figs 2 and 3. From 1836 to 1910 the only class represented in any strength on the Watch Committee and amongst the magistrates, was that of the merchants and shipowners. The first female member is not recorded until 1905. Despite schisms over waterworks, over sanitation improvement, and more relevantly,

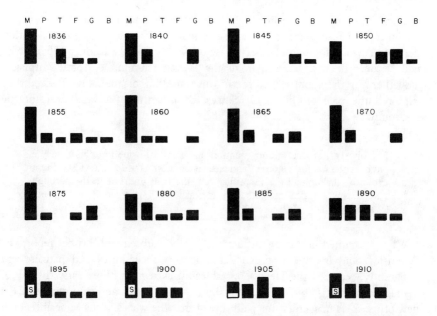

Fig. 2. Occupation of Liverpool Watch Committee Members, 1836-1910.

over the control of vice and over the promulgation of temperance, the male merchants maintained a general unity over the objects of police work.

Whigs and Tories alike were committed to the routinization of police work as the practice of control at the interface of the secondary economy. The policing function was to regularize, map-out, define and patrol the boundaries, both

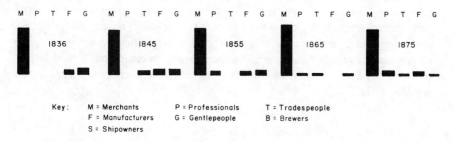

Key: M = Merchants     P = Professionals     T = Tradespeople
F = Manufacturers     G = Gentlepeople     B = Brewers
S = Shipowners

Fig. 3. Occupation of magistrates, 1836-1875.

physical and social, of the lower class communities. In the construction of the organizational form necessary to these functions, there was close collaboration between the developing police expertise of Whitty and the leading Liberal who had become the first Chairman of the Watch Committee, John Walmsley. Together, in the months before the inauguration of the New Police, they explored the pale of the lower classes, documenting the conditions of the residuum:

> I resolved to arouse public attention and stimulate public opinion to the pitch necessary for vigorous and decisive action. To do this, I set about exploring through all their ramifications, the dens of crime in the borough . . . it was a loathsome task to undertake but I pursued it to the end. (Walmsley, 1879, p.80)

Whitty claimed a major influence on the subsequent crime report by Walmsley, and on the proposed detailing of police duties and patrols, and apparently, received the Head Constableship as reward. This early display of managerial expertise by Whitty contributed to the status and importance of the new office. The new chief was paid three times the wages of his Superintendent deputies, and was allocated free housing, thus emphasizing that while the Head Constable might be the servant of the Watch, he was perceived considerably differently from his men.

During the first eleven years of the force, the constraints, and directions by the Watch were severe. A sub-committee of the Watch met daily to supervise police operations. During the first five years, the Watch issued an average of one order a week for the direct placement of police officers.[14] These commands which were, indeed, imperatives, stemmed directly from requests for police services from local property-holders, from shopkeepers, from residents, from theatres and circus proprietors, and from other committees of the Council. Judging by the street addresses of these requests (W.C. Orders) the demands on the police apparatus flowed directly from the wealthy elite, and the associated trading class. The New Police were used directly to demarcate the territories of the dominant classes in the city—the merchants, the shopkeepers, and the new professional and white-collar strata—from the territories of the poor. The preponderance of requests (some 90%) and subsequent commands—were for the control of the streets, and associated recreational contexts. For example, on 3rd March, 1837:

> . . . that the Head Constable gives particular directions respecting the disorderly persons congregating nearly all night at the bottom of James Street, and also of the disorderly company all night in the back part of the White Bear, Public House, Dale Street, and the Tap of the Commerce Inn,

in Davizes Street, reported being full of company on a Sunday during divine service. (W.C. Orders)

The subjects of police work—"disorderly boys", "children trundling hoops", "rough characters", "prostitutes", "hawkers", "Arab children", and adults playing "pitch-and-toss"—were penalized as the source of mercantile discomfort. In the transmission of those complaints, the Watch Committee (or rather the Daily Sub-Committee) was little more than conduit through which class demands were articulated into practice. The only resistance (as recorded in the Order Books) by the Watch, is to those requests for police services which the members considered were directly related to profit-making activities.

Police operations throughout these early years were effectively under control of the mercantile class. However, no specific policies emerge during the period apart from via the general standardization of police work as street patrolling and cleansing. It was the regularization of street activities, which was demanded, and the notion of crime contributed only marginally. While there clearly were, as Gattrell says of Victorian policing, ". . . random police forays into the back streets . . . to reap reach harvest of casual offenders who were there for picking, who had always been there, and who unlike their contemporary counterparts, had no cultural camouflage to protect them" (1980, p.265) in an echo of Mayhew routine police work was confined to encounters with participants in the secondary economy, or with casual labourers, as they occupied in work or in recreation, the streets bordering the commercial and middle-class residential districts. Despite this pervasive degree of direct control by the mercantile class, there is some early indication of attempts to eliminate the discretionary powers of the chief officer (". . . that the Head Constable report all cases, where information have been ordered by the Committee and which are not sent before the Magistrates, with the reasons for not sending them . . .".[15] But in general, apart from the responses to individual complaints and except when new tasks were added to the police function (such as the inspection of Lodging Houses) the New Police were largely left to conduct their duties as their commander thought fit. Although occasionally subject to rebuke by the magistrates over the reliability of their evidence or their mode of operation (for example, in the controversial use of plain clothes officers to inspect Licensed Houses), by the late 1840s police officers occupied a law enforcement domain with wide boundaries.

Due apparently to the commercial requirements of their business life (Watch Committee members, like their Freemen predecessors found policing duties an inconvenient interruption in their work-life), to the uncontroversial (to the merchants) features of police work, and to pressures for autonomy from within the police organization, the Daily Board was abolished in 1847. (A visit to the neighbouring Manchester Police, at the instigation of the Liverpool Head

Constable, had demonstrated to the satisfaction of the Watch that the police could function without daily directive control.)

By this date, the middle of the nineteenth century, the Watch Committee had found itself preoccupied with a range of disparate duties. It had responsibility for the new Fire Police. A sub-committee dealt with Hackney Carriage supervision and regulation. The Watch issued licenses to the Badge-Porters—the baggage handler of the new railway and docks, and sundry other responsibilities had accrued to it, within the general "policing" or regulative function. The priorities of the Watch Committee had become the general control and organization of the city, not the specific duties which fell within the contemporary conception of police work.

The direct political relation between the police and the merchant class was however confused. On occasion, the Head Constable might feel able to defy a direct order from the central pivot of mercantile political rule, the Mayor's office. As early as 1841 (6th February), Whitty was sufficently self-confident to defy an order by the Mayor banning a meeting to be addressed by the Chartist organizer, John O'Connell. Even where there was a measure of agreement between chief officer and Mayor over the desirability of a particular action, the former might take the initiative. For example, in 1867 (12th February), head constable Greig attempted (unsuccessfully) to prevent a series of anti-theological

TABLE I

Written Orders by Head Constable, Liverpool Police 1852-1861.

| Subject | Number | % Age |
|---|---|---|
| Organizational directives | 113 | 41 |
| Dock Patrols | 32 | 12 |
| Police mis-conduct | 31 | 11 |
| Social service work | 14 | 5 |
| Fire precautions | 14 | 5 |
| Traffic control | 12 | 4 |
| Political and religious processions | 11 | 4 |
| Vandalism | 8 | 3 |
| Street disorder | 6 | 2 |
| Licensing problems | 6 | 2 |
| General nuisances | 6 | 2 |
| Sabbath disorder | 5 | 2 |
| Precautions against thieving and crime prevention | 6 | 2 |
| Escaped prisoners | 2 | 1 |
| Character of police | 2 | 1 |
| Thanks from public | 2 | 1 |
| Promotions | 3 | 1 |
| Street obstructions | 1 | 0·3 |

Source: Head Constables Order Book

(and feminist) lectures to which he personally objected. Only late in the day did he invoke Mayoral approval for this entrepreneurial use of legal powers.

Evidently by the 1850s police work had become so routine as to make intervention by the Watch remarkable. Table I documents the total written orders given by Head Constable to his men for a nine year period.[16] The vast majority of directives related to mundane issues such as style of dress, rest-days, and use of truncheons. Secondly came the particular duties of the Dock police, with statements on police behaviour to civilians, and the transmission of complaints individual police officers. Crime, street disorder, and various duties regarding general nuisances received little attention. Either, the street police enjoyed considerable discretion or, as seems more likely, police street work and action against the street populations had become ritualized, by organization and by practice. Already the parameters of police work had been institutionalized. Within those occupational limits, there was little reason by the local ruling class to dispute police operations. Police functions—the patrolling of the streets, the supervision of the visible signs of the secondary economy and of street recreation, as well *as occasional* pursuits into the back streets after a suspected felon—was accepted by both police organization and by Watch Committee, and the grounds for direct intervention by the latter were minimized.

While as Table II demonstrates, there continues to be a stream of letters to the weekly Watch Committee, seeking police presence on the streets and outside the churches and chapels, the matters were increasingly "referred to the Head Constable for attention" by the Watch. That attention, judging by the previous

TABLE II

Demands of Watch Committee Action and Police Deployment,
Liverpool 1836-1872.

| Communication | Number | % Age |
|---|---|---|
| Disorderly street behaviour | 131 | 23·6 |
| Sabbatical disorder | 90 | 16·2 |
| Insulting or incompetent police Officers | 84 | 15·2 |
| Traffic—carriage obstructions etc. | 59 | 10·6 |
| More police required (unspecified) | 36 | 6·5 |
| Street traders (complaints about) | 35 | 6·3 |
| Thieving | 34 | 6·3 |
| Brothels and prostitutes | 29 | 5·2 |
| Vandalism | 15 | 2·7 |
| Gambling and games in streets | 9 | 1·6 |
| Public houses | 7 | 1·2 |
| Night-soil in the streets | 7 | 1·2 |
| Failure to act against strikers | 4 | 0·7 |
| Others | 14 | 2·5 |

Source: Liverpool Watch Committee Mins

table, could at most have resulted in only verbal instruction by the Head Constable to his officers but, in general, these letters do not appear to have been taken as seriously as the earlier direct demands on the Daily Sub-Committee.

After the first few years, the Watch does not seem to have taken much notice of individual letters calling upon police deployment. It rarely requested evidence from the Head Constable of police action, nor did it return to the subject of previous requests.

Further, there is no substantive evidence of the Watch Committee, using the various organizational devices at its command — powers over finance, over promotions, and over discipline — to exert constraints over the Head Constable. Within the compendious content of the formal records, there is no suggestion over the first 75 years of policing of a Head Constable being directly controlled through the financial power (Chapter 4). Similarly, not until the 1930s is there an example of the Head Constable's candidates for promotion being turned down by the Watch Committee. While occasionally the Watch might allow an appeal by a constable against the chief officers' disciplinary action (or more commonly vary the punishment), in nine cases out of every ten throughout the period, 1836-1910, the Watch seems simply to have confirmed the Head Constable's decisions and thus to have reinforced his authority over his officers.

What this summary evidence on the relationship between the police organizations and the Liverpool and the merchant class (as represented through the organ of the Watch Committee), demonstrates is the lack of intervention in policing affairs. After the direct control of the early years, police work became institutionalized with set patterns and fixed practices. Given its agreement with the general functioning of the police, there was no reason why the Watch should interfere. Even during a period in which there was rather more commotion over particular police practices (between 1870 and 1890) a leading member of the Watch could comment dismissively "The work was of a very routine character" after fifteen years service (Forward, 1910, p.100). But in the middle of this "routine work" the authority of the Head Constable was expanding. By turning to that more controversial period, it is possible to illustrate the major strands of that enhanced managerialist authority.

## The Development of Autonomy — The Order to "Proceed against Brothels"

The references by Fosdick and Marshall (quoted earlier) to the direction of the Liverpool Head Constable by the Watch Committees are intended to make different points. Fosdick, in what has become a standard reference point within police orthodoxy, argued that that the head Constable was little more than a tool in the hands of an instrumental and self-motivated Watch Committee. Marshall, referring to the same incident, is concerned only to document an instance in which a Watch Committee contravened the traditional common law discretionary authority of the police constable, by using its powers of sanction under the Municipal Corporations Act. Both, however, imply that on that occasion, the relationship between the Head Constable, Captain Nott Bower, and the Watch Committee was one of unquestioned obedience.

However, the history of that incident suggests a much more complex relation. The instructions to "proceed against all brothels at present known to the police without any delay" and "that such proceedings shall be by way of prosecution and not by mere removal . . ." (W.C. Mins 10th December, 1890) reflect the development of autonomy, not the maintenance of subordination. To understand the background to this apparently definitive control over the police by the Watch Committee some recounting of the background to the case is necessary.

Arguments over beer-house inspection had for many years split the Council and the Watch Committee. The assumed connection between vice and the inspection, or lack of inspection of beer houses (Walmsley, 1879, p.85) had divided both Liberal and Tory fractions almost since the development of the New Police. It had on several occasions been the subject of disputes between the Watch Committees and the Head Constable. The issue of police inspection has also been the grounds for a number of attacks on police evidence by the Licensed Victuallers. In a long report in 1852, the Watch Committee had attributed the vice of the city to the proliferation of beer-houses, and had proceeded to blame the Magistrates for what the Watch described as an over-generous licensing policy (Midwinter, 1968, p.19). The issue had precipitated a running feud between the Justices and the Watch Committee.[17]

For many of the complaints to the Watch Committee, beer-houses were the source of vice and prostitution. Further, it was argued, the illegal profit from the use of the public houses by prostitutes, went to finance the development of brothels.[18]

The campaign against public houses had climaxed in 1878, after considerable pressure from the Liverpool Vigilance Committee (an anti-vice and pro-temperance group), with the Watch Committee ordering the Head Constable to delegate public-house inspection to a selected group of police officers. It reached a further summit when, after a Liberal victory in the Council elections, the whole Council turned itself into the Watch Committee in order to ensure closer supervision of police prosecution of publicans and brothel keepers. ". . . the Watch Committee and the police came to be persuaded that it was their duty not merely to arrest and prosecute drunken persons but to keep a watch upon those publicans who permitted or encouraged drunkenness . . . the police gradually undertook (amid much criticism) the function of driving open vice from the streets" (Muir, 1907, p.326). However, in 1880, fresh local elections removed the temperance majority and the Watch Committee reverted to a smaller and more quiescent membership.

However, during the 1880s, the pressures against vice continued, culminating in a detailed petition from four hundred and fifty ratepayers (W.C. Orders, 3rd December, 1889) which reiterated the view that the public houses were the source of profit for vice and that the police were at fault in not prosecuting the publicans.

*Sensible citizen* — "Say, Captain, can't you give some attention to the Duchesses in the Carriage? The Drabs in the gutter have had enough of it."
*Captain Nott Bower* — "I take my orders from the Watch Committee."
*Sensible citizen* — "Ah!"
*Captain Nott Bower* — "Yes."                                    (from the *Liverpool Review*, 1891)

In reply, the Head Constable provided a complex document that both defended, his discretionary practice, and the rationale for his organizational autonomy. He listed seven criteria from an 1871 Police Instruction Book for determining the appropriateness of prosecutions of brothels — the discretionary determinants. He argued as an expert that prostitution was better controlled by localizing it than by arbitrary prosecutions that dispersed the phenomena over a wider area. He claimed from experience, that both his own and the "unanimous views of the oldest and most experienced officers in the force" that suppression was impossible in a seaport. Finally, he claimed as a legal functionary, that he had not the statutory right to prosecute in many cases.[19] In summary, he utilized all the elements essential to the development of autonomy in the presentation of his case — *legal discretion as a constable under traditional common law, professional expertise, experience as the practitioner* and *judicial knowledge* of the nature of law. Early police managerialism was constituted by these elements.

However, in the short-term, despite this defence, and the Watch Committee's support at the time, he was only given a year's grace. Further petitions (W.C. Orders, 20th May, 1890, and 1st December, 1890) together with a change in the composition of the Watch Committee led to the eventual order against brothels. (But even then the motion was passed with a bare five-four majority, with several members abstaining.)

The Head Constable complied with the direct order and immediately brought large numbers of prosecutions,[20] but the resistance was not at an end. Organizational opposition from within the force hampered the implementation of the policy. But more critically, for the dominant class in the city, counter-petitioners (W.C. Orders, 12th and 19th January) appeared emphasizing the economic consequences of the new policy:

> A deputation in regard to the police raids on immoral houses is to wait on the Watch Committee . . . composed of shopkeepers, and other tradesmen and businessmen from . . . the district raided under the new regime . . . to represent to the Watch Committee that the raids on immoral houses only serve to increase the social evil by distributing it over a wider area and that the raiding of such districts . . . where for many years past the evil has been centred, and allowed to grow unchecked, disorganises businesses and will prove financially disastrous to shopkeepers of the neighbourhood. (*Liverpool Review*, 17th January, 1891)

This business opposition, while not immediately successful, when conflated with the organizational resistance, and the importance of prostitution, within the secondary economy, to the form of labour in the city, ensured that the policy of prosecution of brothels could not be successful in the long-term. In other words, although the Head Constable lost the immediate battle, the case demonstrated both the composition of his developing managerial status, and the extent to which the policing problematic — the policing function — could not be determined by directives from the Watch, as representative of the dominant class, but was related ultimately to the nature of the economy of the city, and the balance of economic forces within it. The mode of production, especially the dependence of the merchants upon seamen, created the demand for prostitution, and the profits from prostitution promoted the well-being of small-scale capitalists in the city. Policing was related to the balance of class forces, in the long term, and the chief's legal relation (his discretionary powers under common law — Chapter 5) in particular, facilitated him taking advantage of that balance.

## The Construction of the Managerial Role

By the time Nott Bower left the force for the Commissionership of the City of London police, the relative autonomy from the dominant mercantile class of chief police officers in Liverpool was assured. The record of the activities of his successor Dunning[21] demonstrates the reinforcement of the police managerial attributes.

That officer in response to calls for police services (for example, Head Constable's Report Book, 12th July, 1904) and in his balancing of the "public interest" (Head Constable's Report Book, 21st September, 1904), demonstrates discretionary powers, professional expertise, police experience (he had been Nott Bower's Deputy), and an ability to interpret legal statutes to his own advantage. Within the parameters of the economic structure of the city, the independence of the chief police officer was already considerable before the outbreak of the first World War.

However, when Rathbone, a leading local merchant and social reformer, opposed earlier attempts to force the Liverpool police to act against the beer-houses, he pointed obliquely to the constraints on that autonomy:

> When attempts are made to enforce laws for which the moral sense of the community has not been sufficiently prepared, they have increasingly been disobeyed and evaded, respect for the law weakened, illicit drinking, and all kinds of fraud and deception increased, and the police demoralised".
> (Rathbone, 1905, p.252)

If one substitutes for Rathbone's "moral sense" a notion of economic determinism in relation to the connection between the mode of production of the city and the forms of recreation and of street economy, and for "the police demoralised", an appreciation of the organizational, occupational and discretionary resistance of police officers, of all ranks to unpopular legislation, then the constraints on the chief officer become clear.

By the 1900s, the Head Constable of the city exercised considerable latitude of decision-making based on expertise, discretionary powers, experience, and knowledge of the relevant statutes. But he was confined to a limited autonomy. He was restricted first by the relation between the mode of production and the objective character of the police problematic, and secondly, by the extent to which orders transmitted by his office were subject to interpretation and discretionary enforcement by rank-and-file police officers.

Finally, the argument in this chapter has in part been addressed to the conventional thesis that political intervention was a major feature of the relationship between Head Constables and Watch Committees in the nineteenth century. The evidence on that point is confused because the relationship itself is more complex, and subject to continuing development. At the outset, the Liverpool Watch Committee and the dominant mercantile class directly controlled the local force, but within a few years police operations had become routinized and most issues of contention had disappeared. The police institution functioned as the body charged with separating-out the "criminal classes" from the "respectable classes" and eased the social and economic life of the mercantile class, while becoming organizationally more and more independent of that class.

However, on occasions, in relation to particular matters such as vice and alcohol, the Watch—or rather the class that it represented—disputed aspects of the police function. But the Watch Committee's interventions on those matters were not successful in the long term owing to the economic relations within the city on which both the merchants and the police depended. The central contradiction, that a merchant class required casual labourers and in various other ways, spawned a secondary economy which posed problems of street disorder, remained. The merchants' livelihood required the disorder they wished the police to quell, or at least keep out of sight. This contradiction created the political space within which the chief police officer and his juniors developed their increasing independence of action.

# Notes

1. This strata of lower white-collar workers is particularly important in the police history of the city in that it regularly provided the reserve of special constables for use in conflicts between the police and the lower classes.
2. Liverpool fences were described by Walmsley, the first Chairman of the Watch Committee, in his major report on crime in the city (see later), as the primary cause of vice and law violations.
3. An 1842 study by John Finch claimed that a large part of the population of the Vauxhall area had no *visible* income, supporting themselves by pawning, prostitution, or "charity". (F. J. Finch, *Social Statistics of Vauxhall Ward*.) See on this Tobias (1974).
4. Perhaps an over-rated point. Muir (1907) notes that 1-in-4 of the population in 1824, is recorded as having been treated in the city dispensaries.
5. See Miller (1977) for London evidence of police concentrations on these boundaries in the 1830s and 1840s.
6. See, for example, on this point, the *Liverpool Chronicle*, 3rd March, 1836.
7. Brooke (1853), using contemporary newspaper accounts, gives a vivid and detailed account of this first recorded labour conflict in the city's history. Shipowners, faced with a surplus of labour, withdrew one-third of the promised pay to the sailors on a vessel. The latter occupied the ship in protest but a number were arrested by the

Liverpool constables. Other seamen struck in sympathy and marched to the Cotton Exchange to protest. Several of them were killed by shots from the merchants in the Exchange. The enraged sailors brought up ships' cannon to bombard the Town Hall and occupied the town for a week before being dispersed by outside militia.

8. Robinson (1978, pp.133-4) makes the point that many of these comments reflect the "... scent of upper-class contempt of lower-class life and may actually hide dissatisfaction with the close association between the constable and his assigned victim". Phillips (1980, p.160) offers a reasoned defence of the constable in the Metropolis.

9. Soon after the Municipal Corporations Act, 1835, the local Tories formed a Tradesmen Conservative Association, and the Liberals, a Tradesmen Reform Association (Fraser, 1975).

10. Compare this comment with the reference to Walker (1977) (Chapter 8) on police service work in the nineteenth century. Miller (1977) documents Edwin Chadwicks's emphasis on police service work as the way to legitimacy.

11. Dowling, the Superintendent of the Docks Police, became his deputy in 1837, and later Head Constable himself. One-third of the Inspectors of the New Police were drawn from the Night Watch.

12. Liverpool Watch Committee Minutes, and Orders to the Head Constable, 1836-1851.

13. Significantly, the first major labour-capital disputes in which the police were engaged, involved not industrial workers but trade unionists in the transport field — tramway workers in 1879 and seamen and transport workers in 1910-11.

14. Between 1836 and 1841, 243 direct operational commands were issued by the Watch Committee to the Head Constable (W.C. Orders).

15. The Watch Committee temporarily attempted to stall the development of the chief's autonomy. On 8th August, 1839, for example, it reprimanded the Head Constable for taking independent decisions over street patrolling.

16. This data is abstracted from an analysis of the sole surviving Head Constable's Order Books in which the Watch required him to note all orders given to the force.

17. Examples of conflicts — Watch Committee v. Head Constable over beer houses, 2nd February, 1841; Licensed Victuallers v. Head Constable, 8th June, 1848, 29th December, 1859; Watch Committee v. Magistrates over Licensing, 1st May, 1852. (W.C. Mins.)

18. In an extraordinary case in 1859, the Head Constable had been bound-over by the Magistrates, at the request of the Society for the Prosecution of Places of Vicious Resort for note "... prosecuting the owners of disorderly houses" (W.C. Orders, 1st April, 1859). In 1862, the Magistrates initiated a controversial experiment of free licensing in order to destroy the monopoly value of licenses and thereby to decrease the assumed availability of profit for vice investment (Rathbone, 1905, p.253). On the specific accusation of Watch Committee partiality over vice and drink prosecutions, see Waller (1981, p.106).

19. From H.C. Report Book, 23rd December, 1889, "Report on Houses of Ill-Fame".

20. The statistics on prosecutions of brothel keepers show the dramatic, if temporary, effects of the new policy — October (2 prosecutions), November (6), December (342), January (32), February (54), March (61), April (59), May (53), June (60), July (43), August (45), September (61). (Source — H.C. Annual Report, 1891). Although it may have been mere coincidence, the Head Constable took an unprecedented month's holiday, immediately after the passing of the resolution. According to Nott Bower himself, the brothels were cleaned-up statistically, but not in practice (Nott Bower, 1926, p.140). The order was effectively rescinded in 1896 (Cockroft, 1974).

21. Dunning was an extraordinary police officer for his time. His Annual Reports were

primarily concerned with critiques of conventional wisdom over the police role, over reliance on criminal statistics, over the handling of drunks and the mentally ill, and over methods of dealing with juvenile delinquents and youthful traders. Despite the fact that he is mainly remembered in labour history for the police brutality during sectarian troubles in the city in the 1900s, and the savage events of the 1911 Transport Strike (Chapter 7), he stands out historically as a major contributor to the development of police professionalism, and was a protypical "academic" police officer.

# 3 The Chiefs and the Local State Since the 1964 Police Act

The Chief Constable . . . must turn his eyes increasingly towards Whitehall via the Inspector and away from the local authority, which he can use at best as a most useful medium of public relations, and as a quartermaster less tightfisted that the word traditionally implies. (Sir I. Jacob, 'The Future of the Police' Police Journal, 1967, pp.309-320)

## Introduction

In the last chapter, the political relation between the nineteenth century Watch Committee and the Liverpool Police Forces was explored. Examples were given of the conventional wisdom over the intervention of economic and political interests into the policing of the city. It was argued that these interventions after the early routinization of police work, were rare. Where they occurred they related to police practices not to a challenge to the general police function. The traditional commentators, by concentrating on the political relation alone, ignored the crucial issues—the inter-dependence between police form and the local economy, and the slow development of the autonomy of the chief police officer. A similar scheme is adopted in this chapter. Through an analysis of the contemporary relation between the chief officer and the new Police Authority (the successor to the Watch Committee), twin themes are developed. The direct political relation between the functionary and the Authority has been substantially altered. The latter no longer has a specific relation to the economy of the city. Local economic relations are now subsumed under national and multi-national interests.

The determination of police function therefore relates not to particular local problems but to factors beyond the influence of the local elite. The managerial authority of the chief officer has developed considerably compared with that of his predecessors in the 1900s. The chief officer is a major figure in local society. When contrasted with the diminishing economic power of the civic elite, traditionally representative of that local and indigenous capital which monopoly capital is continually displacing, the chief officer's status as an expert on crime and disorder, gives the local police, as an institution, considerable autonomy from city hall.

Academic orthodoxy has sought to legitimize this developed autonomy. According to one eminent legalist, writing in the house magazine of the Police Staff College about the inclusion of magistrates on the post-1964 Police Authorities: "This mixture is intended to ensure that the authority is a-political, but recent experiences suggest that this aspiration is not always fulfilled" (Card, 1979, p.11). The argument was developed that local politicians were interfering too often in the expert province of the chief officer, dealing with him in partisan fashion, just as they treated housing managers, education officers, and other functionaries of the local state!

Marshall (whose work in the mid-sixties represented the classic statement on the constitutional relation between the state and the police) more recently commented:

> . . . suppose that the Watergates, Poulsons, and Clay Crosses are not unique
> . . . an unrepeatable phenomenon. Nobody's faith in councillors . . . can
> be as firm as it was fifteen years ago . . . if . . . in the field of law enforcement
> we have to give a calculated and unprejudiced answer . . . to the question
> whether civil liberties and impartial justice are more to be expected
> chief constables than from elected politicians . . . many liberal democrats
> would feel justified in placing more trust in the former . . . (Marshall,
> 1978, p.60)

These latter views reflect the new consensus. The chief police officer is now seen as an impartial public manager, seeking to grapple with complex but politically unproblematic issues of crime and social order, against a background of partisan ("political") pressure as well as under the handicap of severe resource constraints. In contrast to the chief officer's informed use of discretionary powers, the municipal representatives display political commitment in policing, as elsewhere, within the police institution itself (see, for example, *Police*, 1980, 12), and among academic commentators, the gist of conservative opinion is that Police Authorities are increasingly intervening, in a partisan manner, in ways where they have insufficient technical knowledge and expertise.

In the next section of this chapter the nuances within the various commentaries on the present-day relation between the police and local authorities are outlined. It is argued, however, that these approaches reduce questions over that relation to a discussion of a particular formula—the significance of the 1964 Police Act —and fail to appreciate the structural location of the police apparatus. The second part of this chapter situates the present crisis of the local state, with its direct implication for the police institution, within the context of the national and international economy. The peculiarity of local state—police relations, and the increasing independence of the chief officer, it is argued, can only be understood if three factors are considered: by (i) the rise of the politically interventionist central state, (ii) changes in the organization of local government as a whole (the birth of the corporate manager); (iii) the fiscal crisis of capitalism as it affects the various apparatuses of the local state. All three factors are related together through changes in the structure of capital.

The content and form of the local relation is then examined using evidence about the working of the Liverpool and Bootle Police Authority, the successor to the old Watch Committee, before it was itself replaced, following further reorganization, by the Merseyside Police Committee. It is adduced that while some of the defence of that committee to the chief police offer relates to the latter's scope for material manipulation, the relation between the police committee and the chief officer is also related to changes in economic, political, and organizational forms beyond the confines of the city and, indeed, beyond the boundaries of any interpersonal contact between senior police officers and municipal representatives.

## The Orthodox Analyses: Exegesis and Critique

The general debate in the late 1970s and early 1980s over the relationship of the police to the state and the citizenry has been limited to a discussion of the effectiveness or ineffectiveness of the formulae through which the present relation has been constitutionally constructed. That critique has been constrained by the reduction of that relation to the simple product of legal relations, as embodied (or rather not embodied) in the 1964 Police Act.

Some 135 years after the initial legislation establishing professional policing in mainland Britain, the 1964 Police Act was the first attempt to standardize the relationship between the police institution and the central and local states. Its passage swept away a myriad of random statutes and practices enacted at various times since 1829.

By the 1964 Act, the Powers of the new Police Authorities were limited to five main functions: (i) ensuring the efficiency and adequacy of the local force; (ii) appointing the Chief Constable and his immediate deputies; (iii) determining (in liaison with the Home Office) the size of the police establishment;

(iv) providing the appropriate buildings and equipment; (v) overseeing the complaints procedure.

The Chief Constable was required to provide annual reports to the police authority, and additionally, to prepare occasional reports "as might be necessary" on any matter of operational significance in the police area. But the latter requirement was subject to a proviso. He need not provide the report when he believed it not to be in the public interest to disclose the information, or when he considered it to be unnecessary for the discharge of the police authority's function. (The Home Secretary was to be the arbiter in those cases.)

All other powers were vested in the chief officer. He was to be solely responsible for the direction and control of the force, and for appointments, promotions and discipline of all ranks below Command level. The Police Authority lost its right to hear appeals by junior officers against the disciplinary decisions of the Chief Constable.

Finally, the committee was re-constituted, moving towards the county police practice (the Standing Joint Committee) where half the members had been local magistrates. On the new Police Authorities, one third of the elected representatives were replaced by non-elected justices from the local Magistrates Bench.

Three marginally different (if not exclusive) interpretations have been placed upon the Police Act. Leigh (1973), for example has argued that the lack of power of Police Authorities to influence their Chief Officers, reflects the spirit of the original ethos of policing in Britain. Secondly, a number of commentators, have argued that the Police Act left the substantive power of the local representatives unaffected, because they had always been able to exercise informal influence over the Chief Constable. Finally, the view is held in some quarters that the Police Act was a major step in the reduction of the local community's powers over the police.

Leigh argues that the Act brought to the surface the principles originally embedded in policing in Britain:

> . . . the relative weakness of the local police authorities . . . reflects the fact that it was never intended that such authorities should seek to control the police in the exercise of their functions. The Police Act, by investing the Chief Constable with such responsibilities, responded to the very high value placed upon the principle that the Chief Constable should be free from the conventional process of democratic control and influence in relation to operational matters. (1973, p.867)

Certainly, the precedents of policing in Britain support this perspective. The Thames River Police were accountable only to their employers, not to any elected council. Robert Peel's experiment in policing (in 1814), the Irish Peace Preservation Force, and the later Royal Irish Constabulary, were both governed not by democratic representatives but by non-elected magistrates (Breathnach, 1974). Similarly, the Metropolitan Police Act 1829, itself made no provision for direct accountability. Indeed, the source of the democratic relation, as was seen in the last chapter, came about not through any principle of representation but as a consequence of the determination of local elites to find a more effective way of controlling lower class intrusions. From the police institution itself, a managerialist defence of the perceived intentions of the Act:

> . . . most political demonstrations, processions, industrial disputes . . . involve criminal offences in respect of which a chief constable and his officers have individual responsibility. Few of these operations are suitable for democratic control since situations change very quickly and serious results may only be averted by prompt action by the officer in charge . . . (Byford, 1975)

According to the rigid managerialist perspective, the 1964 Act supported in statute the common-sense assumption that democracy is an unnatural intrusion into the expert practice of social control by professional police officers. The discretionary actions of the chief officers are conducted under the influence of expert training, based on experience, relate to an objective appreciation of all relevant interests, including the appropriateness of the particular legislation. In other words, the Act effected by statute what Nott Bower and Dunning had claimed as their due, at the turn of the century.

A variation on this argument suggests that while, in general, police chiefs are left alone to exercise their professional judgement, they remain open to unofficial advice and "soundings". Police Authority members, irrespective of the Police Act, both before and since, have always found informal channels through which issues could be raised with the chief officer (Wilcox, 1974). Prior to the Police Act, one commentator (Keith-Lucas, 1960) had noted the apparent willingness of senior police officers to take cognisance of a Watch Committee's views, on a matter such as a parking restriction, while denying it the right to intervene in criminal matters. Several Chief Constables have reinforced this point on later years. Byford (1975) in a debate with academic critics on the powers of police authorities, emphasized the informal consultations over minor matters with his East Anglian Police Authority. More recently, Pain expressed satisfaction with his relation with the Kent Police Authority:

> . . . some of the Police Authority held that they should have an operational say but through very diplomatic and open discussion, it was pointed out that the chief constable is entirely autonomous. Now we have in Kent a situation of mutual respect: I'm left to get on with the job. Everyone knows that I can be approached . . . about problems. (1978, pp.6–7)

But this blandness conceals the difficulty of determining which matters can be raised with the chief officer and which cannot. One chief officer may regard most police matters—policy, deployment, or operations—as open to scrutiny. Byford argues that most chief officers do provide considerable information, without it being actively solicited. Kettle (1980d) makes a similar point with regard to the chief of the Thames Valley Police.

But equally, the chief officer may enforce a narrow rule regarding the provision of information. After the "death in custody" case in Merseyside, the Chief Constable ruled out of debate various other incidents in the same police division, apparently unrelated to the particular case. He told the re-titled Police Committee that they should "keep . . . out of his force's business". "He will report to them, he told a meeting of councillors . . . in his own time . . ." (*Economist*, 13th October, 1979).

The Chief Officer controls the supply of information to the Police Committee. He is aware that the police authority is unlikely to use its powers under Section 12 of the Police Act to ask the Secretary of State to order him to provide a Report against his wishes. Only one such case has occurred since 1964 and on that unique occasion, the Home Secretary supported the chief police officer's refusal (*Hansard*, 12th November, 1977).

Finally, one view of the 1964 Police Act held firmly in local government circles is that the statute significantly reduced the effective constraints over policing. The Willink Commission, despite fulsome opposition by the municipal authorities, had assumed unquestioningly that they would play a lesser role in the future. Progress in policing meant a reduction in the formal rights of the local police authority.

While the Commission re-affirmed the local organizational structure, of the police institution (while encouraging some force amalgamations), as well as confirming the conception of the police officers as a citizen-in-uniform, it proposed that the local political relation be reduced to those ". . . matters affecting the public interest . . ." which were construed as ". . . the regulation of traffic, political demonstration, strikes, processions, and public order generally" (Marshall, 1978, p.58). From the Commission's perspective, crime had grown, and crime control techniques had correspondingly become more complex. Local authorities were no longer competent in their understanding of the phenomenon, and were too parochial in their concerns to be able to offer anything positive to contemporary police crime-work. Local control had been relevant to the parish pump policing of the 1860s but not to the national crime problems of the 1960s. But, on the other hand, the common law tradition required some local continuity.

The conclusion was drawn by local authorities, that irrespective of the delineation of the relative powers of elected representatives and police chiefs, in the Act itself, the body of argument in the Report was directed against them. When coupled with the change in the composition of the Police Authorities, and the diminution in the specific rights over the force, in the Act, the net effect was to relegate the Police Authorities to a lesser role.

But the outcome of the debate about the Act was not entirely negative from the perspective of the Police Authorities. While some members subscribed to the "informal channels" thesis, others (Simey, 1979) argued that the Act's failure to clarify the relative powers of chief and Police Authority (particularly over the confused divide between operations and policy), was actually a source of strength. A politically conscious Police Authority could exploit the vagueness of the Police Act by requiring explanations of most police work in its area. The operational designation could be limited to the detail of situational encounters with the public while the rubric of policy could be vastly extended. Explanatory accountability powers were of some significance. If only Police Authority members recognized their right to "call for reports", they would use them. The problem of local control of the police was not so much lack of power but rather ignorance of the existing power of explanation.

Despite this optimism, these latter arguments are constricted by their a-historical and a-structural character. They reduce the problem of the political relation of the police apparatus to one of interpretation (or to a re-worded Police Act[1]).

There is no acknowledgement of the historical development of police autonomy, nor account of the implications for the relationship of changes in the local state, central state relation since the development of the early police. Nor is there any consciousness of class relations of both police institution and Police Authority. It is naively assumed that at some golden age in the past, local communities controlled their own police, and a democratic relation existed between the two.

The alternative view is that irrespective of changes in the appreciation of their powers by Police Authority members, the economic and political changes ensured the decline of the strength of the local political relation.

Developments in the interventionist practice of the central state, the enhancement of the urban managerial (or corporate management) role and, fundamentally, changes in the economic relation of the city, are the central factors.

## The Demise of the Local Political Relation

### The corporate manager and the decline of the local state

The orthodox critics of the Police Authority—police institution relation ultimately flounder because of their failure to locate changes in a larger context.

In this section, the direct relation between the chief police officer, as a state functionary, and the local police committee, is placed within the political and economic changes in the central-local state relation. In the nineteenth century, as was demonstrated in the last chapter, police functions were structured by the mode of production in the city. The dependence of the merchant class in Liverpool upon casual labour resulted in police organization taking a particular form—the confining of the lower classes to their areas of habitation, and attempting to constrain those aspects the secondary economy, and of street recreation, that impinged upon the affairs of the respectable classes.

The policing apparatus in the 1970s, in the city, reflected styles routinized in the early years—the commitment to particular organizational forms, the occupational culture, the type of patrol and of deployment. But the social control that it was required to maintain no longer related directly to the problem of coping with the particular contradictions generated through the city's economy. Three inter-related processes had led to a re-constitution of the direction of police work.

After World War I, the heyday of imperialism (from which the city, through its trading base, had been a prime beneficiary) was over. The Port of Liverpool, and its dependent enterprises, went into decline. The small industrial base of the Merseyside region failed to expand to counter-balance the gradual disintegration of the mercantile economy, and of the forms of small-scale production inter-dependent with it.

Changes in the structure of capital led to a supplanting of the merchant class, as its local interests were slowly subsumed within the wider concerns of multi-national conglomerates such as the Vesteys and Cunard. It lost its internal cohesion and its direct involvement in the economy and social relations of Liverpool. Political decision-making in the city and the conception of the policing problematic related to wider matters than that exemplified by the 1836 desire to keep the lower classes out of Toxteth Park. Political authority became increasingly the prerogative of the central state in a representation of economic interests outside the local context. The local police authority, the descendant of the multi-functional Victorian Watch Committee, lost its powers as part of the gradual movement of political control away from the Liverpool Cotton Exchange to the Boards of the multi-national companies.

Secondly, that disintegration of a quasi-autonomous local political structure was accompanied by the rise of a creature foreshadowed by the personages of Nott Bower and Dunning. In the past the local merchants had attempted to rule directly but had stepped back as they became assured that their local agents were committed to the efficient administration of their interests. As the structure of capital became linked at the national and international level, so did that form of delegation increase. Local decision-making increasingly fell into the hands of functionaries ultimately accountable to corporate bodies beyond the boundaries of the city. Within the police apparatus, as in other arms of the local state, urban (or rather, corporate) managers assumed key roles.

Thirdly, underpinning the later deterioration both in the city's economic position, and in the flexibility of the decision-making process, was an alteration in the base of the local state's revenue. Financial decisions were becoming increasingly constrained by a diminution in the economic source from which revenue was drawn as the central state reacted with constraints to the developing fiscal crisis.

Two types of institutional political change have occurred since the Municipal Corporations Act 1835 (the legal base of local political power). Increasingly, services formerly provided by the local state have become regionalized or nationalized. Secondly, those services, and the few remaining under direct local control, have undergone a process of standardization.

During the nineteenth century, following the precedent set by police development, a variety of service functions accrued to the local state. Through a process of functional differentiation, separate welfare, sanitation, and education departments were set up. In the early twentieth century, local responsibilities for health insurance, for planning controls, and for the provision of housing had been added.

Simultaneous with these developments, local provisions of certain commodities had developed in private entrepreneurial hands—the transport, electricity, coal, and gas companies. Apart from the railways, which had been regionally owned from the outset, the local bourgeoisie had constructed an economic base in the supply of the essential services.

But while these agencies continued to proliferate, as the apparatus of the local state became more intrusive into civil society, a process of state standardization heralded the shift in the fulcrum of power. For example, within the police institution, the early vague requirements of local forces by the new Inspectorate of 1856, were considerably tightened by the post-police strike Desborough Committee of 1919[2]. A concurrent process of systematization, (the price local authorities had to pay in return for central government grants), occurred throughout the other apparatuses of the local state. In other words, while the activities of the local state appeared to be consolidated, throughout the period leading up to the World War II, a shift in power was discernible towards the central administration.

Concurrently, the local base of the private services was disappearing with their absorption into larger capitalist enterprises. This latter centralization process was expedited in the immediate post-war period with the nationalization of key economic areas, and with the implementation of tighter state controls, over the range of welfare provisions. Changes in population distribution, in transport facilities, and in housing policies resulted in large provincial conurbations, no longer susceptible to cohesive local government. Like mediaeval parish churches, now stranded in the midst of depopulated ecclesiastical districts, local councils had retained in essence, the structures and boundaries recognized by the Municipal Corporations Act 1835. The populations had either fled to the new suburbs or been pushed by slum clearance schemes into the housing estates, over the old council boundary.

The central state responded with policies of regionalization and unification. The number of local councils was reduced by three-quarters by the 1972 Local Government Act. Larger corporate units replaced the old municipal governments. There were similar developments in the health service, in particular, and in the provision of police (see Chapter 6), of transport, of education, and social welfare agencies as the services were matched to the new council boundaries.

During these later changes, an ideology of managerialism was spreading. Prompted by the requirements of the new conglomerates for executive delegation, and by the adoption of the Labour Party in the early 1960s of Croslandite conceptions of the relation between the technological revolution and social structure (the replacement of economic classes by status groups stratified according to technical skill), corporate management (Cockburn, 1977, pp.15-19) pervaded the domain of the local state.

Encouraged by the administrative recommendations of the Maud Committee, 1967, the structure of many local councils was gradually altered in a way that devolved substantial decision making powers on the new council executive —the professional planner, housing managers, city engineers, and so on. While the police institution was not directly affected by these internal changes in the structure of local government, an occupational ideology of man-management percolated through the Police Staff College, into the receptive hands of an organization striving to achieve the economic and status rewards that traditionally accompany the possession of "professional" skills. The corporate manager movement influenced, if only indirectly, changes in the self-conceptions of senior police officers. This new variant on managerialism was juxtaposed with the developed rationales for autonomy of the chiefs—discretionary authority, professional expertise, work experience, and legal knowledge. Moreover, their local authority paymasters had similarly come to accept delegation to the new corporate managers. Professional elitism (Cain, 1972) in the police service encountered a favourable local climate.

But these twin processes—political centralization and the development of corporate managerialism—appeared notionally to have an opposing impact, upon the local managers. Political centralization and standardization entailed, by definition, tighter control by the central state over local society. However, corporate managerialism, could be signified as a form of autonomy from both central and local direction. Urban managers, trained in unique skills, brought to the social arena particular expertise, which informed their decisions over the provision of service, and consequently, their functional autonomy. Two denials of the countervailing character of these different forces are possible. The institutional reply would document the ideological and social background relation between the new urban managers and the dominant economic classes. However, although that argument is touched upon later (Chapter 6), the primary constraint over managerial autonomy at the level of the local state, relates to what O'Connor (1971) has called the "fiscal crisis of the state". Local managers are limited in their decision making by the economic contradiction facing an advanced capitalist state, simultaneously committed to preventing a reduction in the rate of profit as well as to preserving the services that ensure the social reproduction of labour. The revenue that the state can raise through taxation declines, O'Connor argues, as the cost of local services increases. Urban managers are trapped between the hammer of diminishing state revenue, and the anvil of the demand for more extensive local services.

The state undertakes three forms of expenditure—social investment, social consumption, and social expense—which may be separately related to central and local government.

Social investment involves those functions necessary to improve the productivity of labour. Private industry benefits from the provision of physical assets, such as roads and communication which are a cost on the state not on industry. It also benefits from human investment—the price of education and training, for example, are borne primarily by the state, not by the employer. Social consumption relates to the conditions of the reproduction of labour. The quality of labour is improved by state subsidies of housing schemes, and by state contribution to health, insurance and pension schemes. Human capital—labour —is provided at a cheaper rate to private industry through state subventions.

Finally, the profitability of productive industry depends upon the maintenance of social order. Two types of agency, legitimating and coercive, are responsible for that stability. Welfare agencies ensure social cohesion, by tending the social residuum—the old, the unemployable and unemployed, the physically handicapped and socially handicapped. The police, the legal, and the penal apparatuses constitute the coercive long-stop, when legitimacy fragments.

The urban managers are constrained by the increasing costs of these forms of expenditure. The functions are essential to the accumulation of profit under the capitalist state, but their cost escalates as the receipts from taxation diminish. Police officers may be hired out to control private functions but, in general, there is no direct return for police services. A major contribution to the increase in costs stems from the social expenses area. The residual population that cannot be absorbed by production constantly expands due to changes in the method of production. More complex productive techniques lessen the demand for labour. Consequently the legitimating and coercive agencies are required to spend more.

However, at the same time that innovations in the method of production lead to less labour being required, and makes that unemployed labour more expensive to maintain, changes within international capitalism lead to a diminution in the state revenue. As production is switched from high-cost labour countries to low-cost countries, the ability of private industry in the advanced capitalist state to pay taxation decreases. There is a smaller tax revenue base from which the state is to pay for the increase in social expenses.

The crisis therefore has two effects. Because in Britain, tax revenue is differentially collected by central and local state there is a disproportionate effect. The local state relies primarily upon revenue from direct taxation through rates, assessed yearly on private householders and on private business. It is hit by the decline in revenue more severely than the central state, and comes to depend upon central state subsidies for the support of the local services. The price it pays for that support is that of increased direction of the local society by the central state. The municipal representatives, and the local business interests lose their power.

Secondly, the central state itself does not escape from the fiscal crisis unscathed. With overall tax revenue diminishing, it is compelled to be more selective in social expenditure priorities. It necessarily intervenes more frequently in those forms of service provision that had previously been determined locally, in order to ensure the most effective response to the economic crisis.

The results of this for the urban manager are clear. His autonomy depends upon freedom from economic constraints. But the development of the corporate manager as a functionary on the local government scene in Britain, coincided with the intensification of the fiscal crisis.

However, paradoxically, particular forms of urban manager may temporarily benefit from the crisis. If the central state response, given its perception of the social form of the crisis, (the conjunctions perhaps of racial and economic tensions), is in terms of coercion rather than legitimation, the various social control apparatuses will benefit at the expense of the welfare agencies. Or, to put it another way round, the functionaries at the urban manager level in the control apparatuses may find their freedom of action extended while others, in Departments of Social Service and of Education, will face greater restrictions. Gough, for example, in a critique of changes in the British welfare state has argued:

> . . . (At) the same time that most areas of expenditure were being cut back, certain items continued to expand, for instance, the police . . . what we are witnessing is not so much a *cut* in total state spending but its re-structuring in a specific direction (Gough, 1979, p.173)

Gough states however, that class struggle, including working-class and trade union opposition, may slow down the re-structuring process.

But conversely, the process of re-structuring may also be expedited. If the functionaries are able to dramatize the connection between the organizational goals, and social values within the dominant ideology, greater expenditure and more autonomy may be obtained. For example, (Chapter 9) chief police officers by public pronouncements are able to relate the police institutional problematic —expansion and autonomy—to a social concern with crime.

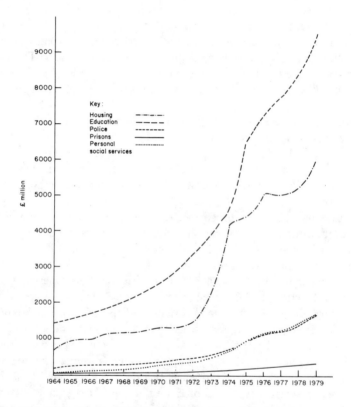

Fig. 4. Changes in State expenditure, 1964-1980. Source: national income and expenditure.

However, the most recent data, Fig. 4, throws little light on any such changes of state policy. Patently from the available information (1979), the intention to re-structure Social Expenditure, from welfare legitimation, to coercion, has not yet shown up in the analysis on government financing. Expenditure in the late 1970s by the state, was increasingly at identical rates in the Personal Social Services and in Policing.

While, at this date, there may have been no relative expansion of policing resources, the declared intention of the central state to switch resources, enhances the independence of the police institution at the local level from financial restraints. Secondly, the rise in the general corporate management role, when combined with the development of the particular attributes of police management—discretionary power, professional expertise, work experience and the legal relation—boosts the self-confidence and relaxes the structural restraints on the chief officer at the apex of local police resources provision. Finally, the more general disappearance of the political authority of the social classes represented through the local state, affects controls over policing in the same way that it has affected the structure of local authority controls over welfare, housing, and other forms of local service provision. Nevertheless although local government re-organization towards corporate management, and the increase in political intervention are important, the primary factor affecting the increased power of the chief police officer lies in the re-structuring of the social expenditure of the state in relation to the developing fiscal crisis. Moreover, all three processes are underpinned by changes in the requirements of different forms of capital—from city merchant house to monopoly-productive capital and finance capital in the terms of multi-national conglomerate. Managerialism, political centralization, and the determination of economic priorities, are complexly related to that economic process of which the changes in the structure of local authority in Liverpool provides one of the most graphic illustrations.

In other words, it is argued that the decline of the police authority power since 1964 cannot be attributed to the mystifications of the 1964 Police Act. The only effect of the Act was to formalize the lack of power of the local authority—to give constitutional form to a situation which had other deeper structural causes. Political intervention by the central state (itself the consequence of changing economic relations); the rise of corporate managerialism as an important specific post-war ideology; and the way the central state is committed to re-directing resources in response to the fiscal crisis; are the primary sources of the enhanced autonomy.

The chief officer may use his managerial skills to underline his authority at the inter-personal level, but his freedom to wield enlarged power relates to the economic and political demand at the level of the central, not the local state. While in practice the two demands may largely coincide so long as policing remains principally directed at the same target, i.e. the marginal strata outside the primary economy, none the less the complex relations of the central state now affect policing ideology and policy, as well as organizational form. No longer is policing susceptible to the general direction of a *local* political class. Indeed as has been indicated, it is increasingly difficult to identify a local mercantile class with any real power base: and similar fates have befallen the local productive industrial bourgeoisies of other large cities.

In the following section, using information drawn from the study of the Liverpool and Bootle Police Authority (Brogden, 1977), the post-1964 relation between chief officer and police committee is demonstrated, while the evidence gives some support to the orthodox critique that the chief takes advantage of the lack of expertise of the members of the authority—the inter-personal argument —the structural base of the relation is also apparent.

## The Political Relation in the 1970s

In the mid-1970s, the city police force had several other distinctions to its credit. Its fame did not rest only on its status as the first of the provincial forces nor on its major contribution to the 1919 Police Strike. By 1975, the recorded crime rate in the city was the highest in mainland Britain. The number of police employees per population, and the cost of the force per capita, were similarly the highest in the country.

The city, which was suffering more from the developing economic crisis than any comparable municipal unit, in terms of the rate of unemployment, paid more for its police force, despite the increasing social malaise. Paradoxically, the local state least able to bear policing expenditure was burdened with the most intensive commitment to that institution. The local police apparatus, therefore, formed a highly visible display of state expenditure, particularly in comparison to municipal expenditure on housing, and, to a lesser extent, on education and on social services.

The crucible of economic dissent was therefore potentially the local police committee (now the paymaster of a combined force, formed from the two neighbouring forces in 1968). The police authority was the undisputed forum for decisions over police resources. The city finance committees appeared never to challenge its financial judgements. Unlike some other police authorities it did not delegate decision-making powers to sub-committees. The study[3] focussed on three separable issues—the location of the police committee within the wider historical and contemporary complex of local state relation; the financial authority exercised by the committees; and the form of material manipulation and control of information in the course of its deliberations.

## The Relation of the Committee within the Local State

In the nineteenth century the predecessor of the local police authority, the Watch Committee, had been the major instrument of social engineering and social control in Liverpool. It had rested at the centre of the apparatus of the local state, as a channel for the general demands of the dominant merchant class.

In the 1970s while it now basked in the reflected glory of those early years, it demonstrated, in membership selection, in the attitude of other councillors to the committee, none of the substantive attributes of the Victorian Watch Committee.

Membership had changed substantially from that of the Victorian Watch. The most obvious difference between the 1970s and the nineteenth century composition was in the elevation of the strata of small business proprietors and of self-employed professionals. Substantive occupational comparison was not feasible however because of the possibly misleading effects of age (over a third of the members had retired from employment). The Authority of 27 members included nine members (some retired) from the ranks of small businesspeople. Seven members fitted into a "professional group", including two retired army officers. Only three members chose to classify themselves as manual or ex-manual workers (despite the fact that the Labour Party was the majority party on the Council itself). The other members were drawn from a medley of occupations across the range of white collar positions and included two housewives. There was no obvious difference between the occupations (or former occupations) of the magistrates as compared with the committee as a whole.

A selection formula with a primary criterion of age and party seniority had resulted in a committee membership mainly characterized by gerontocracy (nearly half the members were in their late sixties or mid-seventies) and attitudinally, by elitist conservatism.[4] Age and length of party service appeared to determine membership of the Police Authority to a much greater extent than on other council committees.

A status prize for local councillors, nomination to the committee, was seen as an accolade given to them for long obedience and service to their respective parties. For example, according to one member when interviewed:

> I think that a tremendous lot of politicians thought that if they could get on the authority they could be a magistrate—they could get some kind of honour after a few years' service

As a premier committee, membership brought obligations as well as status. Principal amongst the latter, was that of avoiding party political dissent amongst themselves, or between members and the chief police officer. Despite disparities between the members in political commitment, there had been no disputes of any significance for a decade or more:[5]

> Conflicts on the Police Authority? Never! Always been plenty of debate—we get very worried about officers' illnesses and whether they should get paid or not. The Police Authority always gives a great deal of thought to the large number of police on duty—we give a lot of thought to the families

Similarly, criticism of the chief officer was out of order, for example, according to a long-serving Chairman of the Fire Brigade Committee:

> We would often over-ride what the Chief Fire Officer wanted. We would never do that with the Chief Constable

Usually, the Education Committee was the reference point but in all cases, whether it was Social Services, Transport or Planning, the chief officer was subject to more criticism by the same personnel who, on the police committee apparently lost their critical faculties.

Within the network of local government committees, the Police Authority was important only by virtue of its fading glory. It was far removed from the key position in the local state occupied by the Watch Committee a hundred years earlier. It was also remarkable as the committee in which the corporate manager, the Chief Constable of the city, was granted the maximum deference and autonomy.

## The Financial Constraints

Given the economic pressures on this local state, it seemed reasonable to expect that a substantial proportion of the Authority's time at the six-weekly meeting would be devoted to budgetary matters. Hart (1951) for example, had argued that the primary bone of contention between the old Watch Committees and the chief police officer would normally be over the financing of the force. But in the city, while the local authority members of the committee were conscious of the budgetary restraints on the overall council budget, they made no challenge to the demands of the chief police officer.

The Police Authority gave minimal attention to the police estimates, for negotiative and structural reasons. The form of presentation, together with the members' perception of the establishment's apparently inflexible determination prevented any serious attention to police costs. As one member phrased it:

> The chief constable never needs to justify his resources . . . all the figures are there . . . we're all laymen. We can't quarrel with the figures.

Blumberg made the point elsewhere:

> Like any other bureaucracy the police are under constant pressure for public funds. No argument for public funds is more persuasive than a battery of statistics which, valid or not have a way of off-setting anticipated criticisms. (1971, p.60)

Members were not disposed to quarrel with requests, so meticulously supported by a mass of criminal statistics.

If the Chief Constable argued, as he invariably did, for a relative increase in manpower and financial resources, his implicit and sometimes explicit justification in terms of an increased crime rate was accepted. If the recorded crime rate rose, *ipso facto*, according to the Police Authority, police spending had to correspondingly expand.[6]

Requests for extra resources was accepted without question: "The first thing we take into account in considering the request for resources is that we are below establishment". It was manifest that the authority spent only a minimal amount of time in discussion of the police estimates. Gordon draws a similar conclusion on Scottish Police Authorities:

> . . . the police authority is little more than a paymaster for the force, providing the necessary finance and physical facilities, but having little control over how such resources are used. (1980, p.80)

Similarly, Kettle has illustrated how the Thames Valley Police Committee, in one incident, not merely agreed to support a raised establishment, when the item was not formally on the agenda, but gave the Chief Constable and the Committee Chairman, wide discretionary powers to meet the resulting additional costs (1980d).

Lack of action by these committees on the financing of the police was a consequence of two factors. Organizational negotiative techniques by the Chief Constable's office ensured a lack of knowledge on the key item of establishment construction. Police authorities were kept unaware of the detail of their financial powers. But in addition, where they recognized their financial controls, they chose not to use them.

The authority of the chief police officer, his corporate management status, his specialist knowledge of the threat to social order, and his ambiguous legal position, together combined to restrain the authority from intervening in the allocation of resources to the force, despite the developing fiscal crisis of the local state.

## The Structuring of Information

Information that passes from the chief officer to the Police Authority is negotiated, interpreted. Financial information was presented in such a way as preclude any opposition. Similarly, any potential threats to the image of the force must be discounted. Manning (1971) for example, has argued that the public's experience of police work is rarely gained at first-hand. Police authority members depend upon the production of police news by information, either directly from the chief officer, or indirectly from the local media (which in turn relies upon police co-operation in its production).

The authority has no administrative staff of its own. Senior police officers understandably manipulate information in order to gain general public support, and specifically, Police Authority acquiescence.

For example, in 1979, when a national controversy developed over the use of a clause in the 1824 Vagrancy Act[6] against young people (particularly black youths) in the inner cities, in response to pressures from outside the city, members of the authority uniquely "called for a report" on local police practices. The Chief Constable duly presented statistical evidence to demonstrate that there was no excessive use of that legislation in the city. However, he did not inform the members of the regular use in the city of powers that existed under a local bye-law, similar in form to the "sus" law. Alternative evidence, not proffered by the chief officer, and not available without his co-operation to the Authority members, reveals the regular use of the alternative police powers (A. Brogden, 1981). The Chief Constable's presentation of the case defined the parameters of the problem and effectively dismissed, by lack of disclosure, the possible critique. He formulated the boundaries within which the Police Authority's requests were negotiated. A major ilustration of this negotiative process lies in the handling of "complaints against the police". Under the 1964 Police Act (later reinforced in the 1976 Police Complaints Act), the record of all formal complaints, by members of the public against individual police officers, and the results of the sequential investigation, must be regularly laid before the police committee.[7]

Complaints are not only potentially damaging to the careers of individual police officers but they also threaten the image of the local force itself. They pose a major problem for any senior officer concerned to defend and enhance that image. This was particularly true in this city where the level of complaints was normally significantly higher than in most other police areas.

The suggestion that police officers act on occasion to the detrimental interest of certain members of the public could have unfortunate consequences for a Chief Constable wishing to depict the force as a model of efficiency and of impartial expertise, and intent on safeguarding the annual estimates. Various devices are used to minimize those effects — some (organizational) are effectively built into the structure of internal police investigations (Russell, 1976a) — and others (inter-personal) relate directly to the initiatives and negotiative skill of the chief officer and of his administrative staff. The chief uses two major techniques in his Report to the Committee to de-legitimize the complaints — by portraying police officers as "Hamlet-like" (Cain, 1973) victims and by interposing complaints with commendations.

The first procedure is one of situational manipulation — the police officer, not the complainant as victim. In the 1972 Report, for example, of the 591 complaints, only 43 were upheld after internal police investigation.

This innocuous piece of accounting was followed by a detailed statement which "located" the problem for the police authority members. Many complaints were withdrawn because they "were of a trivial nature, more often than not arising from a misunderstanding". The thorough investigation of complaints causes considerable extra work for police officers. Many members of the public complain "merely to bring their feelings to the attention of the police officer in question". Others are made "with a view to delay or even prevent criminal proceedings being taken against the complainant". These complaints have a very unsettling effect on police officers who, fortunately, have become used to this constant sniping "as an expression of the changing values of our society" (Annual Report, 1972, p.37). Similar processes of de-legitimization—the police officer not the complainant as victim—can be seen in the 1974, 1977 and 1979 Reports (which despite changes in chief officer, use almost identical wording).

Secondly, the chief uses a juxtaposition device to minimize harmful imagery. According to one magistrate member: "The record of police complaints comes to the committee but it is more than counter balanced by the presentation of the record of public gratitude to the police". Immediately after listing (as he must, by statute) the results of the complaints investigation, the Chief Constable reads out to the members of the Authority, letters from the public, expressing appreciation of the services of police officers. For example, at most public demonstrations, there is usually an "impartial bystander" whose letter of commendation negates any accounts of alleged police misconduct.

The inversion of victim, and the juxtaposition device buttress the predisposition of the Authority members not to query the policies underlying the decisions of the chief.

While the primary example of the structuring of information lay in the field of complaints, the same form of control was present throughout Police Authority deliberations.

Marshall described the local police authority as being concerned only with "paying, preaching and public relation" (1965). In this study, one councillor depicted the functions of the meeting as dealing with the "weak, the lame and the lazy"—officers handicapped by illness or injury, or unwilling to vacate police housing:

> There's nothing meaty about the agenda at all—medical matters, awards to police officers, the closure of police stations, the annual inspections—we never discussed the actual operations of the police

The agenda—devised in a prior informal meeting between the Chairperson and the Chief Constable—was dominated by matters peripheral to police practice. A magistrate member expressed himself strongly:

> The basic function of the Police Authority is the pensioning-off of old officers and the like—we are never more than on the fringe of any activity of the police . . . I regard this committee as a complete waste of time . . . .

Information was structured, either in the form of presentation, or by exclusion, to avoid critique. The Chief Constable's office effectively controlled the issues under discussion and pre-empted the decision-making process. As Moodie had claimed, in an earlier commentary on the lack of accountability of the police institution (1972), the only information freely provided was that which was legally necessary or which conferred positive benefits upon the police image.

## The Practice of Local Police Management

This study suggested several conclusions. Members of this police authority, which (given the serious local effects of the fiscal crisis), should have been the most probable forum for criticisms of the demands of the local police chief, displayed none of these symptoms. The police chief ran the Police Authority rather than the other way round.

The evidence goes a long way to repudiate the orthodox defence of the post-1964 political relation between chief officers and local police committee. As far as this committee was concerned, despite the major economic problems of the city, the police institution was sacrosanct. It was above criticism. The idea of political intervention in police work was absurd. But while it's easy to dismiss that conservative view of the political relation, what of the orthodox critique? What, moreover, of the applicability of this evidence to other Police Authorities?[8]

Certainly, much of the material summarized in these last pages can be adduced to reinforce the orthodox critique. Most police authority members were totally ignorant of their powers and of the nature of their financial control. They had minimal knowledge of either police institution or of the functions of police authorities as laid down in the Police Act, 1964. But that argument is insufficient. Why did local authority members not carry over to the police committee some of the critical approach which led them to make demands made of other chief officers? Although constitutionally the Police Authority is a peculiar committee, residing in the limbo between central and local states, legal and constitutional quibbles were small beer to politicians who in the past had fought their way up the local political ladders. The difference in outline relation between the police corporate manager (give or take a uniform or two) and the Police Authority, and the Chief Fire Officer and the Fire Brigade Committee, was not that great. There was no substantive reason for that major difference in the functional relation — not even the presence of the non-elected magistrates.

It is true that the chief officer was able to display particular managerial skills in constraining the discussions and questioning of the police authority members. But it was their predispositions and those of the Council colleagues to accept without opposition those manoeuvres of the chief officer that ultimately counted. The chief's claim to professionalism and his practical experience of the work under his supervision were significant. But the primary determinates of his autonomy lie in two material areas — the legal and the ideological. The unique feature of the chief police officer as a corporate or urban manager is that, while constrained by political and economic factors like other chief officers within the local state, he has access to a source of autonomy that, on occasion, can override immediate restraints. His legal status as a constable under common law grants him unique discretionary powers. When combined with the legal knowledge necessary to his managerial function, he has considerably more independence as a resource provider in the local areas than any other urban manager.

Secondly, what was also obvious from the 1977 study, was the extent to which the chief police officer's interpretation of his task as the maintenance of social order — was shared without any qualms or quibbles by the Authority members. There was an essential ideological relation — a relation of consent between the two sides.

In the succeeding chapters, the other factors that contribute to the relative independence of the chief police officer are examined. Chapter 4 documents the other side of the political relation — the connection between police institution and the central state. In Chapter 5, the legal relation (which had over-awed the police authority members in the 1977 study) is explored. Chapter 6 considers the solidaristic effects of the chief officer's peer group on the political relation with central and local states. Finally, in the remaining chapters the ideological relation which constituted a major source of autonomy for the chief *vis-à-vis* the committee, is dissected.

# Notes

1. See the outline of the unsuccessful Police Authorities (powers) Bill 1980 — *Police* magazine, **12**, 2.
2. The Police Act, 1890, which had introduced national standards for pensions, was the first substantive move towards central co-ordination but the 1919 Desborough Committee which introduced wider measures of standardization, was the major step.
3. The study encompassed all debates on police matters, recorded over a five year period. All available documentary evidence for that period — Police Authority Minutes; newspaper reports of the committee proceedings; the Chief Constable's Annual Reports to the Authority; and the exchanges between the Secretary to the Authority

and to the Home Office—were analysed. Two-thirds of the membership—magistrates and councillors—were interviewed after their retirement from the committee (owing to local government re-organization and force amalgamation.)

4. See Saunders (1980, p.227) for an account of the effects of the drastic change in the composition of one local council.

5. The only conflict of note on the authority in the previous *fifty* years had been the unsuccessful attempt by the old labour leader, James Sexton, as a member of the Watch Committee, to compel that body to hold an enquiry into a police assault on another labour leader, William Braddock, in 1930. Braddock himself later became a member of the Watch but his experiences at the hands of the police, were not reflected in the subsequent Watch Committee meetings.

6. Section 4, Vagrancy Act, 1824 (i.e. being a suspected person loitering with intent to commit an arrestable offence). Abolished in August 1981, but replaced as a consequence of police pressure with similar, if more narrowly defined, legal powers.

7. For a critique of the Police Act, 1976, see Leigh (1976), Cain (1977), and State Research Bulletin, 6, 1978.

8. After a substantial swing to the political Left in local elections in 1981, there was a significant change in the membership of many urban police authorities. The increased Labour representation, coinciding with the severe manifestations in the cities of the fiscal crisis, resulted in much more severe criticism of chief police officers by those bodies than hitherto but no substantive change in their powers over the police institution.

# 4 The Central State and the Negotiation of Resources

> At the same time as the number of forces has diminished drastically, governmental control, control exerted through the power of the purse and the Police Inspectorate, has increased very considerably. (Bowden, 1978)

Where the diminution in the local political relation of the police institution has been acknowledged, it has been conventional practice to argue that the power of the administrative agencies of the central state has been relatively increased. Central direction is assumed to replace local control. Williams, for example, commenting on the impact of the Police Act, 1964:

> . . . a substantial measure of central control is provided for by giving the Home Office important powers . . . very extensive influence . . . over all police forces: both in the exercise of his express powers and by virtue of his central and co-ordinating role. (Williams, 1974, p.192)

This view has been shared not just amongst the more conservative commentators but also underlies much of the more radical critique of the police-state relation. Gordon (1980, p.83) for example, in his study of the political relation of the Scottish police, suggests that the Home Office Inspectorate and the Scottish Secretary of State, have assumed much of the power lost by the local Police Authorities.

These accounts clearly have substance. Through its central co-ordinating role, as well as through the body of Inspectors of Constabulary, the Home Office as the agency of the central state wields considerable influence over the police institution. More directly, the financial strings are of importance. Through the medium of the 50% grant that the central state makes to the local authority, the Home Office, as the direct channel for political policies over policing, has substantial potential sanction.

However, the degree of directive influence exercised over the police institution, from the central complex of political relations is open to question. There is more assumption than evidence. It will be argued that the appearance of a movement towards central direction has all the qualities of a chimera.

In this chapter, the form of relation between the police institution and the central state will be examined. The primary focus will be on the way that through time the development of the local managerial role of the chief officer is reflected in his relations with the central state apparatus.

One important way in which this changing relation can be illustrated is through the process by which resources are negotiated. If, as many commentators note, the major impact of central control over the police relates to the financial constraints, in the continuing discussions between local Police Authorities, chief police officers, and the Home Office, over resource allocation, one can expect to locate the dynamics of the political process. In particular, if, as was contended in the last chapter, there has been a substantial increase in recent years in the autonomy of the chief officer, then a degree of police independence in the acquisition of resources should now be visible.

This process of resource negotiation is critical to the political relation between the police institution and different social classes. Where resources are tightly defined and monitored centrally — where, for example, a fixed formula governs resource provision — the police institution is in a directly dependent relationship. Where, however, the factors determining resource provision are vague, and subject to modification by the police institution itself, a more independent relation can be said to exist.

The first part of this chapter is devoted to an account of the historical development of the political relation between central and government, and the police institution, as illustrated by changes in policy over the control of police manpower allocations. The recent evidence on manpower expansion is derived from reported negotiations between the three parties — the Home Office, local police authorities, and the police chiefs. The resulting documentation of the growing power of the chiefs *vis-à-vis* the central state in those negotiations is further illustrated by the weakness of the two major instruments by which the Home Office seeks to affect the police institution — the Police Inspectorate and the Home Office Circular. Finally, the other forms of control by the central government over the police institution are outlined. It is concluded, however, that the demonstration of the lack of control by the Home Office, and by the legislature, does not of itself prove the existence of police interests distinct from those embedded in the other state apparatuses.

## The Relationship Prior to World War I

The struggle for supremacy over the New Police between central elite and local elite was, as Chapter 2 indicated, a conflict which for many years resulted in local dominance over the police institution. Throughout the first 80 years of the police institution in Britain, the Home Office (the conduit for central direction) was, in Critchley's words' ". . . content to see nothing, hear nothing, and do nothing—unless correspondence came its way, and then it did as little as possible" (Critchley, 1979, p.98). Until the First World War, the Home Office acted as little more than a clearing-house for crime information and as the vehicle for the administration to local forces of relevant Parliamentary statutes (Donajgrodzki, 1973; Hart, 1951). Until the County and Borough Act, 1856, apart from a yearly request for the provision of the criminal statistics by the Borough forces, there was little contact between the central state and the local force. An early attempt by the newly formed Inspectorate in 1839, for example, to provide general guidance on force establishments and police costs[1] foundered for lack of comparative information (the Inspectors had no statutory rights of inspection until 1856) and lack of power.

There were a number of interventions by the Home Office on the occasion of local disturbances but normally its response to such affairs was simply to recommend an increase in police numbers (Hart, 1955).

The 1856 Act established a quid pro quo. Local Watch Committees were finding policing an increasingly costly affair. The Liverpool force, for example, had trebled in number over those first two decades. Financial assistance was sought from the centre. Conversely, the central state was developing its more direct interventionist role—prompted by labour disputes, the Chartist troubles, and by the need to provide the stable conditions for economic production throughout the country. In return for a yearly grant (25% of pay and clothing costs, raised to 50% in 1888) the local elites agreed to a measure of Home Office supervision in the form of two Inspectors (soon increased to three).

But in the focus of the work of the new Inspectors lay the seeds of later police managerial autonomy. The Inspectors were appointed to increase the efficiency of local forces. But practically the only tool open to the Inspectors to achieve that end was to recommend an increase in police numbers (Parris, 1961). The smaller the police-population ratio, the more efficient the force.[2] Inspectorate pressure was more effective in expanding establishments than in affecting other aspects of police work (Martin and Wilson, 1969).

The establishment sizes of local forces were soon tied to population figures. The police-population ratio provided an accessible indicator. It also offered a basic organizational feature around which other facets of local policing could be structured. In effect, intervention by the Inspectors in attempting (unsuccessfully) to relatively standardize the police-population ratio gave them—or rather the Home Office—an administrative lever. Grants were payable on the basis of manpower expansion in response to Home Office request.

While there was a residue of opposition after 1856 to Home Office Inspectorate intervention (in Oldham ". . . the Mayor directed the Chief Constable to take a posse of policemen to the city boundary to prevent the Inspector of Constabulary from entering . . ." Wren, 1971), by 1890 all 183 forces were grant-aided and subject to Home Office inspection. The urban bourgeoisie surrendered some autonomy, for a price.

In general, however, between the County and Boroughs Act, 1856, and World War 1, Home Office intervention in local forces was minimal. While the Home Secretary might be concerned with points of principle—the refusal of arms training to the Cheshire force, for example, more often than not he ". . . displayed a like indifference to local authorities (simply) seeking advice" (Parris, 1961). To Tobias, however, this non-intervention owed more to intent than to indolence. "In the boroughs he had influence rather than authority, because successive Home Secretaries were determined not to attempt to interfere with the independence of the local authorities" (Tobias, 1979, p.115). The trivial character of Home Office intervention in the latter part of the last century is illustrated by the following (total) communications to the Liverpool force in an average year (1879-80).

> *28th September:* Circular requiring information on indecent assaults on children.
> *12th March:* Forms for the annual Criminal Statistics and details of grant.
> *28th June:* Circular on extradition of foreigners.
> *5th July:* Correspondence initiated by the Watch Committee on the question of new Constables, swearing an oath to the Queen.
> *16th August:* The Inspector of Constabulary supports a request by the Head Constable for an increase in the force establishment. (L.W.C. Mins)

But in fact this lack of central intervention is not surprising. Given that during this period both central state and local state represented the interests of the same class, an entrepreneurial and locally based bourgeoisie, there was no stimulus for intervention (apart from at times of crisis). Consequently, the period before World War I was marked only by advances in the standardization of pay, clothing, and pension arrangements. But the major effect of the period had been to couple the interests of the Home Office with those of the Chief Constables—a developing transfer of power from the legislative to the executive. The chiefs had learnt to play off the Home Secretary against the local Watch Committee.

## The Relation Between the Wars

Prior to 1918, Watch Committees exercised (in theory, if not always in fact) control over the size of their local forces. Assuming that the force met the Inspector's criteria for efficiency, a local force could be increased or decreased on its own authority. But in 1918, it was made a condition of the Treasury Grant that numbers as well as efficiency be subject to Home Office direction. Borough manpower was to be controlled in the way that county establishments had always been.

The police strikes of 1918 and 1919 precipitated crises over the control and organization of local forces. In Liverpool, a major factor contributing to the strike by half the city police force had been the differentials in pay (Bean, 1980). Standardization, it was argued, would eliminate some of the peculiarities which had contributed to the unrest. The major report by the 1919 Desborough Committee resulted in new uniform measures and in more centralized administration. The Home Office's co-ordinating role, which had developed during the war-time period as an emergency measure, was institutionalized, with the formation of a new Police Division. The Police Council, set up at the same time to negotiate pay structures depended upon Home Office organization. The police crisis of 1919, and its demonstration of the distinction between local bourgeois control and the new developments in labour organization (particularly in Liverpool) precipitated central state intervention. Only an administrative agency of the central state could counteract the potential for national organization of unionized police officers. Economic conflict speeded up the intervention process.

Manpower requirements were similarly being subject to more scrutiny. Following in the footsteps of many predecessors, the 1920 Inspectorate Report attempted to provide a standardized formula to cover beat operations. However, the Report concluded, as had its successors, by noting that the precise policing requirements for different areas inevitably depended upon subjective factors. The exact requirements for police officers rested ultimately upon professional local expertise. Any attempt to apply symmetrical allocations of police officers to different areas was "eyewash". Within that bald statement lay a key to the independence of chief officers.

The Home Office remained reluctant to intervene in the immediate post-war period. When the Geddes Committee in 1922 recommended a formula for establishment construction, (based on acreage, rateable value, and population) the Home Office demurred. It rejected the argument claiming that this would carry central control too far and, further, that it would be unsatisfactory to define establishments without reference to special local conditions and the ". . . wishes of the inhabitants" (Hart, 1951).

In this instance the Home Secretary stepped back from a confrontation with the Watch Committees over the extension of central control. But in doing so it reinforced what became a lynchpin of the negotiating strength of the chief officers in later years—the reference to the peculiarity of local conditions. This subjective factor, when coupled with the expanding notion of managerialist expertise, effectively frustrated any direct control over the detail of police resources, from outside the police institution, in the following half century.

During the period leading up to World War II, Home Office intervention developed spasmodically. Principally due to the economic and political unrest of the twenties and thirties—the General Strike of 1926, the large-scale unemployment of the 1930s (particularly the emergence of the Unemployed Workers Movement-Hayburn, 1972) and the rise of a native Fascist movement—central state influence on the police institution became more pronounced. All these events could only be controlled by the state through a co-ordinated response across traditional police area boundaries. The Home Office became increasingly concerned with developing its own machinery for promoting national police policies and centralized co-ordination. According to Martin and Wilson (in their later study of police manpower), the Inspectorate worked hard during the inter-war period ". . . persuading the police authorities of rapidly growing boroughs that establishment and expenditure must keep pace with population" (Martin and Wilson, 1969, p.34).

Similarly, the financial crisis which hit the Northern industrial cities and towns especially hard, in the 1930s, made them particularly dependent upon the Home Office grant and, therefore, on satisfying the urges of the H.M.I.C.s Where unemployment benefits came out of the same rate pool as the police costs, as the St. Helens Watch Committee had found in 1927, few local authorities could afford to defy moves towards central direction (see Chapter 1, Note 5).

There are of course, different views on the reasons for police expansion, and of the increasing importance of the Home Office during this period. Sir Arthur Dixon, a key civil servant attached to the Home Office during the period attributes the readiness of local Watch Committees to comply with Home Office pressure to what he regards as a commitment to progress.

A more go-ahead Police Authority (or a well-to-do Authority with a go-ahead Chief Constable) might ask for an increase in establishment whether to improve the beat strength because of the growth and spread of the population or to provide staff for new developments in supplementary aids to police work . . . (Dixon, 1966, Chapter 25)

More obviously, the between-wars economic and political crises could be dampened nationally by co-ordinated action, and by Home Office reliance on a sufficiency of local police resources. Political and economic factors weakened

Watch Committees as the Home Office responded to crises with more administrative input. By 1939 ". . . the Home Office had built up a position of quite remarkable influence in police affairs . . . Thus it had worked itself into a position of great power without formal responsibility" (Critchley, 1979, p.219). Reaction to political and economic crises, changes in the structure of capital, the territorial aggrandisement of an expanding state bureaucracy, the decrease in economic and political powers represented through the local state, together contributed to an administrative re-shuffling of influence over the police institution from the local state to the central.

But this development in the executive power of the Home Office was also a stepping stone to more local autonomy for the chief officers. As Jessop has argued, administrative changes of this type can signify fundamental changes in policy and in the level of decision-making:

> . . . as the rule of law is replaced in the interventionist state by administrative discretion, the impact of 'routine' administration tends to become . . . far-reaching and significant. This effect is reinforced through the increasing involvement of officials in the formation of policies and programmes. (1980, p.62)

The diminution in the general powers of the Watch Committees, was compensated by an increase not just in the influence of the central state officials in the Home Office but also of the chief police officers. In particular, once the subjective determination—"local conditions"—of police establishments had become institutionalized, substantial powers over resources fell into the hands of the chiefs.

## Post-War—negotiation via formulae

The Second World War had similar effects on policing to its predecessor. Problems of war-time co-ordination, and of post-war force re-construction (for example, as police officers, returning from military service replaced the auxiliary police) constituted the organizational problematic.

But the more general canvas on which police–state relations were being drawn related to other factors. In the long-term, the same processes of executive delegation by capital that had provided the political space for the expansion of managerial autonomy in the local state were at work. The post-war rise of A.C.P.O. (Chapter 6) was the major outcome of that process. However, in the short-term, ". . . there is no doubt that the police were in some ideological disfavour, both governmentally and popularly . . ." (Taylor, 1981, p.41). Amongst other factors, the restoration of a "Blimpish" controlled, military-ranked force, contrasted unfavourably with the work of the Auxiliaries during the war (ibid).

Police resources were scrutinized more closely. The size of the force nationally actually fell from 64 000 to 60 000 in the decade up to 1949, and police costs, as a proportion of state expenditure, nearly halved in that period (Martin and Wilson, 1969). Successive investigations into police resources, however, reinforced ultimately not Home Office control, but the managerial authority of the chiefs.

For example, the 1946 Police Post-War Committee argued that considerations of resource requirements should take account not just of the guiding criterion of population density but also the ". . . characteristics of the population as judged by its record of crime and disorders . . ." (quoted in Gray, 1978), as well of the factors of road mileage, and of rateable value. In the reference to population characteristics, the Committee paid due deference to the professional interpretations of the resident experts, the chief officers.

The addition to the formulae of the crime rates highlighted the changing organizational feature of police work. Prior to that date, crime-work represented merely one aspect of police public order duties. Post-war it became the defining feature of organizational practice and success. Crime rates provided a measure of organizational efficiency (replacing the nineteenth century use of the population index, whose static quality would now impede rather than justify expansion). Crime rates had the additional advantage, from a police standpoint, of being partly capable of control by the organization itself. Crime rates are shaped by policing and statistical practices as well as by extra-organizational events. The emphasis on crime rates reinforced the image of the local forces as formal organizations, with specific goals, and of the professional and expert status of the organization's head, the local police chief. Organizational indices of the efficiency would in future be coupled with socially constructed crime rates.

Although the general unreliability of the recorded crime data has been thoroughly documented in numerous sociological texts, the use of those data by the chiefs to justify police expansion, can best be criticized in the words of Head Constable Dunning, in his 1909 Report ". . . directly you judge the efficiency of anybody upon criminal statistics which can be affected by the exercise of discretion entrusted to him, you tempt him to shape his action, not so much to fit the requirements of the individual case, as to fit nicely into the position to be presented at the end of the year".

This increased influence of the professional experts in determining resources is illustrated further by the Dixon Report[3] on manpower distribution in the Metropolitan force (1949). That report included a caveat with its recommendations on formulae. The latter should be subject to "what the public expect, what the public purse can afford, and what will seem reasonable to those directing policy . . ." (p.270). The balance was to be given to the chiefs. Professional expertise from within the police institution, not Home Office policies, came increasingly to dominate the allocation of resources to the police apparatus.

The application of either formula to the provincial forces was resisted, however. The Home Office prompted resource standardization (even with the subjective qualifications of the record of criminal statistics and the reference to local conditions) remained unacceptable to the growing authority of the Chief Constables. Even in the Met., the Dixon formula soon fell into dis-use.

Nevertheless the obvious disparities in the sizes of the provincial forces and the rising cost of policing to both local and central states throughout the 1950s ensured a continuing search for some universally applicable formula. The Home Office, the Treasury, some Members of Parliament and a number of local Watch Committees (the latter increasingly conscious of their diminishing control over police spending) were becoming sensitive to the escalation in police costs. For example, the Parliamentary Select Committee on Estimates, 1958, called for a comprehensive review of police establishments, pointing to major disparities in the number of police per population, in apparently similar localities.

The central state was losing directive control over police resources (Figs 5 and 6 document the expansion during the last quarter of a century). While most forces, by the time of the 1962–3 Willink Commission, operated versions of the post-war formula, the notion of "local conditions" always affected the final statement of resource requirements (Martin and Wilson, 1969) and the consequent autonomy of the chiefs to decide their own resource requirements was confirmed. Authorized establishments continued to be constructed through a bargaining process in which individual chief constables played off the Watch Committee against the Home Office.

Reflecting both the general pressure from the central state for control over police costs, and the emerging managerial powers of the chiefs as a body, a working party of The Association of Chief Police Officers (A.C.P.O.) made a further attempt to determine the criteria on which police establishments and costs should be based.

In a Report compounded by evaluative reference to areas where there was a "generally amenable population" and where "communities with varying social customs and different standards had inherited different traditions of police protection . . ." (p.9); A.C.P.O., after what by now had become the normal tour of potential criteria for establishment construction, concluded that ". . . any formula which is put forward must be sufficiently elastic to permit of variations to meet local requirements and opinion".

The subjective—or rather the professional—judgement of the chief officers, his autonomy over resources, was to be institutionalized as the final arbiter. The Home Office was constrained in its attempts to define appropriate limits for local forces by its increasing wariness of the lobbying power, as well as the professionalism and managerial expertise of the local chief officers. Later attempts

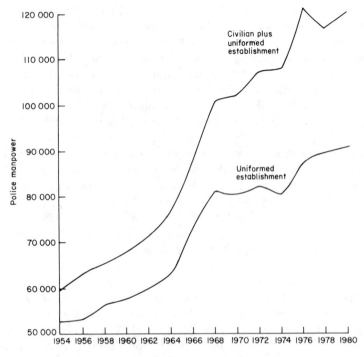

Fig. 5. Changes in police manpower, 1954-1980. Source: adapted from *County Council Gazette*.

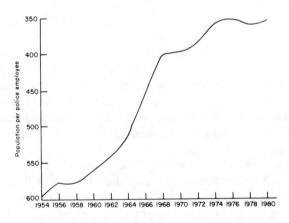

Fig. 6. Changes in police: population ratio, 1954-1980. Source: adapted from *County Council Gazette*.

by the Home Office Research and Planning Branch (1966 and 1969) (Bunyard, 1978) met little more success.

The more general failure of the Home Office to counter the independent power of the chiefs, which had grown while that of the local Watch Committee had declined, had been recognized by the Willink Commission. The Home Office was, in effect, chastized for its lack of combatancy in the Report.

Superficially, the Police Act, 1964, enhanced the powers of the central state. The Home Office was given the powers (like the new Police Authorities) to call for Reports from the Chief Constables, the right of veto over the appointment of the command-level officers, the duty to compel the retirement of inefficient Chief Constables, and the prerogative to set up an enquiry into the policing of any local police area (Section 4). It also gave the Home Secretary the responsibility of improving police efficiency nationally ". . . by developing co-operation between forces, providing common service arrangements and amalgamating police areas . . ." (Critchley, 1979, p.294).

The major formal consequence of the Act was a re-assertion of the principle of administrative infiltration. The Home Office departments concerned with police affairs multiplied (F1 to F7 Divisions).

There was a general spread of the various common services financed and administered by the Home Office. Out of the Home Office funds came the costs of the Police National Computer; the Forensic Laboratories; the seven Police Training Centres, the Police Staff College; the office of the Regional Crime Squad Coordinator; recruitment publicity; and a proportion of the requirements of the Police Council (Negotiating Board). But whereas Cain (1972) argues that these developments, amount to a hidden control of the police by a central state which publicly is not accountable—this being a form of control ideally suited to the requirements of international capital which is not represented in or by the legislature—it is contended here that the police chiefs were increasingly independent of all controls by fractions of the capitalist class. In particular, the control of the central state over local costs, did not increase.

During the late sixties, the large city forces (which had consistently failed to recruit up to their authorized establishments) were required by decree of the Home Secretary to lower their sights to some five to ten per cent below those establishments. When eventually the authorized establishment levels (distinguishing it from the permitted establishment allowed during the short period of control) were reached, forces were empowered to expand beyond that level. This process of almost continuous expansion was interrupted on two occasions, the two periods of force amalgamations of 1968-9 and 1973-4, when the Home Office gained a temporary advantage in the conflict over resources by the force re-constructions.

In general, however, officials of the central state had become aware of their relative impotence in face of the self-determination of the chief officers. Two

comments, in particular, reflect the rise of the image of the chief as the professional expert, facing the lay political elite. Callaghan, for example, as Home
Secretary in 1968 remarked

> I cannot regard the existing level (of police manpower) as particularly realistic
> and because of the introduction of new methods it is not enough to say that a
> particular force is well below establishment. I want to know whether the estab-
> lishment really fits modern policing. (*Hansard,* 15th February, 1968)

In 1974, the Secretary of State at the Home Office admitted:

> . . . despite attempts over a number of years, it has not been possible to find
> any arithmetical formulation on which police establishments can be based . . .
> Determination of the general level of policing need is therefore a matter of
> judgement based upon one hand of the Police Authority, aware of the needs
> and resources of the area, as guided by the professional advise of the chief
> officer of the police, and on the other hand, of the Home Secretary, aware of
> the needs of the resources of the country at large and guided by the pro-
> fessional advice of the H.M.I.C. (quoted in Gray, 1978)

As the last chapter demonstrated, the reference to the Police Authority above,
is a euphemism for the Chief Constable. The Home Office practice had essentially, until the late seventies, been that of accepting through a process of
ritualistic negotiations the slow, but steady, expansion insisted upon by the
police institution. (Table III documents some of the resultant incongruities in a
comparison of provincial forces.)

The concept of a police establishment has come to signify not just the decline
of the rights over resources of the local Police Authority but, more significantly,
the decline during the post-war period of Home Office influence over the police
institution. Judge (1972) reinforces the view that the Police Authorities rarely
challenge the professional judgement of the Chief Constables and adds:

> Establishments in each force are, in truth, very much a matter of the chief
> constable's personal evaluation of his needs . . . there is little evidence that
> Inspectors of Constabulary apply a critical yard-stick to demands for higher
> establishments . . . (Judge, 1972, p.17)

In other words, irrespective of the formal representation of Home Office
powers in the Police Act, and the subsequent increase in the size of the Police
Inspectorate, the size of local police forces and the statement of resource
requirements by the police apparatus, relates more to what the Home Office
describe as ". . . professional judgement" (quoted in Brogden, 1977), the power
of the chief police officers, than to political determination.

TABLE III
Disparities in cost and size between provincial police forces in England and Wales, 1980-81 (actual strength).

| Police area | Net cost per 1000 pop. (£) | Acres per officer | Acres per officer + civilian | Population per officer | Population per officer + civilian |
|---|---|---|---|---|---|
| *Metropolitan* | | | | | |
| Greater Manchester | 20 710 | 46 | 37 | 386 | 307 |
| Merseyside | 24 806 | 35 | 29 | 333 | 263 |
| Northumbria | 17 891 | 412 | 321 | 455 | 355 |
| South Yorkshire | 16 807 | 135 | 105 | 459 | 357 |
| West Midlands | 18 590 | 34 | 26 | 412 | 317 |
| West Yorkshire | 18 603 | 99 | 78 | 408 | 312 |
| *Non-metropolitan* | | | | | |
| Avon and Somerset | 17 153 | 407 | 310 | 451 | 344 |
| Bedfordshire | 16 173 | 279 | 207 | 514 | 380 |
| Cambridgeshire | 15 046 | 772 | 579 | 541 | 406 |
| Cheshire | 14 985 | 312 | 248 | 504 | 400 |
| Cleveland | 19 362 | 98 | 77 | 390 | 307 |
| Cumbria | 18 649 | 1517 | 1188 | 429 | 336 |
| Derbyshire | 16 791 | 357 | 246 | 499 | 344 |
| Devon and Cornwall | 18 048 | 377 | 279 | 501 | 371 |
| Dorset | 16 721 | 558 | 420 | 499 | 376 |
| Durham | 17 546 | 453 | 322 | 459 | 326 |
| Dyfed-Powys | 15 172 | 2869 | 2356 | 455 | 373 |
| Essex | 14 583 | 342 | 259 | 532 | 403 |
| Gloucestershire | 15 166 | 581 | 472 | 443 | 359 |
| Gwent | 16 530 | 350 | 279 | 451 | 360 |
| Hampshire | 14 906 | 337 | 265 | 514 | 404 |
| Hertfordshire | 15 677 | 240 | 173 | 527 | 391 |
| Humberside | 18 758 | 435 | 329 | 434 | 329 |
| Kent | 15 752 | 322 | 232 | 526 | 379 |
| Lancashire | 18 048 | 239 | 179 | 437 | 327 |
| Leicestershire | 15 544 | 367 | 277 | 487 | 367 |
| Lincolnshire | 17 327 | 1137 | 936 | 445 | 338 |
| Norfolk | 13 885 | 1065 | 857 | 527 | 424 |
| Northamptonshire | 14 941 | 596 | 450 | 523 | 395 |
| North Wales | 16 196 | 1203 | 929 | 462 | 357 |
| North Yorkshire | 16 612 | 1515 | 1155 | 483 | 368 |
| Nottinghamshire | 17 844 | 244 | 185 | 435 | 330 |
| South Wales | 18 283 | 181 | 136 | 421 | 315 |
| Staffordshire | 15 309 | 320 | 240 | 476 | 357 |
| Suffolk | 15 460 | 839 | 611 | 514 | 374 |
| Surrey | 16 577 | 233 | 180 | 463 | 362 |
| Sussex | 16 154 | 332 | 251 | 455 | 345 |
| Thames Valley | 13 595 | 459 | 328 | 588 | 420 |
| Warwickshire | 14 934 | 535 | 423 | 535 | 423 |
| West Mercia | 15 054 | 952 | 711 | 516 | 386 |
| Wiltshire | 15 048 | 835 | 634 | 500 | 380 |

Source: adapted from County Council Gazette.

Clearly, this overall picture of the power of the chiefs as the local managers to determine resources is not absolute. That autonomy is structured by two crucial factors—the general commitment of the political interests represented through the state to support for the police institution, and the extent to which chief officers can legitimize their construction, their image, of police work as being in the "public" interest. In the first case, the chiefs cannot utilize resources which damage the long-term interest of the dominant economic forces. Logistical and organizational factors aside, no police chief could switch resources from the investigation of lower class crime to a blitz on company fraud.

Secondly, the professional, impartial, image of the chief officer depends upon public consent. His legitimacy in acquiring resources depends upon the continuing mobilization of support (Chapter 8).

While in the acquisition of resources, the autonomy of the chiefs from political pressures manifest through the Home Office is most apparent, the instruments of domination of the police institution, by the Home Office, are themselves of a frail character. The practice of control through the Inspectorate, and through the medium of the Home Office Circular, similarly suggests little intent to exert influence over the police institution.

## The Police Inspectorate

The Inspectorate forms the major link between the provincial forces and the Home Office. Its advice is crucial on policy formation in that Ministry. In its contact with the police chiefs it interprets the framework of state policy on the implementation of law. Individually, the Inspectors play a trouble-shooting role for the Home Secretary (dealing, for example, with enquiries into the local forces on his behalf in South and West Yorkshire in 1981). But as the chiefs construct a more independent position within the state apparatus, the influence on that corporate body of the Inspectorate, seems to be waning.

For a period after the Police Act, 1964,[4] the Inspectorate as an instrument of the Home Office appeared to be achieving an ascending authority in police affairs. The Act had enlarged its numbers (there were ten Inspectors, instead of the previous three, by 1968) and had expanded its functions. The Inspectors were no longer to confine themselves to the ". . . merely regulative functions of inquiring into the state of efficiency of each force and the conditions of the cells and lock-ups . . ." (Critchley, 1979, p.187).[5] They were, in future, to encourage inter-force co-operation, to plan strategically for the police service as a whole, and to oversee complaints against the police, in addition to a more intensive role in promoting effectiveness. To one senior civil servant in the Home Office, these new powers gave the Inspectorate the status of an embryo command of a national force (Jacob, 1967), although to a second commentator, speaking as a senior police officer, ". . . the Home Office and the Chief Constables soon discouraged any such tendency . . ." (Wilcox, 1974).

In line with their peculiar quasi-civil status, the regional Inspectors submit reports not to the Home Secretary, but to the Chief Inspectors who then interpret the information on provincial policing for the Minister. The information presented in the Reports has little more than public relations value. Evans, for example, (*The Times'* commentator on police affairs) notes caustically and accurately ". . . a reader of the annual report . . . searches, in vain, for telling new ideas . . ." (Evans, 1974, p.45).

Despite St. Johnston's claim that ". . . the annual inspection is a very detailed affair . . ." (St. Johnston, 1978, p.266) other circumstantial accounts suggest that the Inspectors are limited not so much by the morass of detail on their visits, but by the confines of their own assumptions. As former senior officers in the police service, their interpretations of the activities and effectiveness of local forces is those of the state functionary, not those of the consumer or recipient. What might be problematic to an outsider with a civilian background, and with different presuppositions regarding police efficiency, police function, or about the Complaints procedure, is non-problematic to the former police officer-turned-Inspector. To use an industrial analogy, police forces are highly inefficient (judged by their own contrived clear-up rates (Clarke and Hough, 1980)) and have large and increasing numbers of dissatisfied customers (complainants). But the Inspectors have little to say on the former, and accept the forces' own verdict on the fallibility of the vast majority of their customers/complainants.

However, the quality of the personnel is relatively unimportant when contrasted with the constraints on the Inspectorate as an Institution. The Inspector has no obligations with regard to the accounts of the provincial forces (a function which is reserved for the local authority). His contacts with the force are primary, and encounters with affected civilians—whether the interests represented on the Police Committees or through other bodies—are very much secondary. The inspection time is limited, given the structured form of the visit agenda which puts a premium on topics seen as problematic from within the police apparatus. In recognition of the constraints on the Inspector, one Northern force recently offered to conduct half the inspection itself. And, of course, the largest police force in Britain, the Metropolitan Police, is immune from the activities of the Inspectorate, and indeed, from any outside inspection. As the constitutional justification for the inspection is to assess the case for the Home Office Grant, not to provide a form of accountability, the Met. which is formally directly responsible to the Home Office and does not receive a grant in that form, is therefore not to be inspected.

The determination of the effectiveness of a force, by the Inspectorate, is limited to observable organizational attributes. The scope of the inspections has traditionally been concerned with the procedural propriety of the administration of law enforcement. This has resulted in a general reticence for the Inspectorate to venture beyond the narrow role prescription. Prior to the Police Act for example, Lord Horsham of the Home Office, in a parliamentary debate on allegations of corruption by the Chief Constable of Brighton had said:

> The primary function of the Inspector is to advise the Home Secretary whether the forces were maintained efficiently so that they qualified for the Exchequer Grant . . . It is not the function of the Inspectors to act as detectives . . . it is unreasonable to suggest that the Inspectors should have noted the particular corruption because it is not one of his responsibilities to do so. (*The Times*, 9th December, 1958)

Although the Police Act extended the formal duties of the H.M.I.C.'s to cover the question of the competence of the chief officers, police deviancy which has not been the subject of a civilian complaint, for example, is only relevant to the Inspector's works if it appears to affect overall efficiency.

In effect, the Inspectorate seems to have little clearer idea about the assessment of organizational efficiency that it had a 100 years earlier when that attribute was measured in terms of force size. Chester's 1960 argument that the Inspectors' province should embrace any problems in police work—from deaths in road accidents to police corruption—which might reflect on force efficiency, has not been accepted (Keith-Lucas, 1960).

The old weapon of control by the Home Office, through the Inspectorate, Grant withdrawal, is largely moribund. Always a blunt instrument, it was never clear as to what constituted efficiency, in the assessment of grant-worthiness (Keith-Lucas, 1960). Despite the comments of two writers (Card, 1979; Whitaker, 1979), the Grant sanction appears to have withered away. "Although the Inspectors are concerned with the efficiency of the force, the days when they could or were likely to recommend the witholding of Exchequer Grant on the grounds of inefficiency are over . . ." (Oliver, 1975, p.320; Manning, 1977). Since 1922, Grants have been withheld on 17 occasions, with the threat alone proving sufficient in a further 18. But it has not even been suggested since the threats against York and Stockport in 1965. More importantly, when the Inspector recommended Grant sanction in the past, the intention was as likely to be in support of the local Chief Constable and against the local Watch Committee. It was rarely a threat to the developing autonomy of the chief officers themselves. (On several occasions when the warning was given of Grant withdrawal, on the Inspector's advice, the intention was to cajole a police authority away from appointing its own nominee to a senior post, not to enhance efficiency directly—Keith-Lucas, 1960.) In any case, as the control of operations has been outside the hands of the police authority since the 1964 Act, there would be little sense in using Grant pressure against the Authority, to encourage operational efficiency.

Apart from the Grant, the Common Services Fund (which pays for senior and specialized police training, and for the various centralized squads) is financed jointly by local police authorities and the Home Office. The latter has direct control of this Fund, but any initiatives on such matters as training are normally cleared with the chief officers before being put into operation.

The most effective role played by the Inspectors is in promoting interforce co-operation. The development of Regional Crime Squads, for example, owes much to the activity of the Inspectors. But the promotion of organizational inter-dependence, while it threatened local chief officer autonomy, had the more substantial effect of strengthening the police institution on regional basis, freer from the even nominal supervision of the local police authorities, while no more directly under the influence of Whitehall.

The Inspectors may also be used by the Home Office as organizational entrepreneurs. St. Johnston (the former Chief Inspector) recalls the pressure he brought to bear upon provincial chief officers to form their own Drugs Squads, noting wryly that the subsequent recorded increase in drugs-related offences, may have been primarily due to his entrepreneurship. Grey, a former Scottish Inspector of Constabulary, is generally credited with the introduction of the early Community Involvement schemes.

But those two examples relate to the days before the rise of the major urban and regional forces following the amalgamation of the late 1960s and early 1970s. In the days of borough and county forces the Inspector, when backed by the Home Office and not opposed by A.C.P.O., could pressurize weak Chief Constables into action. But latterly, the powers of the Inspectorate as an institution, have decreased relative to that of the new *corporate managers* of the provincial police. Interpersonal and structural factors have been at the centre of that decline. ·

If as St. Johnston argued, the only *real* power of the Inspectorate lies in Grant withdrawal and the ". . . influence of character and experience" (St. Johnston, 1978, p.262) the effective disappearance of the former leaves only relational influence. But even the inter-personal factors have been modified. In the days when the Inspectorate represented the pinnacle of career ascent for provincial chief officers, the H.M.I.C.s office was imbued with high police institutional status. But with the development of the local fiefdoms of Merseyside, of the West Midlands, of Greater Manchester, and of Thames Valley, the new managerialist chief officers of those forces have already reached their occupational summit. The H.M.I.C.s have come to rank lower within the institution than do the senior local force commanders. The latter have less reason than before for taking note of the views of the Police Inspectorate.

Secondly, the Inspector rarely acts outside the confines of a tacit agreement over what constitutes policing policy between Home Office officials and the representatives of the chief officers. He takes few initiatives. Any policies encouraged have almost certainly already been vetted and approved by Home Office administrators working in collusion with senior police officers. Given the broad commitment of both apparatus to the maintenance of order under the law, there is no foundation for divisive conflict. The chief officers are credited by the Home Office administrators with a professionalism and expertise not necessarily accorded by Ministers to other managers of the local state. Expertise in the context of the legal autonomy of the chiefs, ensures that the normal role for the Inspectorate is as a medium for the communication and implementation of previously agreed policies.

It may be, as Wilcox has claimed, that the only lasting effect of the expansion of the Inspectorate by the Police Act, 1964, has been a relative dilution in the power of that body. While that decline has been of both institution and of personnel, its effects are not of great importance. The major feature of the Inspectorate is that it binds the police institution into a more complex network of administration which serves general state intervention in civil society. But the Inspectors are at the periphery of the web, with the chiefs located towards the centre.

## The Home Office Circular

A number of writers fall back on the second instrument of the Home Office, the Circular, as the major device by which the central state influences the policies and, occasionally, the operations of both provincial and Metropolitan police. About 100 of these missives are issued to the police institution by the Home Office every year ". . . which Parliament has no means of discussing and local councils no right to see . . ." (Whitaker, 1979, p.182).

According to Moodie (an early critic of police autonomy) ". . . the Home Office circular 'advising' the Chief Constables has virtually the force of law . . ." (Moodie, 1972, p.237). To Critchley, (writing of the 1930s) ". . . the prolific 'advice' and 'guidance' contained in the Home Office circulars became a euphemism for 'direction' " (Critchley, 1979, p.219).

But that phrasing fails to distinguish between the different types of Circular — the regulatory and the directive.

Regulatory Circulars embody the Desborough-inherited functions of the Home Office, in line with the decisions of the Police Council (now the Police Negotiating Board). Rates of pay, rest-day allowances, and a variety of standardized information is communicated from the Council and from central government. The Home Office Circular is simply the medium of transmission of agreed information.

Directive Circulars cover new initiatives and the reaction to unusual police-related events. Specialized squads from Drugs to the Operational Support

Divisions were encouraged by such communications. In the 1967–1972 period, in the context of the immigration and race controversies, the Home Office issued a stream of circulars relating to police training schemes in community relations, and on the appointment of police Community Relation Officers.

But in that latter example, the result was mixed. The considerable divergencies between police areas in community relations practices, (as revealed by the 1978 Annual Reports), suggests that if these results are typical, the impact of Directive Circulars is inconsistent. Despite the fact that such memorandum are normally drawn up in conjunction with representatives of the chief officers' association, their effect depends upon the agreement of the Chief Constable, or police Commissioner.

Where law enforcement itself is not directly involved: ". . . the Home Office indicates what steps it thinks might appropriately be taken but the ultimate responsibility is plainly as an operational matter, within the jurisdiction of the Chief Constable . . ." (Leigh, 1973, p.868). Despite Moodie's comment, the expressed view of the Home Office itself on the legal status of the Circulars, regulatory and directive, reflects a different view. Home Secretary, Merlyn Rees, in 1979:

> Circulars or memorandum issued by my Department for the guidance of chief officers of the police do not have the force of law . . . but may, where appropriate, contain advice on the exercise of discretionary powers conferred by Parliament. (*Hansard*, 15th January, 1979)

When new legislation is enacted—or old legislation becomes open to reinterpretation, Home Office Circulars will provide guidance on implementation:

> But the legality of such influence is doubtful. In any case, the policy statement is only likely to be issued by the Home Office after wide consultation. (Williams, 1970)

The authority of the Circular correlates directly with the degree of consultation.[6] For example, the advice of the judiciary is normally sought over Home Office Circulars on matters such as interrogation procedures, and identification practices. Normally, however, the working parties of A.C.P.O. are the major source of counsel. No Circular would be issued from the Home Office against A.C.P.O.'s veto.

The Circular instrument represents the use of a conditional authority. Regulatory Circulars inform local forces of the detail of administrative agreements. Directive Circulars stem from consultative processes and their effect is in inverse relation to the assent of the police institution, as represented through A.C.P.O. Although the latter Circulars may be treated as mandatory by local forces, the source of the authority is not so much the Home Office itself, as the administrative apparatus of the central state, but rather the consultative partner.

The Home Office acts as a clearing-house for views from other parties. It synthesizes a collective account which is then circulated as the policing policy of the state. But that fusion is weighted by accounts whose parameters are determined largely from within the police institution. As in the case of the Police Inspectorate, the Circular instrument represents an administrative envelopment of the police service within the wider context of the routine central state intervention, but it does not reflect any significant directive control from the political elites.

## Parliament and Residual Forms of Accountability

There are a number of other channels through which the previous power of local police authorities may be substituted from within the central state, and which may appear to constrain the managerialist authority of the chief officers. But they affect either peripheral aspects of police administration; are narrowly directed; are untested; or depend upon the willingness of the chief officers to take note of the direction.

For many years the Home Office has exercised disqualificatory rights over the appointment of chief officers and of their immediate deputies. Although as Pain has commented:

> It's a policy rather than a law . . . It had been the case that you could not be a Chief Constable of a force you had joined unless you'd been absent for at least three years since attaining the rank of chief inspector. They've now been modified to being absent for three years since attaining the rank of chief inspector . . . (Pain, 1978, p.7)

the practice has been given a new lease in life.

Intended to prevent local nepotism, its most recent public use was in Cheshire in 1978 to bar a local officer succeeding to a command post. It remains however, a negative sanction of limited impact.

Secondly, the 1964 Act gave the Home Secretary the right to compulsorily retire wayward chief officers. But while there has been a suspicion of such threats in a number of recent cases, there have been no recent dismissals, and except in extreme situations, it does not provide a realistic sanction. (In practice, the only sanction that the Home Secretary is likely to use against a chief officer is, where convenient, to appoint him to the Inspectorate. Although a seeming elevation, it allows the Home Secretary to dismiss with grace.)

The power under Section 32 of the Police Act, to call for an enquiry ". . . into any matter connected with the policing of any area" is also conspicuous by its disuse. In few cases since 1964, has the Home Secretary felt impelled to use this authority, and normally resists Parliamentary pressure to innovate that clause (although revived after the Brixton disturbances of Easter 1981).

The similar explanatory accountability device of the "call for Reports" is also rarely used. Although occasional Reports are delivered to the Home Secretary on particular local police matters, like the Enquiries, demands for Reports from Members of Parliament are normally fended off by the Ministry with the claim that the matter is an operational one (and therefore not the subject of the 1964 Act). The normal response by the Home Secretary is banal and negative (even declining to place the Chief Constables Annual Reports, in the House of Commons library).

These responses, of course, do not deny his constitutional right to call for Reports of for Enquiries, or to give full answers to Parliamentary questions. Rather they indicate two things. Either the Home Secretary is normally in agreement with policing policy, as practiced by the chiefs or, alternatively, the police institution is itself too powerful, as a repository of expertise and of discretionary legal powers over law enforcement, for the Minister to effectively intervene.[7]

Parliament has its own independent power to establish enquiries into aspects of the police institution, as into other areas of public expenditure. The 1979 investigation into "Deaths in Custody" by a Parliamentary Select Affairs Committee was a novel, but necessarily limited, attempt to uncover one part of the police apparatus. This case demonstrated a potential for negative intervention that had not previously been evident.

The appointment of a Parliamentary Commissioner, or Ombudsman (sic), opened a more general medium of public accountability. However, despite the recent extension of the functions of that office to cover all major institutions requiring state expenditure, the police apparatus remains the one major sector specifically excluded from those investigatory powers (although curiously, the local police authority is itself open to that investigation).

Since a 1976 Act, which marginally extended the procedure for the investigation of complaints against police officers, there has existed a narrow avenue of public scrutiny in this area. However, the results of the work of the new Police Complaints Board would have confounded those police officers who led the resistance to it (including Sir Robert Mark, who gave its introduction as his formal reason for resignation from the Commissionership of the Metropolitan Police), and confirmed the negative predictions of those commentators who saw little value in its introduction (Leigh, 1976; Cain, 1977).

The capital itself is still largely governed by the Metropolitan Police Act, 1829. The political relation of the police in London has always been more obscure than in the provinces. The lack of any elected local police authority has always made its accountability to civil society peculiar, even by the standards of the provincial Watch Committees and Police Authorities. Where Members of Parliament seek to conduct the formal functions of provincial Police Authority members, they commonly meet with standardized rebuffs.[8] The Home Secretary, as the police authority himself, maintains a vestige of control by formal monthly approval of the amendments to the general orders and regulations of the force. As Plehwe (1974) argues, there has been an expansion of the autonomy of the Commissioner in recent years. Paradoxically, the Home Secretary's answerability to Parliament for the Metropolitan Police may be greater than his actual authority over the force.

The controversies over the 'sus' laws, the Brixton riot, and the more general fiscal crisis, influenced the new Labour Greater London Council to formulate a more democratic relation with the Metropolitan Police. But it was a move successfully resisted by the police institution with the general support of the key economic and political interests in the capital.

The influence of the central state, in the form of the Home Office, over the police apparatus is residual power. The Home Secretary, or rather the civil servants of that Ministry, can affect those areas of police work which senior police officers regard as uncontroversial. The Home Office rarely has a distinctive collective view of its own. Where it does speak out on legal and policing policy, its arguments tend to mirror those of the police institution (as in the Royal Commission on Criminal Procedure—James, 1979). Its powers are few but where they exist they are not exercised.

But more importantly, although several of the channels of influence are of potential significance—the economic constraint, although never used directly against the police institution by the central state does reflect the ultimate, latent, power of the political class that rules through the state, to affect policing policy and practice—there is no reason why they should be used. In so far as the police apparatus serves the general purposes of the state in maintaining social stability, and in its policies reflects the primary interests of the dominant class, within the law, there is little concern with day-to-day malfunctions in that practice. Any critique by other apparatus of the central state, or by Parliament, that undermines the particular legal relation of the police institution (by exposing police deviance, for example) undermines the general legitimacy of the institution. In the end, the Home Office and the police apparatus are concerned with the same general objective. When Plehwe says of London, that it is:

> . . . reasonable to assume that in practice there has been no serious conflict which would have necessitated a comprehensive and precise delineating of the respective spheres of authority of the Home Secretary and the Commissioner . . . (1974, p.334)

he is documenting not so much the absence of conflict but rather the absence of any basis for conflict between the representative of the dominant political class and the police institution. The political and economic elites do not intervene in the police institution, partly because of the relative independence constructed by the new managerialist chief officers, and partly because there would be no particular advantage to be obtained from using the police institution in partisan fashion.

When Critchley, Williams, and Card reduce the powers of the Home Office to a rump of informal relations [". . . much can be and is achieved by consultation, and informal off-the-record discussion" (Card, 1979, p.11)], they buttress the conclusion that the degree of control between the central state and the police apparatus is relatively unimportant. The police institution, under the guidance of expert managers, services the purposes of English law which in turn, like the other activities of the Home Office, contributes to the maintenance of a particular kind of social order. From the available evidence it is clear that the degree of central direction of the police institution has not significantly increased, despite Bowden's claim, but to challenge that point is perhaps to answer the wrong question.

# Notes

1. This first Inspectorate Report, 1839, epitomized the dilemma embedded in the Home Office — Watch Committee relation over the question of police resources. It aimed to construct a formula on which to base police establishments but concluded by accepting that different areas would require different numbers of police officers. This early acknowledgement of local variations became a basic negotiating tool of the chief officers.
2. See, for example, the Inspector's comment on the Liverpool Police, in 1859.
3. The Dixon Report, indeed, merely rendered in statistical form what was traditional policing practice in the Met. Its assessment of the work of 45 Metropolitan stations did little more than quantify and give apparently objective numerical form, to traditional police work. Routine practice (and the assumptions implicit in that practice) was reified as a mathematical construct.
4. A detailed outline of the functions of the Inspectorate is given in the Royal Commission on Criminal Procedure (1981a, p.45). In fact, by 1981, there were only five Inspectors (regionally based) in England and Wales, in addition to the specialist Inspectors and the Chief Inspector.
5. The following example from the 1856 Report on the Liverpool force typifies the form of inspections during the first century:

> The men assembled for inspection looked exceedingly well, and presented the appearance of a carefully chosen, well-trained and effective body of constables. Their clothing arrangements were in good serviceable conditions; the books appear to have been well-kept, and the men's quarters . . . change rooms, and cells for prisoners, were very clean and in good order. In the opinion of this Inspector, this force has been maintained in a very satisfactory state of discipline and general efficiency.

The present influence of the Inspectorate over the police institution is difficult to assess. By an historical accident—the problem of maintaining individual force inspections during World War I—accounts of the force inspections were no longer published. In their place, appeared an even blander Report of the Chief Inspector which appears to represent a very selective summary, of the Chief Constables' own highly selective Annual Reports. This historical accident has since been legitimized by the Home Secretary (*Hansard,* 27th January, 1980) thus ensuring the disappearance of one public, if limited, check of the activities of the Inspectors, and on the policies, operations, and resources of the provincial police.

6. See for example, Circular No. 74/978 on the implementation of Section 2, Criminal Justice Act, 1977 as an illustration of the way Home Office Circulars are drawn up after consultation with the police institution (in R.C. on Criminal Procedure, 1980. Appendix 14, p.166).

7. Ian Davidson of the *Financial Times* conveys some impression of the interpersonal relation between the Home Office civil servants and the police ". . . in practice, it is clear that the Home Office is not in any sense in charge . . . regardless of its ultimate possibilities, and it is my impression that the primary characteristic of the department in dealing with that kind of hot potato, is that of fear . . ." (*Financial Times,* 28th January, 1980).

8. See, for example, the case, quoted by Plehwe (1974), of the Ministerial reply over the disbanding of police road safety teams, and a later reply from the Minister over the closing of a Metropolitan police station. He could not interfere with that closure, the Home Secretary claimed, because it was an operational matter (*Hansard,* 27th July, 1978).

# 5     *The Legal Relation*

.................................................I said that I
Derived authority for my high office not
From the jerk and whirl of irrelevant faction—
........................... your Democratic Punch and Judy—
But from the law being abstract, extant, placed
(John Arden's Chief Constable Feng in *The Workhouse Donkey*, 1964, p.125)

The primary characteristic of the chief officers as police officers is their control over the use of legitimate force in the maintenance of social order within the law. Police work is law enforcement. But the permissive form of the legal structure, together with the requirement to use discretion, gives chief officers wide authority to maintain social order within the law, and to use (or more commonly to threaten) force to achieve that end.

Fundamentally, however, the defining feature of the police apparatus within the state, is not that of its access to force. Its primary characteristic is its legal relation. A police force is that body constituted to enforce the law. It includes within that legal relation, all the manifestations of contemporary British police work, from the Special Branch to the Juvenile and School Liaison Officers. Wherever and in whatever context, police work develops, the primary concern and justification for its involvement is that of the legal relation.

This legal relation has three particular implications for the police institution in Britain. It provides for a unique dimension of authority. It allows the police institution to refute conventional requirements of political accountability to reference to legal controls. Moreover, it allows a particular ideological relation to be postulated between the police institution and civil society.

The one major feature that distinguishes chief police officers from other managers within the local state relates to the form of control. Housing managers, education officers, planning officers and their equivalents all owe their position and their exercise of authority to political appointment. They are answerable personally for their actions to the representatives of the politically dominant class.

But chief police officers derive their authority as police officers, not from political appointment but from the law. In so far as police powers are original and derive from traditional common law, they possess independent rights of arrest and prosecution-powers which cannot legally be interfered with by political representatives. Unlike housing managers, chief police officers have a legal autonomy from political control and direction. They have the right to make decisions which contravene the expressed wishes of the political leadership.

Secondly, this original authority allows for the development of a surrogate form of accountability. Unlike other institutions, the police apparatus can legitimately justify the absence of a formal political relation—portrayed as partisan—by reference to the legal relation. Within policing ideology the gradual disappearance of the practice of political control is viewed as a progressive reform in the direction of true accountability—the obligation to act according to legal not political direction.

Police professionalism not merely legitimizes this substitution but as an ideology actively promotes the replacement of political direction by a conception of legal control. Police officers, it is argued, can only be impartial in their work when they are formally separated from the political structure and allowed to act independently as functionaries of the law, not of government. In Alderson's words:

> In England, the police are primarily associated with the law of the land rather than with politics. The commissioners and chief constables have an independence which is not a feature of the office of their counterparts in France or in the U.S.A. Thus, the British policeman is better able to adopt a stance of servant of the general public and impartial guardian of the peace. (Alderson, 1975, p.12)

Consequently, this notion of the original powers allows for the construction and support of a particular ideological notion of the relation between the police institution and civil society. Political masters are by definition partisan. Law, unlike politics, is neutral and beyond party dispute. If the police officer derives his legal powers from his status as a citizen, then police power is citizen-power.

The corporate body of citizens is represented as a community. The source of police authority lies in that community. Hence, Sir Robert Mark is able to make his claim:

> the fact that the British police are answerable to the law, that we act on behalf of the community and not under the mantle of government, makes us the least powerful, the most accountable, therefore the most acceptable police in the worlds. (Mark, 1977, p.56)

Police accountability is to the community from which its powers derive. An ideal democratic relation is contrasted with the apparently inferior political manifestation and forms of democracy.

From that position, that new responsive relation, democratic policing can be contrasted with the continuing attempt of "sectarian" elected politicians to undermine the new democracy.

The ideological picture of accountability to the law is bound-up with an apparent duty on police officers to remove all vestiges of political direction and control, which they interpreted as control by constitutionally elected authorities. In this chapter, this conventional account of the legal relation of the police institution will be examined in detail. It will be demonstrated that while some of the points relating the police to the law are technically correct (and that others are not), taken together, they make for an ideological view of policing that ignores the material practice of police work in British society, and represents a partisan conception of police-class relations (masked under the social construct of the community). The legal relation of the police institution occludes both the purpose for which that relation is utilized, and some of the major discontinuities in its content.

The first part of this chapter documents the substance of the legal relation of the police in England and Wales, and exposes the essential ideological function of that relation. The proposition that the police officer has original powers, it is postulated, has an especial value for the function and authority of the chief officer. The notion of the legal relation is then extended to encompass the practice of legal and judicial control over the police institution, and, secondly the prosecution process. It is argued in both cases that within the law police officers enjoy considerable unfettered discretion. A criterion of reasonableness permits significant police freedom of action in the process of arrest, in the presentation of court-room evidence, in the legal form itself, and in the decision to prosecute. In turn, that latitude reflects the unique position of the police as arbiters of legal relations within the class relations embodied in the spirit of legality.

## The Police Institution and the Doctrine of "Original Powers"

### In the office of constable

The orthodox conception of the legal relation gives primary emphasis to the office of the constable.[1] As every police training manual instructs, all police officers irrespective of rank, hold that office. The New Police, although distinct from the medley of constabulary forces that they succeeded in numbers in organization, in command structure, and in demeanour, maintained the same link with the law.

Like the mediaeval constable, the new professional forces of nineteenth century England practiced forms of arrest and prosecution as citizens-in-uniform, rather than as commanded by a particular class, legislative assembly, or chief officer. No superior officer — or for that matter, merchant, manufacturer, shopkeeper, or Members of Parliament — could countermand their discretionary powers as embodied in traditional common law.

According to such accounts (Alderson, 1980), the authority of the modern police officer is citizen power writ large. Contemporary police forces are — *sine qua non* — bodies of individuals holding the common law office of constable. The accountability of the police to civil authorities cannot override the fundamental rights and obligations of policing as embodied in traditional common law. This interpretation of the source of powers and of the composition of the British police has been supported in several modern studies of policing, in the older Royal Commissions, and in a number of twentieth century law cases. To Picton Davies, for example, (in a major study of police structure and organization ". . . the basic powers of the modern police officer flow from his status as a constable, and not from his membership of a police force" (Picton Davies, 1973). For the 1929 Royal Commission of Police Powers and Procedure "The police, in this country, have never been recognised, either in law or by tradition, as a force distinct from the general body of citizens" (para.17). Similarly, in the Willink Report, one encounters ". . . because his (sic) powers are 'original' and not 'delegated', the constable enjoys a degree of independence . . ."

Judicial decisions have given benediction to both the traditional common law powers and to the parish constable inheritance. In the classic *Fisher vs Oldham Corporation 1930*, the plaintiff had been subject to wrongful arrest and sued the local council as employers of the arresting police officer. The court dismissed the case, on the grounds that the authority of the officer did not derive from his employment by the Corporation but from common law. "A constable . . . when acting as a peace officer, is not exercising a delegated authority, but an original authority" (Critchley, 1979, p.271).

Practical support for this ideological location of police powers as original occurred in a 1973 incident — the successful private prosecution of Rees-Davies, a Conservative M.P. (over a traffic offence), by a Kent Police Constable (P.C. Joy) after the latter's superior officer had ordered him not to proceed with the charge while acting as a member of the county force. Joy's prosecution power derived from his common law citizenship not from his membership of a uniformed force. The relationship of the officer to the law was direct, no authority — senior officers or political representatives — could intervene.

But while the principle of the independence of the constable's discretionary power and the postulated link between constable and citizens, have been politically buttressed by a number of Ministerial and Parliamentary statements, several points undermine the credibility of the case.

On these claims of the independence of the constable and of the community link, rest the primary defence of the police institution against political intervention. The notion of community accountability via the conception of the constable as a citizen-in-uniform has been developed as an ideological statement which serves as one major justification of the autonomy of the new urban police managers.

However, the question mark overshadows the contention of a direct line of descent from the pre-industrial constable. The other query is over the contribution of that discretionary constable's authority to the powers of the chief police officer.

## The flaws in the inheritance contention

Concentration on the source of powers, deflects attention from the way the practice of policing has been partially modified by the development of a modern police force paid for out of revenue. There is an economic relation (foreshadowed by the original River Thames police, and by the local Docks Police) between the contemporary police, the state and the dominant economic and political forces, that did not exist prior to the first paid substitutes.

Similarly, this ideological defence of police autonomy does not detail the direct relation between the two general forms of policing, the old and the new, and the process of inheritance. In fact, the legislation on which the first forces were based (the Metropolitan Police Act, 1829, the Municipal Corporation Act, 1835), and the County Police Act, 1839) did not specify the legal position of the new police officers and the source of their powers. Their legal status was left in an ambiguous void. Neither those statutes nor the earlier treatise by the man credited with the first scheme for a professional force, Patrick Colquhoun (1797) gave any attention to the question of whether or not the new forces would require statutory powers, or whether the traditional common law power would suffice. The issue was set aside. The relation between the New Police and their predecessors, as law enforcers was constructed in default.

The General Instructions to the new Metropolitan force, in demanding strict obedience to superior officers, gave no advice on the pursuit of original and undelegated authority ". . . if indeed that was ever intended" (Oliver, 1975, p.316). Certainly, there is no suggestion that the New Police considered that the source of their authority lay outside their posts as functionaries in a peculiarly quasi-military organization (Oliver, 1975). They imposed legislation on the basis of their appointment as constables, and according to the strictures of their commanding officers. Within what in practice, were tight confines, they were encouraged (after the first few years of mass implementation of petty legislation) to use their discretion.

While there are exceptions,[2] modern instructions to new probationary constables rarely acknowledge the pre-1829 ancestry of policing, although they outline both general powers, as well as powers determined by statute. Responsibility to the law is stressed but there are few attempts to relate such powers to the notion of citizens-in-uniform.

The relation between the modern police and the constables, as the Royal Commission on Criminal Procedure points out, is much more complex than that portrayed by Alderson and his colleagues:

> This is too simple a view of the position now. The police officer is . . . subject to a statutory scheme of control by his senior officers in addition to the general criminal and civil law. He does have greater legal powers than the ordinary citizen . . . and he is a member of a large disciplined and technologically advanced service, with all the resources and authority that brings. (1981, p.2)

The police constable is neither a descendant of the parish constable nor is he simply a citizen-in-uniform. The original parish constables' powers were little greater than those of the ordinary citizen. But the substance of the powers of the police officer in the 1980s, quantitatively and qualitatively, extends that legal status. He has more power than his assumed ancestor. Certain acts are incumbent on him but not on the citizen.

While private citizens retain the right to effect arrest and to instigate prosecutions, a police officer enjoys a number of unique rights and duties, imposed by statute. "A police officer has all the powers of a private person to effect arrests but in addition he has certain other powers" (Barnard, 1974, p.35). He/she can, for example, legally break into a private dwelling in a search for drugs. Similarly, the police officer is compelled to take an active as opposed to passive approach to law enforcement. He/she cannot legally walk away from a law violation (Card, 1979). In contrast to the position of the police officer, the citizen's powers of law enforcement are not coupled with a duty to utilize them. Further as Williams illustrates "A constable may arrest if he suspects with reasonable cause that a felony has been committed but a private person may arrest only if that felony has in fact been committed . . ." (1974, p.186). A further distinction between the notion of a citizen-in-uniform and the role of a police officer in a professional force is with regard to the disqualification of the latter. The police officer is restricted in the use he/she can make of information gained in the course of his/her occupation.

> When on duty, a constable obtains his evidence *qua* a constable which on many instances could not be obtained by a private citizen e.g. requiring breath test, demanding the production of certain documents like a driving license . . . he cannot use that information as a private citizen . . . (Gillance and Khan, 1975, p.60)

As a signatory of the Official Secrets Act, he/she may be in breach of the law if he/she passes on information obtained as a police officer. The private citizen is generally under no such duress. Moreover, the police officer is subject to special political and social disabilities. He/she cannot join a trade union, move homes without the approval of the chief police officer, or take an explicit part in politics. He/she is disenfranchised of a number of citizenship rights. While the police officer's prosecutorial powers are undoubtedly derived from a citizen's powers, the P.C. Joy case merely reinforces the ambiguities and contradictions in the practical status of the police officer. In that case, Joy's powers of prosecution were both correctly justified in terms of their derivation but ambiguous in relation to his present status. The powers of police prosecution, of who decides senior, or junior officers, are confused.

The rights of arrest and of prosecution of the constables may, according to some accounts be subsumed under the authority of the chief officer, who under the Police Act, 1964, is responsible for the direction and control of the force. Denning's much-quoted commentary in *Blackburn vs Metropolitan Commissioner, 1968*, supports the view that the police officer has lost his citizen's powers:

> . . . it is for the Commissioner of Police or Chief Constable as the case may be to decide whether enquiries should be pursued, whether an arrest should be made or a prosecution brought

According to Denning's claim, because the senior officer who negated the initial prosecution decision by Joy was acting for the Chief Constable, he acted correctly. The legal right to prosecute had been overtaken by the formal rank structure of the modern police.

Indeed, even if Joy was legally correct to engage in private prosecution against the wishes of a superior, under Police Regulations (the disciplinary rules which have the force of law within the police organization), he could also have been legally punished by the organization for that action. Even in his non-work life, he remained a member of the Kent force and liable to the direct orders of his legal superior (Marshall, 1978).

Within the police institution, there is more confusion regarding the relationship between citizens and police than Alderson allows. G.S. Morris for example, in the *Police Review* said:

> . . . the theory of independent status . . . is . . . incompatible with the contemporary position of the individual constable, who as a member of a disciplined force has only a restricted discretion in performing his duties. (G.S. Morris, 1980)

Oliver, later a Chief Constable himself, notes the disagreement at that level:

> . . . Opinions among chief officers are divided . . . one is of the opinion
> that whilst he cannot order the constable to lay a private information . . .
> (1975, p.316)

he would instruct his Solicitors to attend court to advise against proceeding with
the prosecution:

> . . . another is firmly of the view that he has complete command over his
> constables and that it would be in his right to order a constable exactly when
> and how to enforce the law, any failure being visited by discipline; whilst a
> third takes the view that as far as law enforcement is concerned he has no
> influence over the individual constable's authority. (ibid)

While these opinions may in one sense by unimportant—chief police officers
personal views do not have the weight of established law—they are also
determining. Within the ambiguous context of the dispute over the constable's
legal status, the decisions of the chief officers represent the practice of law.
Where a Chief Constable deems it in his right to override the decisions of his
subordinates over arrest and prosecution, that is the law unless challenged by the
courts.

In this ambiguity lies the strength of the chief officers' position. *They can
legitimately free themselves from political accountability at the same time that they
enjoy the freedom, if they so wish, to enhance their own internal control.* Where a
connection can be constructed between the constable's powers and those of the
private citizen, a notion of accountability to the community through citizenship,
is contrived. Chief Officers, like their subordinates, are freed from controls by
political representatives because of their original law enforcement powers. They
require, indeed, demand the freedom to act according to the traditional common
law powers. Further, they intuit, as it were, the community's opinions on police
work. No partisan politicians intrude between the police institution and its
source—that body of citizens who make up the imaginary community.

Oliver again, putting forward the institutional perspective:

> The principal advantage of maintaining a traditional view of the office of
> Constable is that it ensures that Ministers cannot be accused of using the
> police force as another army of Government and there can be no suggestion
> that political expediency will affect the operational independent status of
> Chief Officers. By holding that a constable has original and undelegated
> authority, it is possible to argue that the public enjoys protection from a
> politically untainted force. (Oliver, 1975, p.321)

Clearly, the alternative view to Oliver's interpretation is that the "advantage" is
the Chief Officer's. The emphasis upon the original source of powers legitimizes
the autonomy of the chiefs as the major figures in the police institution, from

external political controls, and distinguishes them markedly from other managers within the local state.

In other words, although there are major flaws in the claim that the source of police powers lie in the "community" and that police powers are simply a version of the citizen's powers, the argument for that relation is strongly made by chief officers because it has particular benefits for their own autonomy. Their freedom of action, when political controls have been discarded, is justified by reference to the peculiar legal relation of the office of constable.

## The "original" powers of the chief officer

The legal ambiguity of the constable's powers becomes more apparent when related to the office of the Chief Constable.[3] While the relationship between the function of police officers and the role constable has recently been given an ideological boost, the ambiguity of the traditional common law status has had a particular effect on the more specific autonomy of the chief officer himself. Together with alterations in the relation between the police institution and the judiciary, and developments in the forms of internal control, the chief officer's power as an independent functionary has benefited from the vacuum created by the legal confusion. ("The chief officer of police is in effect the beneficiary of the older constitutional assumption . . ." Williams, 1974, p.189.) Historically, three forms of legally sanctioned political constraint have influenced the actions of senior police officers — *direct control, accountability by sanction* (negative accountability), and *accountability by explanation* (or Report). The first of these sanctions, direct control, characterizes the relation between Watch Committee and New Police in the early years, and the occasional later nineteenth century interventions, illustrated in Chapter 2. Irrespective of legal structure — of the traditional common law status of the chief officer as a constable — some early Watch Committees gave directions on general law enforcement policy, on general prosecution policy, on the deployment of forces, and also on particular acts of law enforcement and prosecution.

While, on the basis of the Liverpool evidence, these interventions were rare after the first decade or so, where they occurred they related to a direct contradiction between the statutory powers of the Watch, and the traditional common law status of the constable. The Watch was empowered by the Municipal Corporations Act, 1835 ". . . to suspend or dismiss a constable if they were satisfied that he was negligent or otherwise unfit for duty . . ." (Critchley, 1979, p.272). If the Watch determined, according to its own conception of the police requirements of the borough, that the Chief Constable was not conducting his functions properly, it was empowered to dismiss him. But that dismissal would infringe the traditional common law status, if it had been preceded by direct instructions. Where direct instructions were given, they could lawfully be refused even though paradoxically, the chief officer could still be dismissed for carrying out what he considered to be his lawful duty.

This incongruity allowed for exploitation by the dominant partner. As the Watch Committee diminished in importance, and that of the chiefs, and of the central state increased, the chiefs were able once again to lay claim to the common law as the basis of their status. The constable office, not the power of the local authority to dismiss a municipal employee, became the defining feature of the relation. The chief constable's legal status did not change. Rather the common law status was elevated and re-affirmed, relative to the chief's position as an employee of the local state. Legal contradiction facilitated the modification in the balance of power.

In this development, local councillors and Aldermen, on the Watch Committee were repeating the experience of the local magistrates whose position had similarly been undermined by changing legal practice. Originally, responsible for the early county forces, the magistrates had lost their power in London, in 1839, and more generally by the Summary Jurisdiction Act, 1848. However, the major encroachment on their authority arose from the trend, throughout the nineteenth century, of making arrests on the basis of common law powers, rather than on the production of a justice's summons. The police institution slowly assumed responsibility, itself, for the majority of prosecutions, through the assertion of the traditional citizenry powers.

As the common law principle was asserted, the political and judicial authorities were thrust back on their residual powers. For the Watch Committees and the Home Office, this meant the power of dismissal and of control over expenditure. For the magistrates and the judiciary, the powers were primarily those of the invalidation of police evidence in court. Negative sanctions came to the fore when the unconstitutional power of direct control disappeared. This retreat climaxed with the dismissal of the Chief Constable of Nottingham in 1959, by the local Watch Committee. Precedent (the dismissal of the Head Constable of Liverpool in 1844, and the threatened sacking of the Head of the Birmingham force, in 1880), and statute gave the authority the legal prerogative. But the 1959 dismissal took place in a different structural context.[4] The legal form of the Watch Committee's power remained intact but the relative decline of the local state allowed the Home Secretary to take advantage of the ambiguous legal status of the chief officer and to enhance the chief's independence of action. The Home Secretary's action (he had made an opposite one in 1880) in confirming the priority of the common law office, reflected the changing power relation, not changing law. Legal ambiguity, and the simultaneous publicity given to the apparent contradiction between party politics and impartial law enforcement, were the stratagems by which the autonomy of the chief officer from the local authority was enhanced and institutionalized. The office of constable was reinvigorated to justify the new formal relation. The succeeding Police Act, 1964, formally enshrined that principle in determining the autonomy of the chief officer. Accountability by sanction was ceremonially buried by the 1959 incident and the 1964 statute. As explanatory accountability succeeded, the political, legal relation was constructed through the ideological form of the original police powers.

The Act re-stated and reinforced the common law claims. The original rights and duties of the chief officer were underlined and his powers as a constable extended beyond the traditional police area boundaries. It reinforced by statute the common law powers of law enforcement.

Politically, it distanced the police institution by statute, as well as by tradition, from interventions, in control, and in direction, by external authorities. The subordination of the chief to those representative agencies was reduced to the rump of explanatory accountability powers (as detailed in Chapter 3).

But equally importantly, and paradoxically, at the same time that the Act reinforced his original powers, it subtly diminished those of his subordinates in his favour. The police manager was given organizational authority. The Act made it the chief officer's primary responsibility to "direct and control" his force. "Direction" involved the development of policing policy for the area, and the necessary deployment of the constables under his command in order to fulfil both traditional common law functions and the obligations peculiar to members of a professional force. The notion of "control" encompassed all the supervisory functions — such as disciplining and appointing his subordinates. His organizational power was made more precise. The Act located the disciplinary and internal control mechanisms firmly in his hands, removing the interventionist power of the police authority as a disciplinary appeals tribunal. Finally, it made the chief officer tortiously liable for the acts of his subordinates.[5]

In sum, the relational changes which were formally constituted in the Police Act, 1964, substantially increased the authority of the chief officer, at the same time as they constrained the discretion of his officers in his favour. Policing policy and operational control was firmly established as his undisputed territory. He alone was to be responsible for force deployment. No external influence could intervene between the chief and his officers.

Secondly, he had increased his direct power over the organizational controls — the internal sanctions of promotion, rewards, and discipline. The chief had become the sole intermediary between the officers of the local force and the external authorities. Apart from the minor modifications of the later Police Complaint Act, 1976, the Police Act, 1964 ensured that, in future, relations between individual constables and the paymasters of the force would be only through the office of the chief.

While the chief officer may formally control only the general boundaries of the constable's legal discretion, by deployment of resources, by the implementation of a general policing policy of arrest and prosecution, and by managerial decision-making, he may strongly encourage particular forms of action by his subordinates. His organizational position determines the parameters of the constable's discretion. The use of the original powers argument therefore has two functions for senior police officers. It sustains a professional ideology which legitimizes the freedom of the police institution from political control and replaces it with a construct based upon citizenship — the community relation. It also camouflages the degree of organizational control possible by the office. There appears to be no decisive factor preventing a chief officer intervening in normal practice in the haze of uncertainty surrounding his subordinates' discretionary powers. While there is some material base to the traditional common law argument, it has been used in an exaggerated fashion to construct a legal relation which confers certain benefits on the police institution, and on the chief officer, in particular. It reinforces the image of the latter as an impartial manager.

### Residual legal restraints — the permissiveness of law

The orthodox view of the legal relation of the police institution consists of the thesis that, as all other forms of control are shown to be invalid, the law itself offers the most appropriate and value-free constraint. Within that construction of the law, there are three elements. The dominant theme is that of the "original powers" claim. Police powers are citizen's powers.

But there are two further elements. The first of these relates to the nature of law itself. Implicit in the statement of the law, as the taskmaster of the police is the suggestion that it precludes choice. Expert managerial police officers neutrally enforce concise statutes.

Secondly, as part of the legal relation, the judicial institution itself is assumed to prevent police partisanship and to ensure that police conduct adheres to the intent of the law. Police officers, it is argued, like other citizens, are subject to the law of the land. Their practices are kept within the law because watching over them, sit the judiciary.

However, what primarily characterizes English law, and its application, is its permissive and discretionary form. Laws are not imperatives but require interpretation. Mandatory in police work is the requirement to use discretion — to select enforcement occasions and the mode of enforcement. Similarly, the judicial controls. While they ensure that police officers generally obey the law, they are largely permissive towards the police institution where the law is unclear and where the status of the rules is confused.

These two elements of the legal relation can be dealt with together. Judicial constraints on the police institution, and especially on the conduct of chief officers, are indulgent. The two attempts by Raymond Blackburn to sue the

Metropolitan Commissioner over the latter's enforcement policy demonstrated the degree of autonomy in the hands of the latter (Card, 1979). It was established in those cases, that the courts would only interfere with the chief officer's discretionary power on the following occasions: (a) when the chief officer decided never to prosecute a particular category of offence; (b) when he accepted direct instructions from the police authority and did not use his own discretion; (c) when the offences were blatant and the enforcement procedures were lax.

But even in these exceptional circumstances, the judiciary will not take the initiative. It will not act unless prompted by a private citizen or by the Attorney-General. Even when the court does find in favour of such a plaintiff, it cannot order the chief constable to remedy his particular action but can only require him to change his general policy.

The judiciary has one other recognized control over the police institution. It can affect the prosecution conduct of police officers. For example:

> Disapproval of a particular prosecution can be seen or reflected on the strictures of the judges, in the sentences imposed, in the award of costs against the prosecution, and in advice offered for the future. (Williams, 1974, p.175)

Chief officers can be summoned to the courts to justify and to explain law enforcement practices but, again, they cannot be required to alter them. In any case, there are no recent examples of the use of such judicial powers. Explanatory accountability to the courts is practised even more rarely than to the police authorities.

Junior officers are more open to court-room rebuke. The process of arrest, of interrogation, of search and the seizing of goods, provide the opportunity for judicial or magisterial criticism of particular police officers. But rebukes are unusual. The courts act permissively. Griffiths offers one point of view. Police practices, he argues, have "frequently in recent years, stretched far beyond their powers and infringed not only the spirit of the law but its letter also . . ." (1978, p.198).

According to that account of judicial inaction, the judiciary fails to curtail the numerous cases of marginal law violation by police officers — for example, in the presentation of evidence. Moodie, similarly claims that police officers are treated permissively by the courts. For example:

> . . . no action will normally be taken against a constable who contravenes the Judges Rules . . . and a court will seldom disallow the evidence produced thereby. (1972, p.231)

But these views miss the point. The favourable disposition of the courts and the judiciary towards police evidence and police prosecution is not just a by-product, an accidental manifestation of bureaucratic practice in the processing of defendants. Rather it relates to the way the discretionary form of police actions mirrors McBarnet's "spirit of legality" (McBarnet,1978a, 1981). Courts act according to two sets of rules. The formal rules, in statutory form, provides the general guidelines. But within those general rules, there are "common-sense" rules which provide the more specific indicators, in individual cases. The common-sense rules allow the courts to determine the "reasonableness" of discretionary action by the police. "Insofar as the constable can justify his actions in such broad 'common-sense' terms, he is acting lawfully" (Jefferson and Grimshaw, 1981, p.10).

McBarnet (1978a) has documented the way this notion of the reasonable application of discretion is accommodated within the law of arrest. Euphemisms such as "resisting arrest" and "helping with enquiries" are accepted by the courts as appropriate legal forms. Police practices are congruent with the judiciary's conception of "reasonable" practice.

Similarly, the choice of charge fits with the requirement of court practice. The relative freedom of the police to select the charge allows for the legal circumvention of the requirement for a sufficiency of evidence. Cases of "loitering", "breaches of the peace", and so on, are deemed by the courts to warrant only the interpretation of the officer as to the constitution of an offence. According to McBarnet:

> If the police operate at this level with wide discretion, it is not just because they surreptitiously take it into their own hands but because they are formally allocated discretion in what constitutes an offence via vague laws and wide procedural powers. (McBarnet, 1978b, p.89)

The constraints by the courts, therefore, paradoxically maximize police discretion and interpretations. As long as police officers can demonstrate that their action within the permissive form of law, are "reasonable" according to conventional legal standards, there is little intervention by the judiciary with the practices of the police institution.

But it is not just in the relation with the courts that the legal restraints over the police institution are permissive. Police power depends, in part, upon residual legislation which allows police officers blanket powers to deal with any particular cases. The form of law itself, as prompted by the police institution in its construction and retention ensures considerable police autonomy. For example, throughout the history of policing in Liverpool there has existed specific legislation which has ensured considerable police freedom to act arbitrarily against those elements that could be deemed disturbing to the social order. The powers of the original Watch to arrest night-time vagrants were cited in Chapter 2. But the New Police were also given such formal powers — powers that were renewed in 1921, and in 1980, in substantially the same form. The 1842 bye-law, for example, repeated in draughtsmanship, and in intent the powers of the Metropolitan Police, acquired at the prompting of the Metropolitan Commissioners in 1839:

> It shall be lawful for any constable belonging to the police force to take into custody without a warrant, *all loose, idle or disorderly persons* within the borough, who he should find *disturbing the public peace,* or, in his own view, committing *any offence against the Act* or whom he should have good cause to suspect of *having committed or being about to commit any felony misdemeanour* or *breach of the peace,* or to instigate or abet such breach, and all persons whom he shall find between *sunset and the hour of eight* in the morning, lying or loitering in any street, yard or other place within the borough, and not giving a satisfactory account of themselves. (Liverpool Improvement Act, 1842, Section 276)

Similar clauses are later incorporated in the Liverpool Corporation Act of 1921. For example, of several similar powers, it was to be lawful for a constable:

> to arrest and detain . . . any loose, idle, or disorderly person whom . . . he shall have good reason to suspect of having committed or being about to commit any felony, misdemeanour, or breach of the peace, or to instigate or abet any such breach. (Liverpool Corporation Act, 1921, XVIII, Section 551)

Wide-ranging police powers of stop-and-search were incorporated in the succeeding Merseyside County Council Act, 1980. At each period of legal re-construction in the city in 1748; in 1842; in 1921; and in 1980: the general police powers were re-stated. The permissive legal relation, as expressed in these statutory forms ensured that a broad range of police actions, with little burden of proof required in the procurement of convictions, and with the only criterion for conviction, that of "reasonableness" were legally consecrated. The legal relation, through these particular bye-laws defined a variety of selective police actions as legitimate. Constraints over police actions were minimized. Bye-laws, such as these, are the exception not the rule. The reversal of the burden of proof in this legislation is unusual in English law. But the retention of the legislation demonstrates its significance for the maintenance of police power, within the law. It reflects the same spirit of legality, within which McBarnet locates the practices of the courts in their permissive treatment of police procedures.[6]

Where the legal relation of the police institution places the burden of proof on the police, as arresting and prosecuting agency, the courts and the judiciary treat police actions permissively. The legal relation is indulgent. Discretionary action by the police institution is mandated by the courts. Where the assumption of innocence is reversed, as in the stop-and-search bye-laws, the legal form itself releases the police institution, and the chiefs as the key functionaries from restraint. In its combined arrest and prosecution powers, the police institution acts as the agent of the law, within the law. But that relation is not a restrictive one.[7]

# The Power of Prosecution

## *The peculiarity of the prosecution prerogative*

The single feature of the legal relation that distinguished the police institution of England and Wales from the police forces of all other Western countries, is the prosecution prerogative. While chief officers enjoy considerable other forms of authority, by virtue of their office, and by virtue of other constituents of the legal relation, the unique factor is the right to initiate and conduct prosecutions. The lack of an intervening element between the police investigation function, and the determining function of the judicial apparatus, endows those Chief Constables, the Metropolitan and City of London Commissioners with an extra dimension of authority. District Attorneys, Procurator Fiscals, and Juge d'Instructions, have no role within the 43 police forces of England and Wales. The role of the chiefs:

> as prosecutors is one of the most important distinctive features of the police forces of England and Wales; the existence by contrast of a system of public prosecutors in Scotland has been seen as altering the whole relationship of the police to other authorities and to the public. (Williams, 1974, p.187)

The police institution in Britain (with the exception of Scotland) has the largely uninhibited advantage of determining prosecution policies in general, the nature of the charge in a particular case, and, indeed, the right to decide whether or not a charge is actually brought. There is no effective external curb on that process.

> One institutional check upon the exercise of police powers which is common in . . . other jurisdictions, is therefore lacking in England and Wales. (Leigh, 1973, p.865)

This prosecution power is not peculiar to the police institution. Nor is the discretion built-into that prerogative. There are still occasional private prosecutions under common law, the majority of these being by commercial undertakings with only a few by individuals. Other institutions of the state, police agencies such as the British Transport Police, and finance agencies, such as the Inland Revenue, possess extensive discretionary powers, although within a much more narrowly demarcated area (Lidstone *et al.*, 1980). It is not merely that the extra dimension of the legal relation of the police institution is simply one additional form of police authority, but rather that the power of prosecution has become a defining feature of police work in England and Wales.

This power, legitimized by practice, was not part of the grand design for policing as laid out by the Benthamite reformers. Colquhoun, for example, the patron saint of the police institution, (in a proposal that was to be re-stated by the Royal Commission on Criminal Procedure, in 1981), had warned against combining arrest with prosecution powers, at the outset:

> . . . the new vigorous police (should be) strengthened and improved by
> the appointment of Deputy-Prosecutors for the Crown, acting under the
> Attorney-General . . . An Establishment of this sort . . . would be considered
> an honourable entree to many young Counsel; who in protecting the public
> against the frauds, trivia, and devises of old and professed thieves, by which
> at present they escape justice, might keep the rules of justice pure, and yet
> allow no advantage to be taken against the prisoner . . . (Colquhoun,
> 1799, p.227)

As a practice, police prosecution power is both comparatively and historically anomalous.

But the early conflict between central and local elite, that had prevented the development of a national police force from the outset, similarly forestalled any moves towards a national prosecution system. The Home Office, in the nineteenth century maintained similar attitudes to the conduct of prosecutions to that characterized in its relations with the new professional forces. Local prosecution policies were autonomously derived.

In the early years of the urban forces, the majority of prosecutions continued to be brought by private citizens (or by Prosecution Societies) acting on the basis of common law powers. Gradually, however, private actions were inhibited by a number of factors — the cost, the complexity of legal procedures and the duration of both trial and waiting period. Local police forces slowly colonized the prosecution territory. The ". . . police as organised thief-takers found it more efficient to take on the role of prosecutor" (Tobias, 1979, p.126). Police power developed by stealth, and in the name of efficiency. Their power to do so deriving from the common law source. To Lord Devlin, for example:

> . . . every *police* prosecution is in theory a private prosecution; the information
> is laid by the police officer in charge of the case, but in so doing he is acting
> not by virtue of his office but as a private citizen interested in the main-
> tenance of law and order. (Devlin, 1960, p.17)

As elsewhere in police practice, the notion of original powers conferred legitimacy upon state encroachment into civil society. With the growth of the large combined forces of the post World War II era, the form of police prosecution has been institutionalized. The majority of forces in England and Wales now have Prosecuting Solicitors Departments or Sections, staffed largely by civilian solicitors, and headed by a police Superintendent.[8]

The introduction of these formal bureaucratic departments has permitted police chiefs to attempt standardization of prosecution policies internally within the police area and nationally, between prosecution departments, without reference to any non-policing body.

The legislature does however formally limit police initiatives over prosecution in two ways. The office of the Director of Public Prosecutions (D.P.P.) had been created in 1879 as part of an early central state attempt to co-ordinate prosecuting policies and to minimize some of the variation between the existing police areas. The most recent legislation over that office, the Prosecution of Offenders Act, 1979, empowered him to intervene in any prosecution, and to discontinue it if he thought fit. Secondly, a small number of categories of offence must be reported to him by the local police, before prosecutions are commenced. Taken together these two powers:

> . . . gives him the potential for imposing particular prosecution policies on other prosecutors. But the provisions have not been seen by the successive Directors to be used in that way . . . (Royal Commission on Criminal Procedure, 1980a, p.56)

Local police chiefs have exercised the power to determine local prosecution policies largely untrammelled by the D.P.P. (Marshall, 1965, p.116). The D.P.P. acts under the authority of a political appointee, the Attorney-General (who in turn is formally accountable to Parliament). That official too has certain independent powers of prosecution—such as under the Officials Secret Act. Although constitutionally superior to the D.P.P., in practice, the traditional conception of the respective roles of the two central state functionaries has ruled out inter-position by the Attorney-General—the political representative of the governing party does not intrude upon the prosecuting decision-making structure.

The judiciary can also, in theory, intervene in prosecutions by the police institution, but only at the general level. There are no recent examples. In practice, there are minimal political and judicial sanctions over the police prosecution process, a fact recognized in the proposals for a new independent local prosecutorial system, by the Royal Commission on Criminal Procedure in 1980. Although reserve power is held by the legislative and by the judiciary, conventionally, police decisions on prosecutions are not subject to external controls.

## *The debate over the prosecution powers of the police*

When the Royal Commission recommended the establishment of a new prosecutorial system, constructed within the local state (accountable to the existing Police Committees) and formally independent of the police institution, it did so in the face of continuing opposition from the police institution itself. On the basis of that historically developed resistance and the significance of prosecution power for the police institution, the prospects for those proposals are not great.

Within the Report, three distinct issues over prosecution policy are conflated. The fact of police autonomy—the prerogative of the police officers to determine prosecutions independently of other state apparatus or the institutions of civil society—is confused with the organizational problem of police effectiveness and the question of universal standardization of prosecution policies between police areas.

The police institution's evidence to the Commission, contributed to that conflation. Without autonomy, effectiveness will suffer. Standardization is possible because the police institution acts as a unity, independently of outside interference.

For example, the Commission summarises the police argument of a postulated direct relation between effectiveness and autonomy:

> . . . the discretion to prosecute is an integral part of law enforcement. To remove it from the police . . . would be seriously to hamper them in their primary function of maintaining law and order, because it would be likely to diminish the constable's authority . . . removing the decisions from them would therefore be an arbitrary and doctrinaire expression of the public's lack of confidence in their competence and integrity and would be likely to be damaging to morals and hence to law enforcement . . . (p.148)

Similarly, in an earlier critique, Chief Superintendent Bowley of the Police Superintendents' Association related autonomy to standardization. In a vitriolic attack on the ability and integrity of solicitors not attached to the local Police Prosecution Departments, he argued that the case for an independent prosecution department:

> . . . is unsupportable. The forty-three Chief Police Officers, with their association and committees, sensing public opinion and the current attitude of the D.P.P., surely must have as good a chance of achieving any necessary uniformity as any other professional body. (1975, p.442)

The Royal Commission, in its reference to prosecution practices in British

Columbia and in Scotland, patently did not accept that police effectiveness would be diminished by an independent prosecutorial system. In so far, as the prosecution prerogative is necessary to all round police performance, the comparative evidence offers no such justification. Similarly it is difficult to conceive what direct benefits flow to crime control from police direction of the prosecution process. While there is no readily available comparative evidence of discrepancies in clear-up rates and convictions between Scottish, and English and Welsh police forces, the former seem not unduly disadvantaged in crime control by their lack of direct prosecutorial power. But rather more pointed is the justification in terms of standardization. Where the police prosecution prerogative is given substance by reference to claims of standardization, the evidence suggests no great gain through intra-police collaboration. The succeeding evidence of cautioning practices, and of the prosecution of the mass of public order offences, does not readily vindicate the police institution's stand.

## Prosecution Power—the Example of Cautioning

On occasion, the chief police officer (or the Chief Superintendent, responsible for the Prosecution Department), take advice from external agencies on prosecution policy. The more recent, the more controversial, the legislation, the more likely that general prosecution advice will be accepted before proceedings are taken (Williams, 1974).

This advice origin dates from two main sources—the Home Office, and the Association of Chief Police Officers (A.C.P.O.) (*not* from the local police authority). Normally, the Home Office issues advice on the implementation of complex new legislation, as it did with the Children and Young Persons Act, 1969. Increasingly, however, resort for prosecution advice—both by the Home Office, itself, in deciding its own recommendations, as well as from local police forces—is to the specialist committees of A.C.P.O.

This freedom to prosecute unaffected by external constraints does not of course necessarily lead to partisanship by the police institution. The expression of managerial expertise in the prosecution process occurs, for the most part, according to established procedures—a form of "common-sense" wisdom about prosecution develops.

In any case, claims of bias would be difficult to verify. Discrepancies in rates between police areas may relate to other factors than local policy—changes in the number of offences overall, their relative seriousness, or the greater availability of force manpower to deal with the category of offence. Conversely, uniformity of rates between police areas may not demonstrate impartiality. Standardization, according to A.C.P.O. guidelines, is not, in itself, a demonstration of impartiality.

However, there is some inferential evidence that the lack of external constraints on police prosecution policy may lead to localized commitment in those contexts of law enforcements where discretion is concentrated. The more permissive the legal powers, the more probability that chief officers will introduce their own idiosyncratic variations into prosecution policy.

The post-war acceptance of the police caution gave practical effect (in a number of small-scale offences) to the previous, unofficial, police warning, as utilized in several forces. It was recognized in the Street Offences Act, 1959, and the Children and Young Person Act 1969, that police officers should be granted the judicial power to determine the guilt of the accused, under such statutes, without reference to the courts. The Home Office, acknowledging the prevalence of local unofficial cautioning practices, recommended all forces to adopt a formal system. State policy followed police legal entrepreneurship. This recommendation, and the provisions of the two Acts transformed the cautioning practice from one rooted in the constable's common law discretion, to the status of an organizational attribute.

The decision to caution or to prosecute young offenders is ultimately within the prerogative of the local chief officer. The choice of option will be determined not only by the category of offence, the personal characteristics of the suspect, and the processual requirements of successful prosecution, but also by the chief's appraisal of the nature of juvenile crime. In the case of juvenile offences, the use of a caution rather than of a prosecution, may be as much a consequence of the social values of the chief officers as of evidential factors. On some occasions, the choice is the result of definitive stances for or against wider cautioning, on the part of individual chief police officers (Harper, 1975).

Leigh, for example, argues that

> ... the extent to which cautions are used can vary markedly between different police areas, reflecting the different ideological pre-conceptions of Chief Constables ... (Leigh, 1973, p.874)

The chief can influence cautioning practice by various organizational devices apart from formal command. He may delegate the work of cautioning to a single specialized unit, with officers trained and experienced in juvenile work. Alternatively, cautions may be administered by any beat officer. But most important is the general ambience prevailing throughout the force regarding attitudes to young offenders—the ideological atmosphere promoted and supported by the chief officer's views, in internal force orders, in resource commitment, and in public statements. His ideas on both the cause and correct response to juvenile crime filters down to the individual decision-making level, structuring action towards the presumed offender.

Divergent cautioning policies have been noted in several studies (Ditchfield,

1976; Steer, 1970; R.C. on Criminal Procedure, 1980). Variations are often of some magnitude. Harper notes the contrasts in the 1973 figures—in that year, the Dorset and Bournemouth forces cautioned 70% of suspected young offenders, and the Devon and Cornwall force, 68%. At the opposite extreme, with a much higher proportion of prosecution were the Hull force (24% cautioned) and Teeside (16%).

The disparities between a sample of forces in 1977-78 are equally graphic (see Table IV).

TABLE IV

Juvenile cautioning for a sample of provincial force in England and Wales, 1977-1978. Suspected offenders dealt with either by prosecution or caution.

| Police area | Prosecution | | Caution | |
|---|---|---|---|---|
| | No. | (%) | No. | (%) |
| Northumbria | 1164 | 82·4 | 248 | 17·6 |
| Derbyshire | 2511 | 66·7 | 1252 | 33·3 |
| Greater Manchester | 3412 | 60·2 | 5558 | 39·8 |
| Cambridgeshire | 1796 | 60·1 | 1191 | 39·9 |
| North Yorkshire | 1840 | 59·3 | 1262 | 40·7 |
| Merseyside | 7631 | 58·8 | 5351 | 41·2 |
| Warwickshire | 695 | 58·6 | 492 | 41·4 |
| Avon | 3232 | 58·1 | 2328 | 41·9 |
| South Yorkshire | 3612 | 58·0 | 2612 | 42·0 |
| Thames Valley | 3576 | 57·8 | 2567 | 42·2 |
| Cheshire | 2057 | 55·6 | 1644 | 44·4 |
| Leicestershire | 1456 | 55·0 | 1190 | 45·0 |
| Staffordshire | 2022 | 54·9 | 1661 | 45·1 |
| West Midlands | 7311 | 54·7 | 6060 | 45·3 |
| North Wales | 1107 | 50·3 | 1095 | 49·7 |
| Gloucestershire | 1150 | 50·1 | 1105 | 49·9 |
| Norfolk | 836 | 44·7 | 1036 | 55·3 |
| Surrey | 854 | 44·1 | 1082 | 55·9 |
| West Mercia | 2297 | 44·0 | 2920 | 56·0 |
| Devon and Cornwall | 2706 | 43·9 | 3463 | 56·1 |
| Sussex | 1931 | 41·0 | 2166 | 59·0 |
| Dorset | 577 | 38·0 | 976 | 62·0 |
| Dyfed-Powys | 365 | 32·1 | 773 | 67·9 |

Source: Chief Constables' Annual Reports, 1978.

Not that the figures in Table IV necessarily reflect different ideological commitments or images of the young offender, on any punitive–reformative scale. Chief officers with less punitive-orientations may oppose the labelling implications of the cautioning process, viewing the choice as between prosecution and the traditional verbal non-recorded warning. Dyfed-Powys did not necessarily have a more radical commanding officer in 1977-78, than did the Northumbria force.

Nevertheless, there are considerable variations, as represented in Table IV. The Northumbria Chief Constable seems to have favoured the cautioning of young offenders much less than did his peers—the police managers of Dyfed-Powys, of Dorset and of Sussex.

Adherence to the Home Office recommendations varies considerably between police areas. Chief police officers exercise substantial discretion in encouraging or discouraging prosecution decisions. In the course of these actions, and in the promotion of cautioning policies by their control of the organizational variables, they suffer no political restraints. In this instance the legal relation is highly permissive. They enjoy considerable legal latitude in determining juvenile policy.

Presumably, if the chiefs were never to prosecute young offenders, the judiciary might intervene. Similarly, if the Chief never cautioned juveniles, the Home Office backed by local Social Service departments, would bring informal pressure to bear upon the force. But within those extremes, the chiefs enjoy considerable autonomy.

## Standardization and Public Order Offences

Cautioning practices vary according to police area. The evidence in that case suggests no great gain through autonomy of police practice. Similarly, although some of the variations between police areas over the prosecution of public order offences may relate to the peculiarities of those areas, the discrepancies (noted in Table V) do not fit with any notion of internal uniformity. Public order offences depend for much of their recording and prosecution upon police initiatives. Unlike many indictable offences, non-indictable, summary offences, including categories such as prostitution, mis-use of drugs and drunkenness, are particularly susceptible to the policies of the chief officer, to the predispositions of the prosecuting officer, and to local station traditions. "Public order" crimes are crimes without victims, "discovered" only as a result of pro-active policing.

The variations in prosecution rates are substantial for the year 1977-78. Relative to population size, in the *Common Assault* category, only one case was prosecuted in Kent, for every 22 in the West Midlands, 26 in Greater Manchester and Merseyside, and 41 in Cleveland. *Betting and Gambling* prosecutions were six times as common in Merseyside, as in the Thames Valley police area. However, during that year, the Thames Valley force compensated by prosecuting five times as many pedal cyclists as the West Midlands police. Variations in *Indecent Exposure* prosecutions were less common—although the Merseyside force achieved twice as many prosecutions per head of population, as the Staffordshire and Northamptonshire forces. Drunk and Disorderly charges —from simple to aggravated—were a Merseyside speciality. Five times more of

## Table V

Number of offences prosecuted in 1977–1978, for sample of non-indictable offences categories, in nine provincial forces.

| Police Area | Common Assault | Betting, Gambling | Pedal Cycles | Indecent exposure | Simple Drunk | Aggravated Drunk | Drug mis-use | Prostitution |
|---|---|---|---|---|---|---|---|---|
| West Midlands | 199 (199) | 56 (66) | 198 (198) | 171 (171) | 2799 (2799) | 4704 (4704) | 473 (473) | 611 (611) |
| Greater Manchester | 235 (239) | 71 (72) | 312 (316) | 159 (161) | x | x | 877 (890) | 380 (386) |
| Thames Valley | 7 (11) | 14 (21) | 632 (948) | 110 (165) | 533 (800) | 1356 (2094) | 764 (1146) | 0 (-) |
| Merseyside | 232 (401) | 79 (136) | 479 (828) | 111 (192) | 2604 (4499) | 6258 (10812) | 525 (933) | 291 (503) |
| Kent | 5 (9) | 31 (56) | 229 (415) | 110 (199) | 464 (841) | 456 (827) | 211 (382) | x |
| Lancashire | 56 (111) | 13 (26) | 308 (610) | 94 (186) | x | x | 341 (675) | 25 (50) |
| Staffordshire | 39 (107) | x | 148 (405) | 108 (295) | 402 (1101) | 662 (1813) | 154 (422) | 31 (85) |
| Cleveland | 77 (366) | 8 (38) | 87 (414) | 57 (271) | 319 (1519) | 1372 (6534) | 127 (603) | 109 (298) |
| Northamptonshire | 12 (64) | 4 (21) | 45 (241) | 24 (129) | 233 (1247) | 464 (2484) | 45 (241) | 11 (59) |

Note: figures in brackets are number of offences prosecuted, weighted according to population of police area. x = Figures unavailable.
Source: Chief Constables Annual Reports, 1978.

the first category were prosecuted on the Mersey, compared with in the Thames Valley police area and the (mainly) Liverpool force used the *Aggravated Drunkenness* 13 times as often as their Kent counterparts. (Police dealings with the problem of intoxication vary considerably—some forces being unwilling to recognize *Simple Drunkenness* as an offence.)

The Thames Valley police that year seemed most content with prosecuting illegal drug users (five times as many as the Northamptonshire force) and least willing to regard prostitution as worthy of prosecution (remarkably, according to the Chief Constable's Annual Report, in both 1976-77 and 1977-78, the Thames Valley police encountered no prostitution worthy of prosecution, within a population of nearly two million). However the West Midlands force achieved 12 times as many, per head of population, as the Lancashire force. Rates within forces—determined by the Prosecution Department or by organizational tradition—are as varied as are the rates of different forces. There is a lack of uniformity internally, as well as across force boundaries. For example, out of four divisions within the Cleveland force, in 1976-77, the Middlesborough police achieved all that police area's prosecutions for prostitution—72—and successfully repeated the feat, the following year with 109.

The lack of external control over the prosecution process is similarly apparent in the police privilege in the formulation of the charge. Police officers not merely make the decisions whether or not to prosecute but also determine the form of charge. A comparison of the ratios of *Simple Drunkenness* to *Aggravated Drunkenness* demonstrates substantial variation between force practices— Kent 1:1, Staffordshire 1:1·6, West Midlands 1:1·7, Northamptonshire 1:1·2, Merseyside 1:2·4, Thames Valley 1:2·6, and Cleveland 1:4·3. Where the form of deviance may be graded according to its perceived severity, the police institution operates with maximum freedom, subject to the production of reasonable evidence.

There is little empirical support for the twin justification of effectiveness and standardization, for the police prosecution prerogative. While the data on standardization, in particular, are open to a number of reservations, it seems that within the range of non-indictable offences (which of course, represent the bulk of police crime work), little use is made of any intra-police institution comparisons. Police prosecution decisions seem to relate more, by inference, to local force traditions, and to the policy of the chief officer. Autonomy of police prosecution practice contributes a significant dimension of authority to the more general powers of the police institution. Discretionary authority is not merely practiced in law enforcement, and sanctioned by the courts and by legal statute, but also constitutive of the prosecution decision.

Not that the autonomy in prosecution necessarily leads to direct partisanship. In its prosecution practices, as Wilcox (1972) demonstrates, the police institution, as a corporate body, reflects the broad common sense perspectives embodied within the spirit of legality (see Picton Davies, 1973, pp.141-2). In an identical way to the latitude given by the courts to police evidence and to police interrogation procedures, the "reasonable" principle is foremost, in the prosecution decision. The same kind of occupational and class predilections that determine the format of acceptable police evidence in court, define the parameters of prosecution decisions. The exercise of prosecution powers, reflects the spirit of legality—the test of reasonableness. Within the police prosecution officers' conception of equity, justice prevails in evaluating the basis for court action, and is sanctified by the material recognition of the police prerogative.

The defence of the prosecution authority of the police institution has much in common with the defence of the constables lineage. That proposition served to deny political rights of intervention at the same time that it extended the discretionary powers of the police within the law. Similarly, the demands for the retention of prosecution powers that developed on to the police institution in England and Wales, uniquely, and almost by accident, has two functions for the institution. It ensures that the police have unique powers of interposition in civil society. Chief officers as urban managers have a unique source of authority in their powers of law enforcement (as unfettered constables) and of prosecution. Secondly, it assists the political elevation of the police institution itself. The chief officer has no legal rival such as a District Attorney to challenge his jurisdiction over the legal relations of city or town. Similarly, to the array of lower class defendants the Magistrates Courts are (in a restoration of their old urban title), *Police Courts* (Bankowski and Mungham, 1976, p.95). The legal relation of the police institution extends its authority at the same time, that it symbolically enhances the police institution's status as the most visible part of the state.

# Notes

1. Sir Robert Mark's autobiography makes great play with this theme (Mark, 1978).
2. See the appendix to Alderson (1980).
3. Paradoxically, the office of Metropolitan Commissioner does not embody the status of constable.
4. Critchley neatly phrases it "But if the law had not changed, times had" (1979, p.272).
5. While the section regarding tortious liability did not infringe the traditional common law powers of his subordinates as constables (Marshall, 1978), it gave further weight to the chief officer's concern for direct obedience by his officers.
6. See the highly partisan documentary account of the Liverpool police, *Spike Island*, for a demonstration of the importance of these powers to officers of that force.
7. Note the recent apparent extension of police powers by a House of Lords decision (*The Guardian* 26 May, 1982). It determined that a police officer's power of arrest without warrant under Section 28 of the Town Police Clauses Act, 1847 was not confined to cases where an offence had in fact been committed. It was extended to cases where an officer *honestly believed* an offence to have been committed.
8. On this, see R.C. on Criminal Procedure Report, Appendix 22, p.201.

# 6  *The Police Institution*

. . . the Association of Chief Police Officers . . . In this high chamber the
Duke of the Metropolis, the Baron of Manchester, and the Earl of the
Marches of Merseyside consult. Their decisions are sent down by beadles to
the Royal Commissioner on Criminal Procedure and to parliamentary
committees. Home Secretaries attend on them . . . A.C.P.O. does not attend
on governments; governments attend on it. (E.P. Thompson "Law and
Order and the Police", *New Society*, 15th November, 1979, p.379)

Historian Edward Thompson's rhetorical denunciation of the police institution
in Britain is not confined to external critics. Whitaker, in a popular recent
account of policing in Britain, quotes a Superintendent Rowland: "Contrary to
popular belief, we are not ruled by one Queen but rather forty-three Kings"
(1979, p.192). Several such analogies have been drawn between the authority
enjoyed by chief police officers in England and Wales, and the feudal relations of
an earlier social order. However, within those polemics, there are some major
differences.

Thompson portrayed the authority of the police institution as lying in its
collective voice. The corporate unity of the chiefs extends more influence
throughout the state, and into civil society than does the sum of its parts. To
Rowland, (and in a different context, Sir Robert Mark), "Each one is completely
autonomous and few agree with each other" (ibid).

Central to the argument in the present text is an espousal of the first viewpoint. While, on one hand, it is apparent that individual chief police officers, in
their local bailiwicks, exercise substantial discretionary authority under the
rubric of the legal relation, that individuating psychologistic approach is both
evidentially limiting, and theoretically unsound. The activities, idiosyncrasies,
obsessions about particular forms of social deviance, and personal styles of
policing of individual chief officers, are intriguing, and offer an easy target for
radical denunciation. But within the relation between social classes and the state
idiomatic behaviour is largely irrelevant. The Chief Constable of one provincial

force may seek more media coverage than a second, and represent a power in the land via television punditry. However, that public face, easy to portray, and equally easy to ridicule, distracts attention from the collective power of the police institution. Not that the epiphenomena are irrelevant. They provide evidence of the general contiguity between the political and moral stances of individual chief officers and the dominant political culture (Kettle, 1980a; Reiner, 1980a).

But those declamations are essentially manifestations both of the more general intrusion by the police institution into political decision-making within the state, and of the pervasiveness in the moral and social order of civil society of the police as a *corporate* body, and not just as individual interpreters of discretionary legislation.

This chapter explores the corporate character of the police institution — the *collective* authority of the managers and negotiators of the allocation of law enforcement resources and definition of law enforcement in relation to the central and local states. That corporate power is represented in the codification of both the informal relations between the chiefs, and their more formalized membership of their professional body, the Association of Chief Police Officers. It also includes, at a much less substantive level, other forms of structured intra-police relations — the organizations of the lower ranks, the Police Superintendents Association (P.S.A.), and the Police Federation.

The chapter is divided into two halves. In the first part, the various organizational and structural factors that have contributed to the expansion of the authority of the police institution are outlined. Primary emphasis is given to the way the political space, the negotiative autonomy, of the chiefs has been inflated. Political interventions within the state, and within civil society have been reconstituted as police work under a new managerialist heading. The second part of the chapter is devoted to an account of changes in the formal institution of policing. The growth of the Association of Chief Police Officers, in the political interstices between central and local states and between the various legislative and executive apparatuses of the central state is outlined. Finally, similar if not identical changes in the Police Superintendents Association, and in the Police Federation are noted.

## The Chiefs as Negotiators of Law Enforcement Resources

### *The concentration of resources*

Several factors have together contributed to the new authority of the police institution and that of its major functionaries, the chief officers. The rise of

professionalism in senior police work (Cain, 1972); the development of technological expertise; the increased reliance on the police institution by the central
state during the developing crisis of the 1970s (Bunyan, 1976); career oppor-
tunism amongst the senior officers (Russell, 1976b); and peculiarities of the
position of the chiefs in relation to the local media (T. Morris, 1980); are factors
of varying significance and with varying qualities of supporting evidence. But
the most common argument has been one that relates to the twin factors of
*expansion* and *concentration*—changes in the resources at the disposal of the
individual police managers. However, despite the quantitative evidence
upholding that proposition, these latter developments do not appear to have been
of central importance apart from the legal relation of the police institution, as
discussed in the last chapter.

The explanation of the increased autonomy, in terms of resource changes, is
straightforward. The expansion of manpower resources, of police establishments
(documented in Table III), is one of the two major variables. Total provincial
police establishments have doubled in the last quarter century. For every two
police employees (uniformed and civilian) in England and Wales in 1980, only
one was employed in 1955.

The process of expansion has been accompanied by a second process of amalgamation. The Willink Report, 1962-3, advocated a degree of force rationalization,
in the name of efficiency, and as the logical compromise between those factions
of chief officers who wished to maintain the notional local relation of the police
apparatus, and those other chief officers who argued for a national force. The
results of that intervention and the later effects of local government re-organization
are documented in Table VI. Force amalgamations, in the late 1960s, and in the
early seventies substantially reduced the number of local police forces.

TABLE VI
Distribution of provincial forces according to authorized establishments.

| Authorized establishments | 1879 | 1928 | 1959 | 1964 | 1969 | 1974 | 1979 |
|---|---|---|---|---|---|---|---|
| 6-7000 | | | | | 1 | | 2 |
| 5-6000 | | | | | | 2 | 1 |
| 4-5000 | | | | | 1 | 2 | 1 |
| 3-4000 | | | 1 | 1 | 2 | 1 | 3 |
| 2-3000 | | 1 | 3 | 3 | 10 | 11 | 10 |
| 1500-2000 | | 2 | 1 | 6 | 8 | 5 | 7 |
| 1000-1500 | 2 | 4 | 4 | 6 | 11 | 12 | 12 |
| 500-1000 | 4 | 8 | 28 | 26 | 12 | 8 | 5 |
| 250-500 | 16 | 29 | 26 | 36 | | | |
| less than 250 | 194 | 139 | 59 | 46 | | | |

Source: adapted from *Police Force Almanac*.

When the processes of expansion and of amalgamation are combined, the remaining chief officers are seen to have obtained substantially larger forces. In 1963, for example, the average population of the provincial police areas of England and Wales was 316 000 (and that included the mammoth Lancashire force that policed a population of nearly two-and-a half million). By 1978, the average population of force areas was just over one million.

In so far as the individual forces are fewer and larger, the potential influence and actual authority of individual chief constables has considerably increased, a fact recognized by senior officers (Wilcox, 1974, p.145), senior Home Office civil servants (Jacob, 1967, p.314) and conservative police historians (Critchley, 1979, p.300).

Chief police officers, both individually, and as a corporate body, now negotiate policing definitions and practices on behalf of much larger corporate units. Police power—the authority of the command positions—has become regionalized, if not centralized. But the explanation of the new interventions by the chief officers, in terms of the joint factors of expansion and amalgamation is too simple. Similarly organizational processes have occurred within education, within transport undertakings, and within the health service. The police apparatus is not unique in its experiences in the sixties and seventies. The influence of the supreme corporate manager the Town Clerk (now re-named, in the corporate era, the Chief Executive) has not expanded, publicly, to the same extent as that of the local chief police officer.

It is to the unique feature of police authority that one must look for an initial explanation of the rise in police power. As the last chapter demonstrated, the ability to claim a legal basis for the police function confers on it a degree of power and influence which is exceptional. Chief police officers, like other corporate managers, are limited in their public activities by formal accountability to the paymasters, local or national. The legal relation, the claim to a special relationship within the law, partly releases the chief officers from that form of bondage. Police claim, oddly, that they are accountable to a set of rules: not, as other executives, accountable to others for the way they administer a set of rules. That claim to a special relationship, when combined with the lack of specificity over police function (the absence of strict demarcation between combatting crime and pronouncing on perceived social deviance) is the lubricant which permits the gradual broadening and pervasiveness of the authority in this singular type of corporate manager. The expansion and concentration of police resources, together with the varied factors listed earlier, are only of significance in explaining the broadening of the political space of the chiefs, when combined with the legal relation.

## *Political space and the negotiation of law enforcement*

Chief police officers are the negotiators of law enforcement resources. They operate in the political no-man's land within the balance of class, sectional, and organizational pressures. They equilibrate interests according to the nature of the constraints. While the internal organizational restraints may be more complex and demanding than in previous years (Chapter 9), the external demands on policing have radically altered the political space of the chiefs.

In the early days of policing, the nature of the external demands was relatively uncomplicated. Liberals and Tories of nineteenth century Liverpool might differ over particular police practices, but they were in general agreement over the primacy of the policing function—confining the lower classes. The chief was situated at the nexus between the demands of the mercantile class, and the spasmodic resistance of the lower classes with only occasional interventions by such strata as the shopkeepers.

But in the 1980s, various factors have schismatized the external pressures on the chief officer, and have consequently expanded the area of his political space as a negotiator.

The class demands are more diffuse. The local urban bourgeoisie is more fractionalized and no longer directly identified with the demands of capital (as conveyed through the central state). The rise of organized labour, and of the political articulation of working-class sentiment through the Labour Party, and the complexity of the various economic and political relations at local level, have together by their very divisiveness, diminished the directive pressures on the chief. The immediate demands are fragmented. His political space as a negotiator is consequently enhanced.

Secondly, those demands are no longer interpreted for him by a mediating body which could both filter and focus the pressures. The effective disintegration of local police authority influence has ensured that there is no longer any co-ordinating mechanism for the varied local fractional pressures on the police institution. The old Watch Committees fulfilled that role. With its disappearance, the police chiefs now select the legitimate and filter out the illegitimate ones for themselves, using their own criteria.

Together, these two factors, when combined with the changes in the structure of police resources, and with the latitude of the legal relation, have contributed to an enhancement of the negotiative autonomy of the chief police officer.

This negotiation role in the allocation of resources constitutes a political function. The negotiation of "public" demands for particular forms of law enforcement, and the success of the police chiefs in expanding the capacity of the police apparatus, is (given the pervasiveness of the police institution through civil society, and its centrality to the powers of the state) a political activity.

The enhancement of the negotiative role has meant the concomitant commitment of the police institution to political decision-making (Hall, 1980; Kettle,
1980c).

Within the police institution, this form of political negotiation has been
re-constructed through managerialist lenses. Not that such interventions within
the political arena of law-making were simply post-1964 phenomena. Rather the
style, the legitimizations and, most importantly, the potential influence behind
the statements has vastly increased. As early as 1910, for example, Dunning, the
Liverpool Head Constable, commenced a detailed attack on new legislation in
apologetic style:

> The duties of the police to whom politics are so properly taboo, concern
> many matters of social interest . . . makes it somewhat hard for a policeman
> to give out the opinion formed without being taken to agree or disagree . . .
> (H.C. Report, 1910, p.22)

By 1980, the managerialist exposition is more self-confidently expressed. Chief
Constable Imbert, for example, arguing for more police control of public
meetings:

> You may argue that this places chief constables in a political arena . . .
> I believe the contrary: investing the powers in the chief constable would
> remove the sensitive issue from local politics and place it in the arena of
> public order . . . it would be a responsibility of their making instead of as at
> present . . . on purely political grounds, and one which could be coloured
> either by the politics of the local authority, by the politics of the person
> organising the procession, or indeed, by both. The policeman's only
> motivation is peace and good order; and in my view the decisions not to
> ban must be taken on public order grounds and not from a political con-
> sideration. (quoted in the *New Statesman*, 11th April, 1980)

Other senior officers are unabashed at recognizing the political nature of the
negotiator's space. Myers of the North Wales force, for example,

> . . . on these grounds of being long established, of being accepted in this
> country, and envied by the rest of the world and by the solid contribution
> over the last 150 years, that I claim that the police has a right to contribute.
> What is more important to it, is that it is entitled to have its voice heard,
> attention paid to it . . . (A.C.P.O./Association of Municipal Corporations,
> Conference, 1979)

Such statements, and the developing practice of commenting on particular social
and political matters (from the size of electoral deposits to the subject of trade
union power), both reflect and justify that expansion of the political space of the
police managerial negotiators. They permit more latitude in relation to the

internal audience—the police organization, and they allow for the construction of a surrogate form of accountability, which bypasses the institutional framework.

As negotiators, the chiefs face two ways. They confront not only an external audience—the consumers of law enforcement services—but are also concerned to maximize their influence over the labyrinthine organizations of which they are the titular head. That fealty will only be forthcoming when chief police officers appear to be speaking up for their staff. External pronouncements are made in the face of an internal audience.

The larger the force, the less likely that the junior ranks will be bound to the senior by personal ties, and the more probable that they will depend upon public defences of their values as the basis of organizational cohesion. The processes of amalgamation and expansion affected the degree of solidaristic relation amongst the rank-and-file as well as the power of the chiefs. Ritualistic public statements of police organizational creeds cements force unity. The political manifestations have a primary function in relation to the external audience. The media punditry by chief officers establishes a direct, if one-way, connection between police institution and social classes. A proxy form of accountability is constructed. Given the decline of the residual democratic relation, police chiefs construct a placebo, a surrogate democratic relation that helps to legitimize the expansion of their political space.

These political interventions are commonly dressed in the allegorical language of moral concerns. Expressions of political values are couched in the style of Delphic utterances. Note for example (amongst many similar instances), the classic statement of James Haughton, in the 1974 Presidential address to A.C.P.O., prophesying the collapse of civilization, and calling for the restoration of civilized standards of:

> integrity, loyalty and self-discipline . . . Co-operation and compromise can no longer be expected and blackmail in one form or another has become the accepted way of life . . . We are in a "Nero-Rome" situation with too many fiddlers while the country is being burned and blasted to death . . . People are yearning desperately for leadership

The expression of such moral views, reflecting the new political territory of the chiefs has a further function in relation to their autonomy. According to Bowden:

> Where the police become active a politico-moral censors, their political penetration of society is enhanced. By disguising political statements as views on social morality . . . they can enlist the moral support of the population, their task of control becomes easier and less politically expensive . . . there will be less likelihood of resort to coercive weapons of control. (1978, p.81)

Of course, verbal, moral, and political interventions by chief police officers, while they may demonstrate their increased freedom in the allocation and use of law enforcement resources, remain essentially epiphenomena. They are surface manifestations of structural change that only take on significance when expressed through the collective actions of the police institution as a corporate body. These public demonstrations of the political space of the chiefs only become effectively focussed, given substance, when they assume institutional form. Social values are metamorphosized from the idiosyncratic views of the negotiators of police resources, to political action, in the context of affiliation to a centralized but relatively independent police institution.

## The Institutional Form of Police Independence

Police authority may be narrowly confined—by the enforcement or non-enforcement of legislation by a provincial chief constable. But it only has significance in the inter-play between class forces and organizational features when embodied within the police institution—when exercised as corporate action. Only in that second form, does police power represent an expansion of the state apparatus into civil society. Three intra-police organizations provide the institutional base for those incursions—the Association of Chief Police Officers, the Police Superintendents Association, and the Police Federation.

### The Association of Chief Police Officers (A.C.P.O.)— origins and structure

Very little material is publicly available about the operations and intentions of A.C.P.O. Despite the adoption of a ". . . deliberate policy to come out into the open more . . . attempting to influence public opinion and the courts via the media" (*The Guardian*, 19th February, 1979), and its dependence upon state funding (£46 000 for the national secretariat in 1978, a proportionate figure locally provided by a police committee for the Presidential functions of the chief officer, plus the conference expenses of individual officers), it has continually resisted suggestions that it became a statutory body. In the Edmund-Davies Enquiry of 1978, it argued strongly for the retention of its voluntary, and hence confidential, status.

Unlike the Police Federation, it is not liable to any external body. It need provide no information. There are no political constraints on its members (except those that relate to their individual positions as police officers). Decisions by the various A.C.P.O. committees, and attempts to influence other aspects of the state or of civil society, are revealed only when its council deems it appropriate.

A.C.P.O. has all the trimmings of a powerful secret society—financed through the central state but not directly beholden to the paymaster. A.C.P.O.'s origins lie within three separate institutional structures—the elderly County Chief Constables Club, the Chief Constables Association (set up in 1896) and the Home Office Central Conference. The County Chief Constables Club was founded in 1858, primarily as a social forum for (as its name implies) senior officers from the County forces. Toward the end of the century, a separate association was established for the Chief Constables (and their immediate deputies), from the cities and boroughs. The two organizations remained distinct, given the peculiarity of their relations with their different political masters. In the Edwardian period, relations between the urban chief officers and local Watch Committees were those of professional expert and local paymaster.

County chiefs remained part of a set of feudal style status relationships which survived the feudal economic and political relations, with appropriate deference to magistrates and landowners. Values and attitudes of the two organizations reflected their different class relations. Both organizations, however, were independent of the Home Office. The third root of A.C.P.O. emerges from the World War I. The conditions of that period pressed the Home Office into setting up co-ordinating local conferences for Chief Constables, in different parts of the country. In 1918, the Home Office organized what was to become an annual Central Conference with the aim of providing a more direct link between the district conferences and the central Government, and which became a centre for interforce co-operation and a clearing house for the "exchange of ideas and experience" (Critchley, 1979, p.183). These meetings were directly supervized by the Home Office. Ministry officials chaired the discussions, determined the agenda, and included the H.M.I.C.'s as part of their representation.

During the course of the initial meetings, the police officers came to appreciate their own disunity in the face of the representatives of the legislature. Consequently, from 1922 onwards, the two Chief Constables' associations developed the habit of holding their own meetings two weeks prior to the Central Conference. At these pre-emptive encounters, differences could occasionally be reconciled, and a common front constructed, as a potential foil to Home Office proposals. A.C.P.O.'s direct line of descent is from this meeting, and its later more political role has its seeds in this early attempt to distance senior police officers, as a unified body from the Home Office. Being legally barred from discussing employment conditions, the preparatory meetings had only two functions—the pooling of expert advice on police matters to inform the debate with the Home Office, and secondly, to construct a measure of autonomy from external, especially Home Office, influence.

The decline of the influence of the local land-owning classes on the county police brought the class relations of the two chief officer associations into relative congruence. In 1948, outside pressures (particularly the strictures of Lord

Oaksey) resulted in a marriage of convenience, and the formation of the present Association. (The County Chief Constables' Club continued with an almost entirely social function, having reached the status of annual announcements in *The Times'* social column.)

The year 1948 was a watershed in the development of the independence by the chief police officers. In the 1920s, the dual organizations had functioned as staff associations—company unions, with the right to discuss any matter, apart from conditions of service. From that stage, they had marshalled themselves, by the 1930s, into focii for senior police opinion (particularly the urban officers' organizations). During the pre-war period, they contributed specialist advice in limited and in uncontentious areas—such as the 1938 Memorandum on the Prevention of Road Accidents.

The inauguration of A.C.P.O., however, saw a transition to a more political stage—that of a political lobby within the state apparatus. This was a gradual development, enhanced in 1968 by the re-constitution of the organization with a full-time secretariat. At the 1949 conference, A.C.P.O. limited its political input to debates on the utility of capital punishment. By 1978, speakers were calling for an increase in the electoral deposits of candidates.

Its 1948 constitution and statement of aims summed up the transition from staff association to pressure group. Formally, A.C.P.O. was to carry out five functions—to promote the welfare and efficiency of the police service; to safe-guard the interests of members; to provide opportunities for internal discussions of matters affecting policing; to give advice to other bodies such as the Home Office, the local Watch Committees, and Royal Commissions on subjects related to the police service; and finally to provide social amenities for members.

These aims encompassed the activities carried out in the earlier stage, while laying the foundations for future political intervention. They are administered via a complex organizational structure. A.C.P.O. holds regional meetings, in its eight districts, four times a year. From these sessions, resolutions and views are forwarded to the central A.C.P.O. council. This latter consists of the Metropolitan Commissioner, the elected national officers and the regional secretaries. In turn A.C.P.O. council organizes an annual conference for the whole membership. (A.C.P.O. has a membership of just over 200, comprising all those officers above the rank of Chief Superintendent in England, Wales, and—since the recommendations of the Hunt Report, 1970—Northern Ireland. Scotland has its own association which sends fraternal delegates to the A.C.P.O. council.) In addition, apart from the continuing Central Conference relationship with the Home Office, A.C.P.O. holds regular conclaves with the local authority associations, meetings used by A.C.P.O. to cement relations with local political elites, and as a public platform for senior A.C.P.O. opinion. At national level, A.C.P.O. operates a decentralized committee structure. These committees consider specialized police interests such as traffic, communications, computer development, technical services, police training, and general services. Further *ad hoc* committees are set up as required by the council — for example, on the development of police establishments, in the field of public order, or to give evidence to various Royal Commission, and to other public bodies.

## A.C.P.O. — *the political apparatus of policing*

In its acquisition of corporate, collective authority, the police executive reaches a further stage in the transference of political power from the local merchants and industrialists of nineteenth century Britain, to capital interests centred outside the political realm of the nation-state.

The indisposition of the Liverpool merchants to the immediate control of the local police had marked to the first step in the transfer of a limited authority to the new police managers (Chapter 2). The second stage featured the development of capital interests at the national level. The parameters of local police work were drawn up at the behest of economic interests divorced from the immediate concerns of the local bourgeoisie (Chapters 3 and 4).

Finally, with the construction of a unified police executive, the body of police corporate managers, a further plateau is reached. The influences on the general forms and practices of police work derive from the international structure of capital relations. The executive arms of the central state, with the police institution as one of the primary apparatuses, increasingly respond to the long-term requirements of economic relationships transcending international frontiers. There is a separation between the interests of the nationally dominant political class, and the executive that formally serves it, just as the local dominant class lost its specific relation with its police executive. The police institution increasingly becomes concerned with political negotiation, as a body of semi-autonomous corporate managers at the *national* level.

These negotiations have become channelled through several forums. For example, since 1949, its annual conferences have been used as sounding-boards by the Home Office, initially through the office of the Permanent Under Secretaries and later, in 1957, as its stature grew, of the Home Secretary. Appearance at A.C.P.O. conferences has become a duty incumbent upon Home Office Ministers, and one that reflects acknowledgement of the new political constituency. Although the subject of the Minister's speeches are frequently directed towards general law enforcement topics — Butler on organizational developments at the Home Office, on the handling of race riots, on the increase in crime and in traffic offences, on manpower requirements, and the famous "checks and balances" speech on amalgamations, (A.C.P.O. conference, 1964): Jenkins on manpower, and on juvenile crime: Summerskill on the financial stringencies facing state services — they all fit within the wider framework of state policy. Before the rise of A.C.P.O. politicians were never required to justify those policies to the police. Post-A.C.P.O. the freedom of the Home Secretary to act is more limited. Indeed, his appearances at the conference have a supplicant flavour. A.C.P.O. requires that policies be justified to it as a corporate body.

Secondly A.C.P.O. acts as a source of advice and expertise to many Royal Commissions and Parliamentary committees, on occasion, going as far beyond the brief of its particular area of professional knowledge. Pain (1978, p.6) offers a limited view of the machinery

> I'm the secretary of the C.I.D. Committee, so any Bill of Parliament that relates to crime would be examined and discussed and we would make representations before it became an Act of Parliament. We would discuss with the Home Office whether it's a practical thing from the police point of view . . . (quoted in *Law Enforcement News*, 1978)

In recent years, evidence has been presented to many Royal Commissions, some of which have only a tangential relevance to police work. The Commissions on Standards in Public Life, on Mental Illness; on Assizes and Quarter Sessions; on Justices of the Peace; on Civil Liberty; on the Constitution; and on Legal Services; have all received memorandum from A.C.P.O. Battered wives and inveterate gamblers have similarly been paid attention.

It was instrumental in the formulation of issues for the Royal Commission on Criminal Procedure in deferring the balance of arguments as lying between citizen rights and police efficiency. Such a formulation meant that no enquiry into the police task itself was necessary. There were to be questions on the mode of police investigation but no questions on police function or problematic.

But the simple enumeration of constitutional interests does not sufficiently illustrate A.C.P.O's progression down the political road. The trend of evidence to such bodies has been to broaden the scope of A.C.P.O.'s concerns. In particular, A.C.P.O. has sought solutions to police problems in the political contexts. If for example, the police are faced with a problem of disorder at an election meeting the solution, according to A.C.P.O.'s evidence to a Parliamentary Select Committee is to institute a ". . . more realistic level of deposit for parliamentary elections" in order to reduce ". . . the field of candidates, many of whom would appear to be contesting seats unjustifiably . . ." (Kettle, 1979). A.C.P.O. has little hesitation in arguing for political solutions to problems of political order, and consequently adopts its own political stance.

Thirdly, A.C.P.O. is a political entrepreneur. Its committees have taken the initiative in recommending to members, and to the Home Office, the development of particular units and of techniques. It was instrumental in setting up a centralized unit to deal with secondary picketing. Its arguments on the use of specialist units to deal with drugs, and on the use of computers, built up too great a head of steam for any local police authority to do other than offer *post facto* agreement. It innovates in those vague areas where the law is unspecified or the discretion wide—in recommendations on the handling of strike pickets, and on the control of football supporters. Having set the precedent, it waits for the law to catch up. It operates within the permissive space of the legal relation. Fourthly, the relationship between A.C.P.O. and individual officers is important. A.C.P.O. reinforces the corporate identity of the local police managers.

There are varying views on the power of A.C.P.O. to influence the affairs of local forces. According to one chief constable:

> We can pass this sort of thing amongst ourselves. We make a recommen-
> dation to the A.C.P.O. council and the A.C.P.O. council will decide, and
> that's every chief constable. If they accept the recommendations, then we
> will all adopt it. If they don't, I don't adopt it. (quoted in Kettle, 1980d)

The President of A.C.P.O. offers what seems to be an understatement:

> At the end of the day, the Chief Constable does what he wishes in his own
> force and A.C.P.O. has no control over what the Chief Constable does; there
> are no sanctions that can be applied if he doesn't agree with what A.C.P.O.
> does and while the council of A.C.P.O. comes to the decisions on a whole
> range of issues, no Chief Constable is bound by those decisions. But it is
> clearly desirable, that there shall be some sort of common understanding.
> (ibid)

While idiosyncratic chief officers may assign their own interpretation of legitimate public demand, and negotiate their own policing practice, for most senior officers, in areas of doubt and controversy, reference is made either formally or informally to A.C.P.O. for guidance. Where one officer finds himself in the public firing-line, after the mis-handling of an event, A.C.P.O. will step in to provide the appropriate colleague support.

For example, after the clash between the police and anti-fascists in Lewisham, in 1977, a routine meeting of the A.C.P.O. council gave a press conference on the issue:

> The Association of Chief Police Officers . . . wish to associate themselves
> and support the statement by the Commissioner . . . on the responsibility of
> the police to uphold the law and maintain public order independently from
> political pressure or threats from those who wish to use violence to achieve
> their ends. (*Daily Telegraph*, 17th August, 1977)

This statement also lamented the limitations of the Public Order Act and the lack of understanding of most people for police problems.

Actions by Chief Officers in controversial situations can be buttressed, and thereby legitimated, by the intervention of A.C.P.O. Their own colleague support organization is the major *public audience* to which chief constables defer. It is the repository of managerialist expertise. A.C.P.O. wields influence in diverse ways. By combining the individual power of chief police officers at the level of the state, it can both reinforce their autonomy and strengthen the authority of the police institution within the state apparatus, and within civil society. Moreover, agreement among chiefs of police may be interpreted as evidence of the "professional" nature of their judgment. A.C.P.O.'s influence is felt more by implicit threat than by action. Home Office staff and police authority members could make life marginally more awkward for its individual members if they so chose. But the identity of interest between those two bodies and senior police officers ensures that the influence of the police institution is likely to become more extensive.

The police institution in Britain, as represented by its major corporate body has followed the movement from low policing to high policing originally mapped out by Fouché. The staff association for the major-domos of the Watch Committees has been steadily transformed into a body increasingly pre-occupied with the politics of social order in the state. Primarily responsible for negotiating the legitimacy of demand for law enforcement resources, the local police managers collectively assume significant power. Chief police officers have become conscious of their potential corporate power, at the same time, as the objective conditions of their existence—within the context of the economic depression of the early eighties—has made policing more directly related (as Laugharne argued) not so much to law enforcement, as to the defence of the state. A.C.P.O.'s position at the law enforcement nexus ensures that its opinions count.

## The Superintendents and the rank-and-file

Two other bodies formally represent police interests in England and Wales, the Police Superintendents Association (P.S.A.) and the Police Federation. Both are relatively insignificant in comparison to A.C.P.O. Indeed, it has been argued that the fire and fury generated by recent conferences of the two organizations reflects their lack of power to influence events rather than a demonstration of political muscle. Certainly, some of the rhetoric of the P.S.A.'s conferences gives new meaning to the adage, "empty vessels make the most sound".

For the P.S.A. the problem is acute. Without the statutory recognition of the Federation, without independent bargaining rights, before the quasi-military power and public persons of the chiefs, and crucially without the negotiative position of chief officers, with limited controls, but a high level of responsibility for the activities of their juniors, the Superintendents (both as individuals and as a corporate body) have little opportunity to affect the political context of policing. The P.S.A. sums up its own views of its members:

> It has been suggested that the Superintendent's role in the service is best equalled to that of the Works Manager. They are not on the "shop floor". Neither are they members of the "Board of Directors", although we are always pleased to see our members promoted to the "Board". (Edmund-Davies Report, 1979)

In recognition of its lack of public voice, the P.S.A. has made various moves to develop a more cohesive and articulate presence. Following the pattern of A.C.P.O. development, it combined provincial and Metropolitan Super-intendents into a national organization in 1952 (after 33 years) of separate existence. In 1977 it established a (partly) state-financed national secretariat to co-ordinate both its internal operations and its effectiveness as a political lobby.

Much of its strategy has related to (unsuccessful) attempts to join the Board— either by a joint secretariat or by outright merger with A.C.P.O. It is noticeable that the P.S.A. can find stronger reasons for not amalgamating with the lower ranks than with A.C.P.O.:

> Over the years, there have been many suggestions for amalgamating the Association with either that of the Police Federation or the Association of Chief Officers, or perhaps formulating a new Association to cover the Inspectors and Superintendents as an officer class. These have been rejected for many reasons, chief of which must be that any such joining up with the Police Federation or part of it would unbalance the representation of Superintendents' views . . . (Edmund-Davies Report, 1979)

Indeed, there is some evidence that the lack of an alliance with A.C.P.O. relates more to the unwillingness of the latter to act as a groom than to reticence on the P.S.A.'s part.

On the other hand, it has (equally unsuccessfully sought the legal recognition already held by the Police Federation and rejected by A.C.P.O. "It was a question of status. They were of the opinion that their view would be given more weight if they were given statutory recognition" (Edmund-Davies Report). Unlike A.C.P.O. the Association was willing to accept Parliamentary-dictated organizational rules, if that were the price of legal status.

Power for the P.S.A. is limited.[1] Where it gives evidence to Royal Commissions—on Criminal Procedure, Legal Services, Gambling, Criminal law —and provides memorandums on topics as diverse as public order, picketing, football hooliganism, evolution, speed limits, and seat belts—the content has usually mirrored that of A.C.P.O. (although, like its conference speeches, expressed with more vehemence). Where the evidence has differed from

A.C.P.O.'s—for example, over the non-exclusion of the police from provisions of the Sex Discrimination Act—the evidence of the chiefs has had more effect on the final Bill. Its public posture has generally been one of defiance. Unlike the chief officers' association, it tends to react with hostility to existing situations rather than to initiate changes itself. Take for example, the attack by one officer on the suggestion from other groups that prosecution powers be removed from the police.

> We have got to watch for the thin end of the wedge—the small directive which will say that if there is a difference of opinion between the chief prosecuting officers . . . Chief Constable, the C.P.O.'s will prevail. Then we shall have all the authority of night-watchmen and the C.I.D. will be just a load of store detectives. (P.S.A. Annual Conference, 1975)

The vocal conservatism of the P.S.A.—an inarticulate snort at those changes which appear to affect the well-being of the police (and by implication, society) —was loquaciously expressed in the major debates during its 1978 conference. On complainants: ". . . the new system of complaints is an example of a satisfactory system being changed at the request of a small minority of agitators". On training, the Bramshill courses were decried by one speaker as being only about, "how to invite the Reverend Swann round to tea". On policewomen: "Have we got to wait till one of them is the subject of a gang rape or smashed to pieces before the authorities realise what is obvious?". On the tape recording of interrogations: ". . . would be inordinate in expense, would debilitate the investigative role of the police, and at the same time would fail to provide the idealistic requirements of those who demand its use . . ." Finally, in its evidence to the Royal Commission on Criminal Procedure 1979: "If there is to be any definite commitment to law and order in its widest sense, it is almost certain that police powers will have to be increased".

In practice, the only weapon of the P.S.A.—structurally and organizationally castrated—is publicity. Its annual conferences receive almost the same press coverage as those of A.C.P.O. In recent years, it has supported, like the Federation, media campaigns on specific issues. It is recognized at the institutional level by a number of bodies—for example on the Police College Board. But it has little other than formal influence beyond the Page Two headline. Neither master nor servant, the Police Superintendents Association can at most only make a marginal contribution to the development of the power of the police institution within the state.

The Police Federation, although substantially different in breadth of membership and legal status from the P.S.A. is not dissimilar in degree of influence. Given its peculiar origins, in the aftermath of the 1919 Police Strike, it has only recently resorted to political action. Prohibited from industrial action, with an unrepresentative branch structure (each branch committee consists of a similar proportion of constables, sergeants, and inspectors), its members lack the legal power even to determine their own place of residence.

As a political lobby, it has, however, developed a solid institutional base. A large secretariat, a polemical monthly journal, a Parliamentary representative— Eldon Griffiths succeeding James Callaghan), and considerable funds, have provided the Federation with the platform for a direct move into the political arena. Coupling itself to the orchestrated "law and order" campaign of the mid-seventies, the Federation entered on to the political stage with much sound and fury (Reiner, 1979). One outcome, which owed much to the way the Federation synchronized its interests with that of the Conservative Party, was the substantial advance in police pay, relative to other occupations, from 1978 onwards. It contributed to the re-direction of "social expenses" away from welfare towards control. But unlike A.C.P.O. the Federation's political ventures have a certain quixotic character, ". . . tilting at windmills, forever launching grand schemes which have no real chance of fulfilment . . ." (Kettle, 1980a, p.32). The Federation raises issues in the public domain as a substitute for direct access to the corridors of power. When these issues connect with the concerns of fractions of the dominant class, as on law-and-order, the Federation makes progress. When they do not, as in its calls for the restoration of capital punishment for the murder of police officers, it has minimal impact. The Federation's public posturing is an acknowledgement of its impotence in the larger debate, and a symptom of frustration at its contradictory class location (Reiner, 1978). Employed through the state and yet not of the state, it has the power to bring particular topics into public discussion but has minimal access to the executive power to influence the outcome of that dialogue.

Further, the necessarily conspicuous character of its political intrusions may be dysfunctional for police autonomy. When coinciding with other events, such as police corruption trials, they may bring not so much the topic, but rather the police institution itself into the political firing-line. Where rank-and-file officers demand more pay for instance, in the allegorical war-against-crime, their own conditions of service and working-styles, may become the subject of scrutiny.

The Police Federation and the Police Superintendents Association operates in a political limbo. They have access to neither the techniques of the elite lobby nor to the power of mass action. Only through the tenuous ideological connection can they build alliances with the more powerful political groups and social classes.

## Negotiation, Independence and the Police Institution

In the last quarter of a century, the processes of police unification and politicization have gathered momentum. Spurred by the expansion of police resources and through force amalgamations, themselves the product of more decisive intervention by the central state, the police institution is a powerful force at the police manager's elbow.

The course of that development has been facilitated by the growth of the ideology of police professionalism and the construction within the police institution of an array of managerialist attributes, at a time when the local state was abdicating power to the body of corporate executives. But the major lubricant in that process has been the legal relation, which has permitted the police institution to broaden its authority while retaining formal obeisance to the legal order.

The rise of A.C.P.O. has given a measure of coherence to the new police autonomy, and provided a more resistant base to external political authority. The politicization of policing has occurred without any effective opposition from other aspects of the central or local states, or from social classes. A general identity of interest, as well as long-term objective function, now connects the chief officers with the dominant economic and political class. The chief officers enjoy a largely unassailable position of mediation and negotiation over the supply of law enforcement commodities.

Some commentators view this accession sympathetically. Thus one correspondent in the conservative Police Review:

> Almost without exception this power has been exercised benignly and in the broad interest of society, because these interests were easily identifiable and substantially in tune with the thoughts of the officers exercising power . . . (but) . . . the broad interests of society are now less easy to define . . . (Will, 1980)

Where that power is exercised, it is normally in non-contentious situations. It would be difficult to regard advice on seat-belt legislation as an intervention on behalf of an economically dominant class. For the most part however, the power to intervene has not been put into effect. Police power lies in its potential not in its abuse.

The influence of the police institution is wielded in unobtrusive style and according to its perception of legitimate demands. It has responded to a social audience — the "public" — according to the various pressures on chief officers, and according to its own interpretation of the priority and legitimacy of those pressures. The values and political viewpoints of some senior officers have been softened and modified in practice by structural, organizational, and sectional constraints. They cannot act directly against the long-term interests of the dominant class (even if they should wish to do so). Some of their intentions are frustrated by what they conceive of as inadequate resources. And even groups of gay activists campaigning against police harrassment, may make chief police officers uncomfortable about the actions of some of their junior officers.

During a period of prosperity the conjunction between the desires of individual chief officers, A.C.P.O. as a body, and the distinctive class interests has the form of a truce. While the legitimacy accorded to different external demands will vary, chief officers can utilize various organizational devices for maintaining a high level of consent from pressure groups, and from social classes. Local police authorities can be partially satisfied by a return to beat patrolling, critics of Special Patrol Groups can be calmed by changes of name, training and length of duty in the unit, and black community groups can be cooled by invitations to their leaders to give talks on race relations at the local police training centre.

But at time of economic crisis, with its particular manifestations of unemployment, reduced welfare spending, and lower incomes — all factors which hit the lower classes harder than the dominant groups — the distinction between legitimate and illegitimate demands becomes clearer. The ambiguity of values is uncovered. Truces are more difficult to arrange, as the police on one side become more necessary to the defence of the state and the existing structure of social relations. The public order function of the police apparatus is elevated. On the other side, the illegitimate interests have less to gain from the retention of that form of state and social relations.

The temporary consent to the social order, coupled with consent to policing, established during the period of prosperity, slowly dissolves. The conspiratorial political theories of some senior police officers, that can be dis-regarded, when the client-public is not dissatisfied with policing in general, attract more attention partly because they can be acted upon, (more autonomy is the negotiator's price), and partly because the police as an institution becomes more distrusted, as consent dissolves. The major problem facing the police institution therefore, becomes one of maintaining wider public consent, at a period in which its own coercive and political intervention power is increasing.

The final part of this text concentrates on this problem of consent. The next chapter considers the historical development of a consensual relation between the police apparatus and the lower classes. Chapter 8 documents the evidence of consent in contemporary society, exposes the ambiguities in that evidence and demonstrates the continuing requirement on the police chiefs to re-construct that consent through service work. The concluding chapter examines the ideological form of consent, and considers its implications for the determination of police work by the chief officers.

# Note

1. The best example of the frustrated position of the P.S.A. lies in its evidence to the Willink Commission 1962-3. Its evidence to the Scarman inquiry into the Brixton anti-police riots of 1981, suggests a slight diminution in its traditional hard-line posture.

*Part Two*

*Consent*

# 7 Consent: Class Relations in Police History

> ... possibly no other nation in the world could have witnessed, during the progress of a similar crisis, the spectacle of police and strikers engaging in a game of football. (G.W. Keeton, Keeping the Peace, 1975, p.166)

## Introduction

The success of the police institution in constructing a position of relative independence within the state, may paradoxically germinate the seeds of a threat to that independence. Autonomy has bred its own critique of the police institution. When the stability of civil society, and of class relations, depends upon an ideological relation—the notion of democratic accountability and the electoral regulation of the state apparatus—the existence of such a ubiquitous institution as the police which has escaped from that political frame, and which has shrugged off the democratic apparel, presents a major contradiction.

When exposed, the police apparatus' freedom from institutional constraints, is a source of indigestion at the democratic feast. As long as the facade of political accountability was maintained, criticisms were muted, and class relations restrained. But latent controversies and opposition are fuelled by the appreciation of the undemocratic form of a major public institution. Autonomy is a problem for both social classes and for the police institution.

The accusation of a lack of accountability gives vent to two forms of reaction from the police chiefs.

For some, the retort represents a form of paranoia (Cain, 1977), compounded by occupational stress. The motives of the critics are maligned. Lacking the burgess security of professional groups, and being more publicly vulnerable, police officers do not find it easy to shrug off criticisms which established professions might disdain.

Alternatively, a notion of accountability by consent is reiterated. A democratic relation is established by reference to the level of general support in civil society for the police apparatus. Police officers are evidentially conducting techniques of law enforcement and of civil intervention, supported by the vast majority of citizens. Without that approval, the particular style of policing practised in mainland Britain, would be impossible. *Ipso facto*, in a circular logic, democratic accountability is demonstrable in the non-institutional form of general public acclaim.

This reference to public consent to policing is not contrived. It is not an artificial construct, an ideological conspiracy, deliberately manufactured as a rationalization, or a concealment for malifeasant practises, suddenly revealed. Instead, it represents a concrete ideology, a major and substantive view of the relation between civil society and the police apparatus as affirmed by senior police officers, and repetitively reiterated in a myriad public and private statements. The discursive constitution and demonstration by the police of consent to policing provides a fundamental legitimation, both within the police institution and externally, to the policed citizens. When Charles Reith declared: "The chief element in the power of the police is the approval of the community, and their success depends upon their ability to retain it" (Reith, 1940) it was a statement credited, and taken as axiomatic by successive generations of police officers. But only in the last 20 years, has the notion of consent, singled out by Reith as a major feature of the British police system, been advanced to be the defining feature. Concomitant with the enhancement of the autonomy of the police institution, has been the transmutation of consent into the device by which democratic accountability is attested.

As the relationship with Home Office and local police authority is weakened in favour of the police institution, public approval is given added significance. A surrogate form of accountability is constructed out of consent.

Consent uplifts the rhetoric of police language in the service of autonomy. In Mark's words, in an echo of Reith:

> . . . the most essential weapons in our armoury are not firearms, water-cannon, tear-gas or rubber-bullets, but the confidence and support of the people on whose behalf we act. (1977, p.24)

Power flows not from the barrel of a gun, from the police constable's truncheon, or the Special Patrol Group radio, but from the latest opinion poll of public views on the police. According to Superintendent Butler of the Police Superintendents Association: "In Britain, we have always policed by consent; police activity is sustained by the active co-operation of the public or at least by its acquiescence".

In this chapter, alternative perspectives on the question of consent are contrasted through the medium of accounts of the history of police-class relations. In the first half of the chapter, the professional ideology is documented. Certain core assumptions preface that orthodox history. Inter-related premises on the legal and political relation of the police institution, on the philosophic contribution of the English Utilitarians, and on the features of early police organizations, are central to that account of the development of consent. However, within that official ideology there are two historical variants[1] — the Reithian and the institutionalist. The former version claims that after an initial period of hostility, the police institution, as the primary institution of the state, rapidly accumulated popular support from all social classes, through its evident contribution to the common good. The new industrial society was moulded on the police organizational precedent. In the institutionalist accounts, which arrive at the same eventual conclusion about the consensual relation, there is an incremental view, with the police institution as one of several burgeoning institutions of Victorian society.

These histories, the bedrock of the official ideology of consent, are contrasted in the second half of the chapter with fragments of an alternative history. Some of that opposing evidence on the historical relation between social classes and police, is drawn from the same primary sources in Liverpool as the material utilized to document the early emergence of autonomy, in Chapter 2. But most of the contrary material constituting an alternative history is from secondary sources, which if nothing else, demonstrate that a quite different reading of the historical data is possible. In these diffuse, alternative accounts (like the orthodox histories of varying quality), it is documented that by the end of the first century of policing the relationship between the police, the working-class, and the residual groups of the secondary economy, was characterized not so much by consent as by a tentative, negotiated, truce. The lower social stratum, the more probable that that truce was replaced by an undercurrent of antagonism. Conversely, the higher the stratum in the cities, by the end of that century, the readier the residents were to provide active support for the police institution through the adoption of the uniform of Police Specials, at time of crisis — the symbol of conflict between classes, not consent.

## Orthodox Histories of the Police:
## A Discourse of Consent

Histories of the police are legion. They range in quality from the sophisticated work of academics such as Radzinowicz (1956) and Hart (1951, 1978) and of civil servants (Critchley, 1970, 1979) and Tobias (1979), to the personalized reminiscences of retired police officers — Browne (1956), Nott Bower (1926), Moylan (1934), St. Johnston (1978), and many others.

These accounts of police development and of the construction of consent, vary only within the narrow parameters of conservative and liberal assumptions.

At the core of those histories, can be distinguished four discrete elements. They emphasize a legal relation, and an idiomatic view of political allegiance. They assume the primacy of the native philosophical creed of Utilitarianism. They enshrine particular notions of police organizational style and practice. The presumed legal relation between police and public (as depicted in Chapter 5) is central to the histories and to the construction of consent. The police officer is represented as a citizen-in-uniform. As a member of that public, who has been elevated by his peers to an office of law enforcement among them, his authority derives from traditional common law, rather than from statute. This absence of an exceptional legal power, in relation to the citizenry, discursively ensures an indivisible unity between policed and police. Lack of support for the police—the corporate body of citizens-in-uniform—is an anachronism, because the rights and duties of both citizens and police officers are enshrined in the same legal sanctuary.

This legal unity is complemented by a political relation. The local formation of police organizations (Chapter 2) it is claimed, bonded an empathetic connection between police officers and the idealized local communities. Force instructions, the immediate rules enforced by local forces, related to their sense of community needs as much as to the abstract law. Indeed, their legal powers were originally only operable amongst their immediate fellow citizens. Unlike the reserve militia of pre-industrial England and Wales, they rarely served outside their own districts. Although the amalgamations of later years have made this local link more tenuous, the orthodox histories maintain the continuing reality of the political allegiance of the police to their local roots.

Thirdly, the histories imbue the consent thesis with the ethos of Utilitarian social philosophy. The same social creed that produced the Panopticon as the model for Victorian penal reform, had direct implications for the construction of a preventive police. An intrinsic component of the work of Jeremy Bentham, and his influential policing disciple, Edwin Chadwick, was the concern with legal reform—ameliorating, and yet making more effective, the previous forms of crime control. Curbing crime at its source, by prevention rather than by arbitrary *post facto* reaction, maximized what Alderson was later to call the "positive" elements in human behaviour, and minimized the dysfunctional aspects of law enforcement. If crime was caught at the outset, least damage to the social fabric would be done.

That injunction, to intervene at source, determined the organizational practice. It required early intervention (the principle demonstrated in the succeeding chapter), and, as neo-Freudian theories about the importance of childhood for personality development took popular hold after World War II, police involvement in the social milieu of young people—at home, at school, and in recreation. Preventive policing required and mandated police officers to engage in the social life of the community. Secondly, as a corollary, prevention entailed a police commitment to re-direct and to re-construct deviant behaviour. The stricture given by Liverpool Head Constable Greig to new recruits on the way to handle a young child, kite-flying in the city street (by removing her gently to a city park) has gone down in police histories as the epitome of the preventive practice underlying consent.[2] Policing style was therefore vital. The compromise over the New Police between central government and local elites, included principles of police conduct. Deference to their betters and a personal lack of threat (police demeanour)—the unarmed constable—were the personal characteristic required by the consent relation according to the discourse of the orthodox histories. The histories also add a secondary function to the notion of organizational style:

> He must remember that there is no qualification more indispensable to a police officer than a perfect command of temper, never suffering himself to be moved in the slightest degree by any language or threats that may be used; if he so do his duty in a quiet and determined manner, such conduct will probably induce well-disposed bystanders to assist him should he require it.
> (the first Metropolitan Commissioner, quoted in Melville Lee, 1901, p.240[3])

Style was vital to the transformation of passive acceptance to active support. These themes are inter-meshed by the orthodox histories into a specific conception of the relation between the police institution and all social classes. Accounts of present-day police work take as given the assumptions in such accounts. In the work of conservative social scientists, from Gorer (1955) to Banton (1964), in the writings of commentators such as Evans (1974), Lewis (1976), and Whitaker, and in the prefaces of the Chief Constables' Annual Reports, there is an unstated police history based on this consensual reading of the past and a theological account of the evolution of consent.

Common to those orthodox histories are three central themes on that development.

(i) Opposition to the New Police, after the first years, was fragmented and not socially or economically based ". . . only the criminal, the crime industry profiteer, and some of the radical extremists continued to proffer serious opposition . . ." (Reith, 1940, p.69) by the time of the creation of the first provincial forces.

(ii) Any early working-class dissent from policing gradually disappeared during the nineteenth century and, by the Edwardian period, the lower-classes gave general support to the police institution:

> . . . in the early years, the police had to suffer a venomous hostility, particularly from the Chartists and radicals . . . yet in spite of some ignominious episodes when they were attacked, took refuge in the police station or actually

> fled the town, the police gradually became accepted and the idea that they
> represented an instrument of class domination gradually died away . . .
> (Moir, 1969, p.143)

(iii) All social classes were receiving similar benefits from the police institution
by the Edwardian period. Robert Roberts (in his revealing account of an
Edwardian slum) and Critchley, both quote the same 1911 *The Times* leader:

> . . . the policeman in London, is not merely a guardian of the peace,
> he is an integral part of social life. In many a back street and slum, he
> stands not merely for law and order, he is the true handyman of a mass
> of people who have no other counsellor or friend. (Roberts, 1973, p.100)

Where opposition did take a class form, these histories argue, the base was not
economic but due to cultural or geographical isolation. Consequently, it is
claimed the lower class, like the middle-classes before them, through a process of .
cultural diffusion, soon came to appreciate the benefits of the social stability
flowing from a professional police force and from its service functions.


## The Reithians — consent by sacrifice

The most extreme conservative account of the development of consent to
policing is found in the work of Charles Reith, Melville Lee, and their successors
— writers such as Browne (1956), Coatman (1959), Howard (1957), Minto
(1965), Solwyn (1935), and more recently, Thurston (1972) and Ascoli (1979).
Their view of the metamorphosis in police relations with the lower-classes will
be illustrated through accounts of one major incident — the so-called "Battle" of
Cold-Bath Fields. The Reithians share a common conception of society. Social
order is Hobbesian. Man is basically selfish. Without some strong guiding hand,
there would be anarchy and chaos. Fortunately, the police institution that was
developed in Britain in the early nineteenth century, incorporated those
attributes that allowed it to rise above that self-interest. The first constables
appointed by the Metropolitan Commissioners personified the traits that were
essential for social progress and for the construction of an orderly society (Gorer,
1955). Police officers became social unifiers, elevated by their fellow citizens
through their dispassionate conduct.

Consequently, policing in Britain developed a special symbolic character.
On the one hand, the police institution was an impartial referee — a neutral, but
congenial bureaucracy imposing disinterested, yet compassionate, law enforcement. On the other hand, it became a symbol of national unity, summing-up in
its practices and stature, the desirable moral attributes and social behaviour.
While this incarnation of nineteenth century police — class relations has

something of the composition of a caricature, is patently exaggerated, and cannot be taken with much gravity, it has some importance. In the texts of the Reithians, this perspective is the skeleton for an occupational ideology which denies any legitimate disjunction between police apparatus and the subordinated social classes. Where the police symbolize social unity, consent is axiomatic. Only alien elements would undermine the general support for the police institution.

The denigration of original opposition to early policing from groups in the lower-classes is a continuing theme. In Reith's own work (1940), for example, ". . . the unskilled labour classes . . . were largely affected by anti-police propaganda, inspired by Radicals' fear of police interference with their (revolutionary) plans". Howard blames: ". . . the extremists of the National Union of Working Classes . . ." (1957, p.140). In Melville Lee, the initial resistance is the work of "agitators" (p.245).

A major example of this denial of the legitimacy of dissent from the police institution, is the treatment by the Reithians of the Cold Bath Fields incident in 1833.

That clash, between the four-year-old Metropolitan Police and a large working-class crowd, is symptomatic of the material distortion at the core of the consent principle, and of policing ideology. The affair itself is regularly commemorated by police writers, partly because of the death of a police officer in the course of the confrontation.

Thurston, in an extraordinarily partisan account, sets the scene:

> . . . The meeting at Cold Bath Fields was organised by a few obscure agitators for the purpose of organising a National Convention of the Working-Classes, and was an early stirring towards the trade union movement. This half-baked affair attracted public notice and, as well as simple working folk, a number of known bad characters, some of them armed, turned up at the prospect of violence. Colonel Rowan was prepared for trouble and dealt with the gathering with precision and firmness . . . (1972, Introduction)

Again:

> The organisers were obscure and maladroit and the uneducated supporters ready dupes for the agitator. Such a meeting inevitably attracted known ruffians who came for violence . . . (ibid, p.178)

For the Reithians, the conflict between the police and the "mob", and the defeat of the latter, is treated as an allegorical story of the triumph of the forces of good, light, and reason, over the malignancies of barbarism, dark, and irrationality:

> . . . the attempted riot was the Waterloo of the war waged with revolutionary aims by political extremists in London, and finally ended their hopes of success. (Reith, 1956, p.162)

This account has been legitimized by repetition. In a popular contemporary children's text about police work (which draws mainly on Howard and on Melville Lee), one finds:

> . . . the Battle of Cold Bath Fields was a complete victory for the police. Although a policeman had been killed and several injured, there was not one person in the mob who had been severely injured. At long last, the fearful power of the London mob had been destroyed. (Dumpleton, 1963, p.68)

The refusal of a London jury to convict participants in the demonstration, of the murder of P.C. Culley is criticized for its "misguided prejudice . . .". To Browne, the jury's verdict is ". . . scandalous . . . all reasonable people are disgusted . . ." (p.105). Thurston derides all those witnesses, ranging from a clergyman to a cavalry Colonel (and newspaper accounts, from the radical Press, to *The Times*), who suggest that the conflict owed more to police provocation than to conspiratorial violence.

Ascoli uses a David-and-Goliath theme: "A confused running fight ensued in which the police, heavily outnumbered and confronted by armed thugs, behaved with astonishing propriety . . ." (p.155) and proceeds to relate the event to the question of consent:

> Eventually, the mob was dispersed and the police, though they did not then know it had won their final and conclusive victory over the Ultras. More importantly, they had won an even greater victory in the long-term—the seal of public approval. (ibid)

Militaristic metaphors are essential to the Reithians in their portrayal of the good fight between the police and the criminal class, with the symbolic martyrdom of a police officer representing the turning-point in police–class relations. After the performance of the police in that battle, public confidence was with them. The mythology of Cold Bath Fields is a key element in the dramaturgical construction of consent.

However, there are alternative accounts of this conflict. Radzinowicz (whose work contextualizes police development within the larger history of the criminal justice system), lets the participants speak for themselves:

> . . . many charges were levied against the police as a result of this episode. They were said to have been brutal and provocative, many of them drunk . . . The Rev J Parson . . . said that what he saw was an attempt to escape, not to resist by the people: the police rushed from every avenue to prevent them getting away, many (people) were knocked down and men, women and children, indiscriminately struck (1956, pp.181-2)

Thompson, similarly takes the evidence to the jury seriously, and gives the major alternative account to that of the Reithians:

> Attendance at the meeting was not large. The police appeared in great force down every approach (blocking all exits), and on the pretext of seizing an American flag, moved without preamble into a direct attack. In the affray, men, women and children, were beaten unmercifully, casual bystanders and newspaper reporters were bludgeoned, and street traders' barrows and baskets of loaves were strewn across the roads. Somewhere in the middle of the confusion, Police Constable Culley was stabbed . . . (1979, p.380)

The jury consisted of local shopkeepers and none of them apparently had any sympathy for the objects of the demonstration:

> Nevertheless, they unanimously returned a remarkable verdict "We find a verdict of justifiable homicide on these grounds—that no Riot Act was read, nor any proclamation advising the public to disperse—that the Government did not take the proper precautions to prevent the meeting from assembling and that the conduct of the police was ferocious, brutal, and unprovoked . . . (ibid)

Irrespective of the accuracy of these opposing accounts, the affair has two functions in policing ideology. Within the imagery of the Reithians, Cold Bath Fields was a watershed. Before the confrontation, there was large-scale dissent from the new police institution. Afterwards, the way was downhill. The "public" recognized that "right" had won.

Secondly, the accounts of the event serve to define the enemies of policing and, by implication, and obversely, the police themselves. When Ascoli, writing of events 130 years later, refers to the "rats" and to the "militants" of the anti-nuclear Committee of 100, a "new movement of extremists" choosing the "politics of violence" (1979, p.180), he is using language and distortions legitimized and institutionalized by the Reithian version of Cold Bath Fields. For the Reithians, consent to policing was constructed through baptism by fire and the propitious sacrifice of P.C. Culley's blood. Together with the delegitimization of oppositional elements, the Reithian histories structure the historical foundation of the police institution, and endorse a partisan view of police-social class relations.

### The institutionalists—consent by stages

There is a second, more sober strand of police history, that remains within the conservative parameters in its depiction of the growth of consent to policing. With links to Bentham rather than to Hobbes, the institutionalists for the most part seek to relate the expansion of the police apparatus to the more general development of different public bureaucracies of the new industrial society. They portray police reform as one of several social improvements, aimed at lessening some of the social problems resulting from the impact of the Industrial Revolution. They range, in emphasis, from the "great men" theorists such as Hart, via the constitutionalists (Critchley) to the social pathologists (Tobias). To the latter, especially, (following Silver) the police were urban sanitation experts, cleaning-up the malaise of industrialization, urbanization, and the population explosion.

Police development was not important in itself but rather as one of several inter-related reforms. Crime could not be suppressed simply by police action but only in co-operation with the other city bureaucracies—the new institutions of welfare, education, and housing reform.[4]

Social relations between the police and the policed were inevitably hostile at first. The lower classes were not sufficiently well-equipped to appreciate the benefits that police reform would eventually bring to them. Besides, as Chapter 2 demonstrated, many of their habitual activities were such as to disturb the "natural" order of the city. The police therefore were a necessary, front-line, defence until elements hostile to society could be incorporated by education, work discipline, and the ballot box. Repression and confrontation were only significant at the outset, as the police apparatus gave the other institutions adequate breathing-space and opportunity.

The working-class had first to be controlled before it learnt to co-operate with the organic forces of social order. Edmund Chadwick's contribution to the 1839 Constabulary Commission is a primary reference point. That Benthamite reformer

> . . . was a great and prolific inventor of bureaucratic processes and institutions
> . . . new institutional means were a way of curing ills of the old order, and a
> prime necessity at a time of acute social change was to assert tutelary control
> over the working-class. (Donajgrodzki, 1977, p.70[5])

For Critchley, this attempt to ideologically harness the working-class had some of the aspects of a class struggle, as the latter resisted the attempts of the police to channel its activities into legitimate routes. The eventual decrease in violence and the creation of a more orderly society is due as much to the new sophistication of the state's control techniques, (of which the police institution is the most important), as to the process of democratization (Critchley, 1970).

Hart, like Tobias (although they disagree elsewhere) emphasizes the evolutionary and reformative character of police development. Giving great weight to the work of Robert Peel, she depicts police reform as one of several steps designed to mitigate the harshness and arbitrariness of earlier penal and preventative methods. The Peterloo massacre by the yeomanry, for example, had demonstrated the folly of relying on traditional means of social control in the new industrial society.

For the most part, the institutionalist writers describe any continuing hostility to police after the first half century as isolated phenomena, betraying either incompetent police leadership (such as Sir Charles Warren's crushing of a Trafalgar Square demonstration in 1881); inconsistencies in the laws that the police were asked to implement; or the general backwardness and isolation of some groups from conventional society—the costers, the gypsies, the inhabitants of the rookeries, and floating labour populations (such as the railway navvies, Chesney, 1968, p.36; Coleman, 1966). Continuing conflicts derived from communication problems—lack of education, or lack of integration into the primary economy. For the mass of the population, consent to policing was established slowly, as the process of cultural diffusion allowed ideas and new social values to spread from the middle to the working classes, and from there to the peripheral groups. Integration in society was accompanied by approval of the police apparatus as one of several institutions of reform.

For the institutionalists, the police service was gradually accepted in the same way that urban dwellers came to appreciate sanitation, education, and appropriate housing. Responsibility for social control slowly evolved from being a personal responsibility to a service supplied by the local state, to a function of the central Government.

The work of both Reithians and institutionalists contains a measure of truth. For example, the Reithians were obviously correct to suggest that the police officer who delivered winter-relief, within the parochial confines of the provincial city or town, would be more likely to be generally accepted by the recipients of that service than the agent of a centrally-directed gendarmerie who had no local service functions. Similarly, there is some substance in the institutionalist approach. Not all opposition towards the police was based upon class or economic interest, and consent was really developed gradually as more groups became incorporated within the political and social system of developed capitalism.

But there are major problems in their assumptions on the construction of consent. For example, while the institutionalists do not make the mistake of the Reithians in largely ignoring social stratification and economic inequality, they suggest a general withering-away of class protest during the nineteenth century. Class inequality, with its implications for the police role, is relevant only to the Industrial Revolution period. Lack of overt conflict between the police and lower class fractions is mistaken for consent (in the same way that the underlying economic cleavages are generally ignored). The specificity of police action against the different classes is glossed over. The general complexity of the class structure in the Victorian age—the distinction between the "respectable" working-class and the participants in the street economy is similarly obfuscated.

For the most part, the institutionalists share with the Reithians an unquestioning conservatism—the lack of attention to the society that is being policed, and to its inequalities; the identification of the public interest with sectional demands; the denial of the legitimacy of dissent; and the confused notions of the groups said to be threatening the social order—the vague concepts of the mob, dangerously class, and residuum. Similarly, there is a methodological problem in the conventional reliance upon official data sources for accounts of public reactions to the police. Parliamentary papers (as Hart herself has pointed out) may be used as much for propaganda, as for a faithful portrayal of events (Hart, 1977; Storch, 1976).

The substance of consent, particularly the relation between working-class groups, and the lower classes, and the police institution, is therefore more problematic than is depicted in either Reithian or institutionalist accounts.

The evidence is questionable. Consent, as a major prop of the ideologial relation of the police institution must be subject to a more adequate historical appraisal. In the last decade, a number of more radical historians have begun to document fragments of an alternative history—one which suggests that despite the mass of official records—Parliamentary papers, Watch Committee Minutes, and the like—there was a residue of continuing, if spasmodic conflict between the police institution and the lower orders of Victorian and Edwardian society.

## The Class Relations of the Police Institution in Social History

In the work of Miller (1977, 1979), Robinson (1978), Storch (1975, 1976), and, to some extent in Phillips (1976, 1978, 1980), there are the first signs of the development of a more concrete description of the expansion of the police apparatus an account which, unlike that of the institutionalists is primarily concerned to situate the police institution within the networks and complexities of class relations. Their contributions can be supplemented, through the work of historians with wider interests, through the committed biographies of working-class leaders, and through primary material from the history of the Liverpool Police. The evidence from this eclectic selection supports three alternative propositions, in relation to the thesis on policing and consent. Obscured by the orthodox accounts of police history is a different version of the changing class relations of the police institution.

(i) There was substantially more physical conflict between local police forces and lower class groups during the first century of police development than is normally acknowledged.

(ii) Where that overt conflict disappeared, it was replaced not by consent but by a kind of "grumbling dissent". The police institution was accepted in lower class areas, not because it had become any more popular, but because of its organizational superiority.

(iii) There was no single unified lower class reaction. The context and form of working-class encounters with the police differed from those groups outside the primary economy.

The evidence in support of these propositions, refuting both the Reithian and the institutionalist versions of the growth of consent, depends upon an appreciation of the complexity of the Victorian class structure.

By the Edwardian period, varying relations had been constructed between the police institution and the different social classes. The classes represented through the local state in Liverpool, as we have seen, the merchant capitalists, the business proprietors, the professionals, the shopkeepers, and the new ancillary strata of clerical workers, gave increasing assent, a support that was most visible at time of crisis. For the urban industrial workers and their kin—the "respectable" strata of Victorian England—by the 1900s, the relation with the police institution had assumed the features of a truce, grudging acceptance, with occasional direct confrontations in the course of an industrial dispute. For the lower classes, the participants in the street economy, strata of mercurial proportions dependent upon the dominant mode of production in the city, and the fluctuations in employment attitudes to the police institution throughout the first century of policing remained essentially unchanged. They were subject to continuing, occasional, and apparently arbitrary "culls".

## The bourgeois reaction

While there are several descriptions of a direct connection between the new manufacturing and entrepreneurial elites of the industrial towns and cities, and the police apparatus, most evidence suggests that direct interest in the new police institution was abnormal. To the middle-classes, they were not centrally important (as in the Reithian account) but simply one of sundry city bureaucracies instrumental in mapping-out, controlling, and containing the proclivities of the other class. Political and economic crisis, however, brought forth a different reaction.

The very few examples of direct partisanship have been mythologized through repetition. Among the original studies, Phillips, has illustrated the collaboration between the police, the coalmasters, and the magistracy, in enforcing low wages on miners in the Black Country in the 1850s. "There can be no doubt that the machinery of law and order operated to the disadvantage of the working class" (Phillips, 1974, p.159). But even in that case, it was the routinized functioning of the police institution as an agency of control that led to the class co-operation, not apparently any specific pressure from the coalmasters themselves. A ritualized relation, and a generalized consent, seems to have been the norm, after the early years, between the police and the business-class.

Several writers (Chesney, 1968; Cohen, 1979; Hart, 1951; Miller, 1977; Parris, 1961; Thompson, 1979), distinguish the shopkeepers as the strata which maintained consistent demands on the police institution for action against participants in the street economy. Many accounts document the significance of the tradesmen's interests in the development of the consent to policing. Glover, for example, gives the Reithian view (half-way through the century), in commenting upon the relative stability of Victorian society: ". . . the revival of public confidence was no doubt largely engendered by the confidence placed in the New Police by the shopkeepers . . ." (Glover, 1934, p.62). Critchley notes after the dispersal by the Metropolitan police of a Chartist demonstration in 1848: "The crowd dispersed, and that night the middle classes thronged the streets singing 'God Save the Queen' ('But what they ought to be singing was "God Save Our Shops"' muttered the disappointed Chartists)" (Critchley, 1969, p.138). The control and affiliation with the retail petit bourgeoisie may in part account for the repressive consequences of police ideology. Petit bourgeois ideology seems to have replaced earlier High Tory, quasi-platonic, notions of the police as protectors and exemplars.

But shopkeeper support for the police was fickle and conditional. Their properties were in the front-line in any street disorder, as well as in direct competition with the street economy. The significance of the police institution for the tradespeople in time of crisis, is illustrated by this excerpt from a Liverpool account of an attack on bread-shops by:

> . . . A number of half-grown men, women and boys, assembled in Scotland Road and by their presence caused serious apprehension in the minds of the Tradesmen that a repetition of the Bread Riots of 1855 was about to take place, and a very large proportion of those carrying out business in that thoroughfare hurriedly put up their shutters and closed their Shops . . . One man was also apprehended by two Shopkeepers in Canterbury Street for having gone in the Shop of one of them and asked for Relief, and upon being refused, threatened that person that he with others would come and sack the place before the night. When the man was searched at the Bridewell, 3 farthings and five Soup Tickets were found on his person. He was sentenced the following day by Mr Raffles to a month's imprisonment with hard labour . . . (H.C. Report, 13th January, 1861)

The police were a necessary business expense to the shopkeepers. To the other middle-class strata in Liverpool, where it will be remembered industrial capital was of limited importance, crime and disorder were largely experienced at second-hand. The merchants and, arguably, the industrial bourgeoisie elsewhere, supported the police institution primarily because it was the visible representation of a legal order which provided the foundation for a society which had peacefully integrated the middle-classes into the political process (Miller, 1979). Generalized consent to the police institution, related to its impartial practices, routinely sweeping ". . . of the streets with an equable hand, street traders, beggars, prostitutes, street entertainers, pickets, children playing football, and free-thinking, and socialist speakers alike . . ." (Thompson, 1979, p.23) was the attribute of a class whose hegemony rested upon the rule of law.

But at times of tension this general support was given material form. When the social order was threatened, the local bourgeoisie enrolled in their thousands as Police Specials. At those recurrent crises, ". . . the principal reserve for the recruitment of special constables was the middle-class" (Mather, 1959, p.84). No reservations about the police institution were obvious, when the professionals, shopkeepers, and white-collar clerks of the city, donned police uniforms (more probably, armband insignia) to meet the threat to their social and economic welfare:

> Difficulties of recruitment belong the early years . . . a remarkable change in 1848 . . . the almost legendary muster of 160,000 constables in the London area was matched throughout the provinces . . . in Liverpool some 3000-4000 selected from the principal inhabitants . . . (ibid)

Seventy years later, Reith's unity between police and public (or rather one section of it), was never more obvious than during the police strike of 1919. In Liverpool, (the only significant area of strike activity outside London), members of the city merchant houses enrolled, en masse, to support those police who remained at work. "The business interests in the town made it clear to their staff that every able-bodied man . . . was to volunteer his aid" (Judge and Reynolds, 1968, p.74). "Typical of the civilian volunteers who signed up with the Specials were members of the Hightown (a select residential suburb) Sporting Club who enrolled to help the Lord Mayor out of his difficulties" (ibid). The donning of police insignia legitimized class violence. By the time of the 1926 General Strike, the Police Specials had been developed as a directly class-based force:

> . . . it is not considered wise or expedient to attempt to press the actual working classes into the scheme as it might lay them open to the charge of being "blacklegs". The ideal . . . is to have in each business community every young and able bodied man, other than manual workers, ready to protect the city and stand for law and order. (Liverpool Stock Exchange Minutes, February, 1920)

To working-class people, the same crises and the entry of the Police Specials evoked a different response. In 1848, 500 Liverpool dock workers had, according to Mather, given up their employment rather than temporarily adopt police uniform. In 1919, the Liverpool "mob" had ". . . nothing but contempt . . ." for

the Specials (Judge and Reynolds, 1968, p.162). In 1926, during the General
Strike, workers showed more antagonism to the Specials than to the professional
police officers (M. Morris, 1977, p.54). The ordinary police function could be
comprehended as one way a working-man might regrettably better himself
through secure employment. But the middle-classes in police uniform were the
outright embodiment of class interest. Among the latter, they recognized
". . . right-wing elements anxious to do anything to destroy the unions . . ."
(ibid). Consent to policing by the middle-class was that of generalized approval
for a servant institution, which was not so much a model for sober public
behaviour, as a servant which kept the beggars from the door, and the riff-raff
from the streets. It was a consent which related not to a social unity, and an
organic society but was based upon a conception of a class-divided society. The
police institution was significant like other local bureaucracies and deserved
approval not because it symbolized national unity, but because it ensured the
maintenance of legally ordained privilege.

## The working-class relation — the tinder of industrial confrontation

Working-class response to the police institution during that first century varied
over time, by region, and by strata. In general, by the end of that period, the
relations that had developed were not so much ones of consent but rather a
grudging acceptance, a tentative approval, that could be withdrawn instantly in
the context of industrial conflict.

Dissent was readily re-kindled in industrial struggle. In the early years, in
those towns and cities where an industrial base had already been established, the
accounts dwell on the confrontations. The police had been given what Storch
(1976) calls an "omnibus mandate" to maintain social stability, in the service of
the new industrial order. Conflicts between the police and working class groups
were far from uncommon.

As early as the 1820s (and prior to the formation of the New Police), Foster
(1973) credits the Oldham artisans with a consciousness of the political function
of policing. Continuing clashes between artisans and mill-owners over the
control of the police, are documented over a decade. There are a number of
accounts of violent conflicts between police officers and industrial communities
in the early years. Midwinter recounts a series of confrontations in the industrial
towns of Lancashire, referring, for example, to the arrival in Bury, in 1839, of
"a brutal, bloody, bullying, and unconstitutional force . . ." (Midwinter, 1968,
p.3). Storch (1975) and Radzinowicz (1956), document similar anti-police riots
in Leeds, Manchester, Hull, Lancaster, Stoke, and Middleton. Of the conflicts
between the outside "blue locusts" and local cotton operatives in one small

Lancashire town, Storch says: "The events at Colne from April through August 1840 were not so much riots as a bitter war against the police" (Storch, 1975, p.79). The Home Secretary had refused to let the Metropolitan Police help crush a miners' strike in Durham in 1844, because "it has the effect of impairing discipline and sometimes excites a strong feeling against the police." (Mather, 1959, p.109).

While these outright confrontations lessened as the century progressed, and as middle-class support for the police institution developed, a political consciousness of the class nature of the New Police remained. Pelling (1968), for example, notes the continuing political articulation of working-class opposition to the police institution. Prominently itemized, on working-class manifestos through the Victorian era, were demands about the control of the police. But this appreciation of the political role of the new police apparatus, and the realization that their provincial expansion owed much to Chartist threats to the privileged classes (Critchley, 1979), was true of the industrial towns. There is no such indication from the capital itself, and from ports such as Liverpool.

In the latter city, there is only very limited evidence of the police being used against the diminutive industrial working-class, for example:

> On the application of Mr Mair that a police constable be sent under the direction of the Head Constable to Mr Mair's Iron Foundry . . . to protect his workmen during the Turn-out of the Moulders from his Establishment. (Watch Committee Orders, 23rd March, 1839)

However, there are no records of any direct confrontations in the early years and, indeed, the Watch Committee, when approached by an industrialist for assistance in disciplining his work force was likely to turn down the request, or demand payment for those services. Although there is some minor indication of conflict with casual labour (Chesney, 1968, p.37) in the form of the dock workers in the 1840s, not till considerably later did any more precise demarcation of working-class forces develop.

The disputes that had characterized other cities early in the Industrial Revolution, only began to develop in Liverpool in the latter half of the nineteenth century. Unionization, the development of labour organization amongst the docks and transport workers that formed the base of the city's economy, occurred at a later period than in the manufacturing towns.

There is very little evidence of direct police intervention on the side of capital until a degree of similarity developed between the organization of production in Liverpool and its organization in the industrial towns, in the 1870s and 1880s. In the 1850s, only one such incident is recorded in the Watch Committee Minutes. In 1856, the Marquis of Chandos, Chairman of the London and North Western Railway, wrote to thank the Watch Committee, for the assistance of police officers in breaking a strike of railway clerks. But twenty years later the following manifestation, from the Canada Shipping Company, becomes more overt:

> . . . reference to our letters of 7th Feb, intimating that some of our men had suffered intimidation and requesting the attendance of sufficient officers to prevent a recurrence of the same, beg today to thank you owing to the excellent protection offered and the arrangements made by you in our behalf, our men were enabled to continue their work at our Steamers unmolested.
> Now that the strike has terminated, it became our duty to express our entire satisfaction at the care shown by you and your subordinates during that time . . . (Head Constable Report, 25th February, 1879)

[Keeton (1975, p.162) provides some evidence of the clash between the police and the dockers during that dispute.]

By the 1880s, the Liverpool police had the capacity to intervene in industrial disputes outside the city boundaries, at the request of local Watch Committees or magistrates. During the period 1883–1894, the Liverpool Watch Committee sent detachments of police to defend the Caernarvonshire quarries against strikers; across the city boundary to deal with a seamen's strike in Bootle; over the Mersey to terminate a salt-worker's strike in Cheshire: into St. Helens to support employers against local workers; to Trafalgar Square for a political demonstration; and to Lancaster for another local dispute. After its earlier commitment to policing the secondary economy of the city; the rise of organized labour in the transport industry (the police had also been involved in a major tramway strike in the city in 1879) was reflected in a partial re-direction of the force in training and deployment to protect the primary economy. Changing economic relations, the belated formation of a conscious working-class, had its impact on Liverpool police organization and practices.

By the 1900s, confrontations with labour had become more common and more bitter, exacerbated by police involvement in the sectarian troubles of the 1902–1910 period. The major conflict took place during the national transport strike of 1911. While the early period of that strike by seamen, transport, and dock workers, produced comparatively little discord [". . . relations between the Liverpool strikers and the bobbies seldom deteriorated from friendly chaffing, and the Head Constable could tell the Home Office 'No disturbance took place' " (Hikins, 1980, p.106)], the unexpected arrival of police officers from outside the city, took strikers aback by their unexpectedness:

> . . . it seemed obvious to the crowd that the authorities were in league with their employers. There could be no other explanation . . . The Birmingham policemen were received angrily with a shower of fruit and a few stones, and a jeering crowd dogged them all the way to Dale Street. (ibid)

Within a few days, the scene described graphically by the labour leader, Tom
Mann, took place:

> If the worst and most ferocious brutes in the world had been on the scene,
> they would not have displayed such brutality as the Liverpool City Police,
> and their imported men . . . such a scene of brutal butchery was never
> witnessed in Liverpool before. Defenceless men and women, several of them
> whom were infirm, and many of whom were aged, were deliberately knocked
> down by heavy blows from the truncheons of powerful men, and even as the
> crowd fled from this onslaught, the police still continued to batter away at
> them . . . (Quoted in Coates, 1967, p.220)

After that affair, ". . . no policeman was safe from attack . . ." (Hikins, 1980,
p.23). This breakdown of the truce between the Liverpool working-class, as
represented through organized labour, and the police institution was mirrored in
succeeding minor incidents. The following year, for example, there was an
onslaught on a crowd of pickets and bystanders by police officers protecting
strike breakers (the incident had sectarian overtones) in the newly incorporated
city district of Garston. The following is an excerpt from one of thirty similar
petitions to the Lord Mayor, after the event:

> I am the wife of Francis James Smith who is a Scaler. Neither I nor he had
> anything to do with the strike.
> On the evening of 13th August, I heard that my child had gone amongst the
> crowd and I went up to the crowd to see if she was still there . . . I went along
> King Street. When the Constables charged the crowd and the crowd was
> running away because the constables were striking them in all directions,
> I came across my little child and was reprimanding her for being amongst
> the crowd, and I had hardly got the words out of my mouth when a constable
> whose face I know, but whose number I don't know, rushed forward and
> with his baton made a deliberate aim what I thought at my child's head. I put
> my left arm forward to cover the child's head and it caught me just above the
> elbow. The pain was very severe, and as I was stooping down he made
> another savage poke at me in the side giving me a most painful blow with his
> baton . . . as the policemen were charging, they knocked down 3 children and
> stamped on them. They were lying there helpless as I was knocked down . . .
> (Liverpool Trades Council Records, 1911)

For these and similar reasons, by the time of the unique 1919 Police Strike in
the city, there was little sympathy between the police strikers and the mass of the
labour movement. There was approval of neither the police institution as a
corporate body nor of the officers as follow trade unionists, fighting an identical
battle with the employing class. Although there was:

> . . . undoubted support from the trades council, local Labour party and
> executive committees of individual unions . . . In contrast, much of the

> rank-and-file was more cautious of the newly professed affinity of the police
> for the labour movement . . . others were said to view the police strikers
> "with contempt". (Bean, 1980, p.22)

Indeed, according to Judge and Reynolds (1968), not merely did the working-class decline to support the police officers as fellow workers but amongst the lower classes, sectarian divisions were forgotten as they turned on the common enemy—the remnant of non-strikers and the middle-class specials.

After the defeat of the strike, and the dismissal of all strikers (who forfeited numerous benefits), the Liverpool Police became more solidly committed to anti-labour activity. Its depleted ranks were rapidly filled with ex-servicemen, whose own class experiences pre-dated war-time service. This reinforced anti-labour feeling was soon manifest with the ferocious attack on unemployed workers in 1921 (Frontispiece). The old combative mood, which had come to the force during the pre-war sectarian disturbances, and in the 1911 Transport Strike, was re-asserted.

Finally, while direct conflicts between workers and the police, in Liverpool, seem to have been rare during the General Strike, there is evidence of some physical encounters and of a more general underlying hostility. Across the Mersey, for example, the employers' emergency newssheet admits that in the course of an encounter with pickets "truncheons were drawn and freely used on the more combatative ones, who threw themselves on the ground and kicked and struggled . . ." (*Post and Courier Bulletin*, 12th May, 1926). But the more general police-worker relation during the strike appears to have been of a generally pervasive police and Special Police presence, punitive forays against individual pickets, and C.I.D. intimidation (*General Strike Bulletin*, 6th May, 1926).

This picture of episodic conflict between police and industrial workers continuing unabated, is not that of the orthodox histories. The distortion of police-labour history was never more acute than during the period of the General Strike.

In those histories, the same degree of symbolism is conferred on the representation of events during that nationwide cleavage, as had been ascribed to the Cold Bath Fields saga, of 90 years' earlier. Coatman, Keeton, and Howard wax with jingoistic glee in describing events during the General Strike, as signifying the apogee of police acceptance by organized labour. Critchley, (normally, the soberest of police historians) treats the immortalized game of football between strikers and police with due reverence, and as a metaphor of the consenting relation:

> . . . both sides . . . played . . . the game according to unwritten rules, as
> though the standards of Arnold's schoolboys had permeated all classes . . .
> (Critchley, 1970, p.202)

> They emerged from it all with greatly enhanced status, not only as pro-
> tectors of the public, but almost as their guardians, so agreeable was
> their good humour and so implicit was the nation's trust in their impar-
> tiality and forbearance at a time of national danger . . . (Critchley, 1979,
> p.200)

Whether that particular football match was typical of relations between labour and police during the General Strike is difficult to assess. Certainly, there was little evidence in Liverpool of sporting rules governing the industrial encounter, with mutual applause for the winning team. One such football match in Carstairs, where the game was arranged to calm an inflamed situation, resulted in a physical confrontation after a mis-heard jest by one of the strikers (M. Morris, 1979). Elsewhere in the country, there was substantive evidence of violent attacks on strikers by the police (see, for example, Farman, 1974, p.246). Often the lack of overt conflict related to the degree of control exercised by the local Strike Committee, rather than to any consent to police authority.

In practice, overt conflict between an organized working-class and the developing police apparatus, whether in Liverpool (where that class had only latterly developed strength) or more widely, was rare during that first century. But the relation was certainly not the consenting one as portrayed at the end of that period, in the writings of the Reithians, and of the institutionalists. Police actions, particularly in a city like Liverpool which had witnessed substantial police oppression, were always suspect, open to misinterpretation, and subject to widespread rumour. If there existed consent to the police institutions, it was a tentative approval and subject to precipitate withdrawal. However, compared to the reaction and experience of policing of the participants in the street economy, it was a comparatively harmonious relation.

## The street relation — continuing repression

While for the organized industrial working-class in the Victorian and Edwardian cities, conflicts with the police were largely limited to the industrial context, for the participants and dependents of the street economy, clashes continued to be a feature of everyday life. Dissent from policing by the marginal groups encom-passed sundry individual tussles with police officers, and occasional mass anti-police conflagrations that might originate through sectarian or racial schisms.

Closely parallelling changes in the London district of Islington (Cohen, 1979), the nascent Liverpool working-class was gradually separated from the residual groups, and from the participants in the secondary economy. Changes in the labour process deepened that schism. Dock-work was partly de-casualized, and the new ocean-going steamships permitted the concentration of regular workers such as seamen, dockers, and transport workers. A gap of social status, and often of age, sex, and race, opened up between the developing working-class and the residual groups of the street economy and casual workers.

Elements of the Samuel Smiles "self-help" ideology were diffused from the urban bourgeoisie to the artisan class (Miller, 1979). A process of social exclusion (Parkin, 1972) operated to separate-out the working-class through the assignation of deviant definitions. As the labour force became disciplined to the wage, those marginal groups outside the primary economy were discarded and became recognized by the industrial labour force too as legitimate targets for police. Social mobility for the new industrial proletariat was partly achieved at the cost of stigmatizing those strata, particularly the vagrants, the street traders, and the unemployed youths, outside the primary economy.

In this process of social exclusion, the labelling of the marginal groups was reinforced by the expression of bourgeois opinion which strove to incorporate the urban working-class within the institutional framework, partly by segregating the residual groups for special attention. For example, the *Liverpool Mercury's* accounts of the so-called "bread riots" in the city in 1855, distinguished the "lowest class" from the "respectable" working-class (Editorial, 20th February, 1855).

*The Mercury* felt the need to ". . . repeat that the Working-Classes of this city took no part in the disgraceful outrages" (23rd February, 1855). The arrestees ". . . appeared to belong to the lowest and most vicious class of the Irish population in the town" (ibid).

Gattrell notes:

> As the world of the respectable "progressed", the 30% or more at the base of the social pyramid, and from whom most crime was *expected*, were progressively subject to all the control which the ingenuity of Victorian philanthropists and the Victorian state could devise . . . (Gattrell, 1980, p.335)

This process of the criminalization of the pool of casual labour, the lower-classes, and the concomitant de-criminalization of the labouring working-class was facilitated by legal change. The passing of the Habitual Criminals Act of 1869, and the Prevention of Crime Act in 1871, added to the sanitation of the lower orders. In that latter year the Liverpool Watch Committee proposed a new bye-law, specifically aimed at the street people:

> Every person who shall stand, loiter, or remain on any Carriageway or Footway, in any Street, Lane, or Public Place within this Borough, without some reasonable or good and efficient cause, and so in any manner obstruct, incommode, hinder, or prevent the free passage-way along any such Carriageway or Footway, shall forfeit a sum not exceeding £5.

The expansion of police powers at the end of the 1860s narrowly focussed on a specific group (Hart, 1977; Miller, 1979), a focus which in Liverpool, as elsewhere, seems to have had the assent of both working-class and bourgeoisie. Organizational factors within the police institution contributed to an easier relation with the respectable working-class, and to the institutionalized exclusion of the lower classes. The antagonistic milieu of the street for patrolling police officers resulted in practical compromises. If the police officers as individuals wished to survive, and if the police institution as a corporate body aimed to gain a measure of consent, tolerance was necessary. Discretionary law enforcement led to a truce with one class at the cost of joint criminalization of the lower orders.

> . . . a system of informal, tacitly negotiated and particularistic definitions of public order were evolved which *accommodated* certain working-class usages of social space and *outlawed* others imposed a system of unofficial curfew, informal out-of-bounds, to define what were the wrong people, wrong age, in the wrong place, at the wrong time. (Cohen, 1979, p.131; Ignatieff, 1979)

A partial consent was constructed by agreement over the victims. What was liable for police action on the streets of the city slum was not pursued in the stable working-class area. The activities of the lower classes were controlled by what seemed to the outsider to be severe and capricious action by the police institution, but what in practice was the application of a systematic code resulting from that negotiation process.

Controls over and the constitution of outcast groups took several forms ranging from general surveillance to occasional fishing trips (Charles Dickens recounts one such venture in Liverpool[6]) into the rookeries. The "move-on" practice disciplined the city streets.[7] As Jack London recounts in "The People of the Abyss" (p.77) for the marginal groups in London's East End, this particular police power (as enshrined in Liverpool in the 1871 bye-law), was the major form of contact with the police institution. The male reserve army of labour was designated outcast, demonstrated to be unreliable and hence unemployable on a permanent basis, and effectively disorganized internally.

Such was the formative effect of this agreement over victim, together with the continuing commitment of police patrols to the containment function, that the experience of the lower classes at the centenary of the Liverpool Police was little different from that of the earlier period. Street harrassment continued as the major form of contact between the police and the residual groups throughout. Note for example, the flavour of coercion caught by an unemployed Liverpudlian in the 1930s:

> Every day you'd see twenty or thirty men standing on street corners and sitting on doorsteps. Then suddenly one of them would call out 'Aye, Aye lads . . . here's the cops' and they'd all move. The police would walk in

single file on the edge of the pavement and if they caught the men hanging around, they'd book them. (*Liverpool Echo*, 27th August, 1980)

Armed with a variety of legal powers (the provisions of the Vagrancy Acts, the statutes dealing with prostitution, betting and gaming, drunkenness, frequenting, obstruction, and the several bye-laws), police officers had little difficulty in exerting authority over the street people.

### Street people and crime statistics: harassment demonstrates the need for more police

Through such legal resources, the Liverpool police force constructed its arrest rate. Between 1860 and 1930, on average, one-in-twenty of the total city population appeared in court every year, for the most part on those charges where police actions were most permissive and discretionary.

Some indication of the concentration of those charges on the lower strata can be deduced from the evidence on the literacy of the arrestees (from the Head Constable's Annual Reports). In 1863, only 2% (525) of those charged could read and write well (Hart gives a figure of 8% for London). Thirty-eight per cent (10 008) were judged to be totally illiterate. By 1900, the figures had changed little—1% (181) and 23% (4550). (These figures, of course, do not take account of the sundry use of undocumented "stop-and-search" powers and similar authority, on the city streets which were inevitably skewed against that stratum.)

This continuing repression of the residual groups was normally met with resignation. Arrest was an occupational cost of participating in the secondary economy, and a normal risk in the course of street recreation. Roberts, speaking of Edwardian Salford, comments on the (earlier) *The Times* editorial, in terms which could have been equally applicable in Liverpool:

> . . . nobody in our Northern slum, ever spoke in fond regard, then or after-ward, of the policeman . . . Like their children, the poor, in general, looked upon him with fear and dislike. When one arrived on a 'social' visit, they watched his passing with relief. Here was no counsellor or friend . . . one spoke to a 'rozzer' when one had to and told him the minimum. (Roberts, 1973, p.100)

Alternatively, there was the occasional violent reaction, either in an assault on an individual officer, or on occasion, in a sectarian affray that might turn into an attack on the common enemy, on the intervention of the police. An index of "assaults on the police" has been used by Storch (1976) to document the continuity of dissent from policing in Northern England, during the second half of the nineteenth century. There is, however, some doubt about the efficacy of that measure (Gattrell, 1980). More accessible are the accounts of internecine

conflicts between slum dwellers being transformed into anti-police manifestations. For example, the sectarian dispute that had divided English, Welsh,
and Irish Protestants, from the Irish Catholics in Liverpool, throughout the
century, was the spark for numerous clashes with the local police institution.
From the last days of the old Watch (Chapter 2), to the early 1900s, and again in
the 1930s, there were major conflicts between Protestants and Catholics on the
city streets, which invariably reverted to confrontations with the police. The
most notorious series of events were those of the 1902–1909 period (revolving
around the figure of a certain Pastor George Wise). Resulting charges of police
brutality were vented during the unprecedented enquiry of 1910 (Liverpool
Police Enquiry Act, 1910) which despite its general findings (the dismissal of all
complaints against the police), did nothing to assuage anti-police feeling amongst
lower-class Catholics and Protestants alike.

Immediately after World War I, a rather different incident demonstrated the
hostility between the Liverpool Police and the local black population. The city's
major race riot (1919) was significant for, amongst other things, the antagonism
between the police and Liverpool blacks, feelings that are evidenced (in the
formal police records) by the list of injuries to police officers, reportedly, at the
hands of black assailants, (no list of black injuries is appended). The contribution
of the Head Constable to the development of consent amongst the minority
ethnic groups, can be illustrated by a brief excerpt from his starkly racist account
of the affair:

> The Head Constable begs to report to the Watch Committee that for some
> time there has been a feeling of animosity between the white and coloured
> population in this city. This feeling has probably been engendered by the
> arrogant and overbearing conduct of the Negro population towards the
> white; and by the white women who live or cohabit with the black men,
> boasting to the other women of the superior qualities of the negroes, as
> compared with those of white men . . . there have been serious disturbances.
> In nearly all cases, negroes have been the aggressors . . . (Head Constable's
> Report to the Watch Committee, 17th June, 1919)

The succeeding partisan report does little to reinforce the Head Constable's
account although it is apparent that the afffray between police officers and the
black community (one of whom died in disputed circumstances in the event) had
been severe. (The succeeding prosecution of the mainly black defendants, used
this Report by the Head Constable as the primary evidence in obtaining
convictions—*Liverpool Courier*, 19th June, 1919).

The final example of conflict between the police and the residual groups in
that first century of professional policing is taken from a major incident in 1932,
when various forces (including the Liverpool Police) assisted the Birkenhead
Police in attempting to remove unemployed squatters from tenement blocks in

that town. Two days of street-fighting were followed by police attacks upon the occupied houses and flats. Cockburn provides one of several similar accounts of the affair:

> At nightfall, the police were sent into the working-class quarters, smashing ground-floor windows and breaking into houses with what could be hoped was pacificatory violence . . . Sporadic fighting occurred by day . . . by night, these now often being resisted with sticks and iron bars, and heavy showers of stone . . . (Cockburn 1973, p.64)

This Birkenhead struggle has provided a further opportunity for distortion and mis-representation by the orthodox police historians, Reithians and institutionalists, of the relation between the police institution and social classes. Although a major event in the inter-war period, and probably the most severe clash between police and policed in the twentieth century, it rarely rates a mention. Even the local (Birkenhead) police history (S.P. Thompson, 1958) does not refer to the conflict although it was the major event in that force's history since a similar intense (and similarly unreported) confrontation between police and public in Birkenhead in 1862 (*Liverpool Mercury*, 8–11th October, 1862).

The evidence of the relation between police and public, as presented in the second half of this chapter, is undoubtedly as partisan and episodic as in the majority of traditional police histories. But it denies any natural evolution of consent to the police institution in British society, and demonstrates the partiality and selectivity of the orthodox tradition. There was a pattern of distinctive economic class interests, in attitudes to the police, in the first 100 years of the professional forces. From the middle-classes, who experienced policing largely at second-hand, there was a general assent. Between the industrial working-class and the police, after some early political struggles for the control of the police institution, a form of truce developed, occasionally disrupted by events at the economic base, within the direct labour-capital relation. But from that class there was never any specific historical assent to the police institution.

Finally, for the lower classes—participants in the secondary economy, the inhabitants of the streets, the unemployed, the young, and the minority ethnic groups—from Liverpool Irish to Liverpool West Indians—attitudes to the police ranged from the passive to the violently hostile. Consent to the police institution was irrelevant to the residual strata that suffered the brunt of the police working-class agreement over the selection of criminals for the statistics. These groups as victims solved working-class status problems, police organizational problems, and capital's problems of flexibility in the size of its labour force. As outcasts they were not fit for security of employment. They were as police practice and the police working class consensus showed, too unreliable.

In so far as the favoured police notion of accountability by consent depends upon a particular perspective on police history, there are material faults with the presentation of the evidence and therefore with that surrogate form of accountability. In the following chapter, the relation between police and social classes in contemporary society is examined. The present day evidence about consent to policing is analysed, and the various devices by which consent is reconstructed are outlined. As with the historical accounts, the contemporary accounts suffer similarly from distortion.

# Notes

1. Walker (1977) and Manning (1977) make similar distinctions.
2. Address by the Head Constable to Young Men Joining the Liverpool Police, 1872. Critchley was the first of several writers to use this speech as primary evidence of the consensual character of British policing. Greig continues with the classic phrase "A person passing through the hands of the Police recovers his liberty, but his character seldom."
3. Similarly, candidates for the Liverpool Police were to be ". . . well-recommended for good-temper, honesty, and sobriety, all of them points of great importance . . ." (*Liverpool Mercury*, 5th February, 1836). As is noted in Chapter 8, Charles Gorer later claims that this "character" is the supreme virtue and unique feature of the British police system!
4. "Over the centuries, police work was to be expanded by hundreds of other official bureaucracies dedicated to the 'rational' control of the lives of citizens, notably those of the lower classes who might not work willingly, pay taxes, serve in the military, be 'decent' in public, and be 'orderly' at all times" (Douglas, 1971, p.71).
5. Donajgrodzki also cites the contribution of the Victorian mines inspector. Tremenheere, who wrote extensively about the need to develop a tutelary control over the lives of the poor, partly through the work of the clergy and partly through the new police institution (1977).
6. In "The Uncommercial Traveller" (Poor Mercantile Jack).
7. The importance of the "move-on" power is referred to in a variety of texts—from the elderly C.H. Clarkson and J.H. Richardson *Police*, 1889 (p.75) to Storch (1976). The following quotation from the Liverpool Head Constable's Order Book to patrolling Constables, reflects the spirit of that legal power:

> He must observe the practices of those who live on his walk, that he may know them . . . but above all, he must notice all disorderly characters and disorderly homes: first in order to protect unsuspecting persons, and, secondly, in order to prevent crime by impressing bad characters with a conviction that they are known and watched by him. In acquiring this knowledge, however, he must not enter into conversation with such people nor idly chat with any of the inhabitants. Their habits will point them out sufficiently without further enquiry. (Instructions to the Liverpool Police, 1856)

# 8    *Consent, Dissent, and Reconstruction*

> . . . of these extra duties, some may seem to be outside the scope of the police duty proper; but in a great many of these may be traced a distinct connection with that main idea of the prevention of crime, anything which helps the very poor and so relieves them from the temptation to crime, anything which helps to take children of the criminal classes away from evil surroundings, and companions, and while there is yet time, implants in them their instincts of honesty and virtue, is true police work . . . (Blackstone — *Commentaries on the Laws of England.* Quoted — without acknowledgement — in Head Constable Dunning's Introduction to *Instructions the Liverpool City Police,* 1903)

> . . . the Deputy of the Chairman of the Watch Committee was there, and took the opportunity of stating that he was sure that the Watch Committee would cheerfully agree to the Police being the channel for distributing relief as far as it would not interfere with their general duties, he conceived that it would be the means of reaching deserving cases, and create a good feeling towards the Police (Head Constable's Report to the Watch Committee, 27th January, 1861)

The notion of consent is inextricably linked with the performance of police service functions. As police commentators and police officers have been aware from the days of Blackstone to the present, public support for the police institution derives primarily from the supportive actions of police officers, in roles largely unrelated to crime control. The general factotum duties of nineteenth century police officers (as the quotation from the Liverpool Watch Committee above, demonstrates) were rapidly brought to bear upon the problem of marshalling consent to the police institution.

The documentation of the extent of police service work in the academic literature has ensured that its quantity and variety is unquestioned. Punch (as one of several examples) claims in an Essex study that over half the routine calls to the police were for "help and some sort of support" (Punch, 1979, p.106) for personal and inter-personal problems. Bittner in the U.S.A. has made the ". . . inference that no human problem exists, or is imaginable, about which it would be said with finality that this certainly could not become the proper business of the police" (Bittner, 1974, p.30).

Service functions are vital to policing style in Britain and, crucially, to the construction of a surrogate form of accountability through the *consent principle* in recent years. The retreat from Unit Beat Policing, in particular, has permitted the incarnation in police rhetoric and literature of that general community dogs-body, the Reithian "community constable". Police visibility in some lower-class areas has increased dramatically as new bicycles are purchased and Pandas restored to the zoos. Police work, it is demonstrable, is now literally "leg-work" in the service of the community. Independence of the police institution from political constraints is achieved through the medium of the construction of a broad service relation between police and community.

But this rejuvenated commitment by the police institution to the principles of preventive and pro-active policing through many different duties that seem to have little relation to the crime control problematic entails neither an alteration in the class relations of the police institution nor, in practice, a return to a variant of the pre-industrial parish constable. Service work with all its particular benefits, is about the *mobilization of consent* to an established form.

Chapter 7 documented the varying and ambivalent features of consent within the history of police–class relations. This chapter provides a picture of the consent relation in the 1970s and early 1980s, and demonstrates the centrality of police ser-vice work to its construction and maintenance. As was evidenced in the last chapter, the consent relation has dynamic qualities. Changes in the economic and political context affect attitudes to the police institution as they do other relations between soical classes and the state. The police institution can only retain general support (and consequently, its relative political independence) by missionary service work.

The first half of the chapter documents the available evidence on attitudes to the police institution in contemporary mainland Britain. There is considerable, if superficial, evidence of consent at the general level. But below those surface manifestations of approval, there are substantive indications that the ambiguities and caveats in the granting of consent by the lower classes remain present. The second half of the chapter relates the recent expansion of police service work to the reinforcement of consent, in the face of that continuing ambivalence.

## Consent and Dissent — the Ambivalence in Attitudes to the Police

There is a major problem in attempting to assess the relative popularity of the police institution in Britain. Quantitative indicators of support have tended to suppress the nuances and ambivalence in that relation. No qualms have prevented the police institution from utilizing the flimsiest of such evidence as the basis for ideological statements about police–class relations. Alderson (1980), for example, synthesizes the historical accounts of the Reithians with an extraordinary survey by the social scientist Charles Gorer (1955), to produce an eulogy of the consent principle. Gorer's major thesis is that what he calls "national character" — the distinctive personal traits of different nations — develops from the example of the life and personality of those functionaries who contribute most to a nation's well-being, during its course of development.

As an illustration of that peculiar, Reithian, thesis, Gorer refers to the contributions of a notional New England schoolteacher as the personification of the traits of American national character. The police institution, he claimed, played a similar role in Britain.

"Character" was all important. Using the model eulogized by the novelist P. C. Wren (who had immortalized police officers by describing them as ". . . strong, quiet men, calm, unarmed, dressed in a long authority, the very embodiment of law, order, and security, the wonder and admiration of Europe . . ."[1]), Gorer analysed the responses to a questionnaire administered by the novel device of an advertisement in the Sunday newspaper, *The People*. He concluded that "the most significant factor in the development of a strict conscience and law-abiding habits in the majority of urban men and women was the invention and development of the institution of the modern English police force" (Gorer, 1955, p.294). In an echo of the words of Melville Lee (1901, p.240), Gorer claims "What was so really novel about the British police was that the force was recruited entirely on the basis of character . . . the model of self-control which has now become so widespread in English characteristics . . ." (ibid, p.296). The evidential popularity of the police institution, judging by the comments of his respondents, could only be explained through the direct relation between "English" character and the police model.

The Reithians give the historical version of the development of consent. Gorer provides the social scientistic gloss, and Alderson connects the two to demonstrate both the popularity of the police, and the principle of accountability by consent:

> . . . the police as a British-type institution par excellence have gradually modified themselves and have simultaneously caused modifications in public behaviour. This social modification resulted in a remarkably precise juxtaposition of police and public . . . (Alderson, 1980, p.53)

This panegyric (as later reinforced by a contribution from William Belson's study for the Metropolitan Police, 1975) serves to identify the police with a consensual society, whose peaceful modes of behaviour depends primarily upon its imitation of the personal attributes originally used by Rowan and Mayne as some of the criteria for recruitment to the first Metropolitan force. However, while Gorer's deductions from his study regarding "character" and the relation between police and society, may be generally dismissed (even if they are taken seriously by senior police officers), there are alternative indices which produce broadly similar conclusions on consent.

## The evidence of consent

There are several contrived techniques for assessing public perception of the police. The popularity or rating of a local force may be gauged by the rate of complaints against its officers, by the number of assaults against members of the force, or by the proportion of jury acquittals in the face of police evidence. For example, in 1979, the Merseyside force registered twice the national level of complaints, twice the average number of assaults against police officers, and the rate of acquittals in the Liverpool Crown Court was:

> . . . probably the highest in the country, almost twice the national average and easily outstripping the other main metropolitan courts; it compares with 12% in Newcastle, 14% in Birmingham, 17% in Manchester, and 20% at the Old Bailey . . . (*The Times*, 17th April, 1980)

A composite of those indices could be used (as did *The Times*) to give an indication of public support for a particular force but would be unsatisfactory for measuring public support for the police institution on a national basis or in relation to social class. In any case, the numbers of complaints may be a reflection of the effectiveness or ineffectiveness of the complaints system— unsuccessful complaints against police officers may discourage other potential complainants and result in a low rate. "Assaults against police officers" is a notoriously fickle measure and may simply reflect the particular legal resource techniques open to police officers in dealing with potential offenders. Juries convict on the basis of many other factors than simply on "images of the police". In the end, one is forced to resort to the indices commonly used by the police institution,[2] the opinion polls, and those few sociological studies that cast light on police-class relation.

Consistently, over the last 15 years, opinion polls have demonstrated that the police institution has the high standing in British society, portrayed by Mark and his colleagues. In terms of ethical standards, police officers rate highly in comparison with other occupations. As an economic priority, the police institution is elevated. Nor are police officers denied the "common touch". According to one poll, the police have more regard for individual rights than most other institutions.

Gorer's conclusions on the occupational status of police officers are reinforced by recent polls. One survey (Harris Poll, 1969–1971) suggested that for young people, it was the most prestigious occupation. Two polls (Gallup, 1977, MORI, 1980) contrasted the "honesty and ethical standards" of police officers with a variety of other occupations (mainly white collar) and with locally elected representatives. Only medical practitioners enjoyed more support. Of the occupations listed, policing (with the highest proportion of manual worker entry) ranked significantly higher than almost all others. There was no apparent connection between the social background of police officers and perception of their status. The office, rather than the incumbent, determined the prestige of the police institution. These findings endorse the assessment of the public standing of the police as documented in the survey conducted for the Willink Commission over a decade earlier. In that study, over 83% of the respondents professed great respect for the police.

Similarly, Belson's survey of a sample of the Metropolitan population found a very high level of public support for the police. ". . . there was a marked tendency to rate the police highly in terms of personal characteristics and ability such as well-trained, calm, efficient, fair, kind, intelligent, friendly . . ." (1975, p.68). The following year, a Marplan poll produced almost identical findings. Eighty-five per cent of the respondents rated the police as "honest" or "very honest".

In part, these attitudes relate to the form of contact (or rather lack of contact) with the police. Few respondents had encountered the police in any situation with a conflict potential. In MORI's 1980 survey, while only one-in-seven had had no direct contact with the police, the majority of the encounters had been initiated by civilians, seeking assistance. Only a small minority had been accosted by police officers in the course of crime detection or prevention. Of those who had come into contact with the police in any way, 75% expressed themselves satisfied with the way the matter was dealt with. Hostile experience with police officers were very much a minority phenomenon.

Support for the police is expressed in different forms. In a 1977 survey by Marplan, seven out of every ten respondents felt that the public should give more help to the police and all but a minute proportion were ready to assist the police in the case of a serious crime or accident.

A blunter way of documenting public perception of the police is in terms of economic priorities. There is no necessary link between attributing a particular social *status* to an institution, and ascribing to it a similar economic rank. But the police rank high on both social and financial indicators. In the context of government restraint of wages in the public sector, several polls demonstrated public willingness to make the police an exception. In 1977, a large majority of the adult population considered that the police should be treated as a special case for a pay-rise and allowed to exceed the government's ten per cent guidelines.

This view was taken, irrespective of age, social class and of the respondent's own trade union affiliations (Marplan, 1977).

The same poll also showed that whilst two-thirds of the respondents felt that the police should be allowed to exceed the pay limits, they agreed that their own (or their spouse's) pay should be restrained. A further survey reinforced this economic evaluation of policing, in a comparison of police officers with a range of other occupations over the right to exceed the guidelines (Gallup, 1978).

Police officers were clearly the major exceptions to public support for pay restraint. Policing was an economic priority. A similar assessment is documented in a second 1978 survey (Marplan). Seventy per cent of the respondents from the Metropolitan London population expressed the willingness to pay up to ten per cent more on their annual property rates, in order to increase the resources available to the police.

A different type of respect for the police institution in Britain, is shown in a cross-nation survey of attitudes to the police (Almond and Verba, 1963). In a list composed of the police apparatuses of the United States, the German Federal Republic, Italy and Mexico, as well as that of Great Britain, the latter were ranked highest on the two dimensions ("expectation of equal treatment by the police" and "amount of consideration for point of view") by its respective public respondents.

Further evidence of the high ranking of the British police is drawn from a 1973 comparison of different institutions in terms of two dimension—perception of police concern for "individual rights" and "interest in ordinary people" (N.O.P., 1972). From a list of 17 institutions—ranging from the media, to Parliament, and the Queen—the police were placed second only to the local council on the first item, and behind the local council, and trade unions on the second item.

Finally, there is some indication of the resilience of the police image. Media accounts of alleged police violence or corruption, seem to be insignificant [according to one set of polls (Gallup, 1976, 1979)]. After corruption exposes in the Metropolitan police, 74% of respondents professed themselves unaffected in their positive feelings about that force. The later poll (conducted after further revelations) produced an identical result.

Together, the various pieces of evidence—perception of occupational morality, economic priority, and behaviour toward individuals—adds up to a high degree of consent. For the police chiefs in search of a surrogate form of accountability, the survey evidence is readily available. Public attitudes and policing practices do not seem to be far apart.

Fragmentary and episodic support manifestations occur regularly. The murder of three police officers in 1966, resulted in 50 000 letters of sympathy. The shooting of Superintendent Richardson in Blackpool, in 1971, led to widespread commiserations. After the Vietnam Solidarity Campaign demonstration outside the American Embassy in October 1968, 300 000 Londoners signed a petition congratulating the police on their handling of the incident. Serious injury to a Metropolitan policeman in 1980 led to a sizeable public collection. In repeated cases, in recent years, juries have refused to convict policemen accused of corruption, or to determine inquest verdicts against the police interest. Support for the police, however demonstrated, appears to be one of the ways that social classes in Britain cement their unity. Ritualistic offerings to the police institution allows a ceremonial affirmation of common purpose. Public consent to the police, as manifest in the survey evidence, is a product of group celebration, within which the police institution can identify the source of its independent authority.

### The fragility of consent

Given the format of the opinion polls and surveys, these findings on consent are not altogether surprising. Rarely do the polls attempt to relate variations in attitudes, to the question of stratification. Nor do they attempt to distinguish the nuances of perceptions of the police. The relationship between police institution and social classes is much more complex than can be documented through those devices.

However, even within the polls, a different presentation can locate an under-lying dissent. Some of the pointers to the *conditional* features of support for the police will be outlined in this section. However, the omnibus *service* function of police work more than counterbalances the number of antagonistic encounters between police and the incorporated social classes.

Relatively few police duties involve hostile encounters with civilians. Apart from in the enforcement of traffic regulations, the exercise of legal authority by police officers is normally confined to the marginal strata—ethnic minorities, the participants in, and dependents on, the remnant of the street economy, and young people who have always lived a street life in the evenings, and now, with unemployment, increasingly do so in the day as well. Conflict relations are limited to already stigmatized segments of the population.

For the middle class, the police officer bears the hallmark of a valuable social servant (Jackson, 1968, p.118). Views on the police form part of a constellation of attitudes—bestowing general approval on the most visible elements of the state, which by guaranteeing the rule of law, maintain the privileges of that class. But for all social classes, service functions have some value. In Banton's (1964) organic community, the police officer was a major contributor to social inte-gration, performing varied functions interdependent with communal survival. Cain's (1973) pig-licensing rural police officer was no obvious threat to a class of agricultural workers. Escorting children across a busy city street does not engender hostility from stalled motorists. The support for the police institution is not reducible to a crude false consciousness.

However, the argument that the high status of the police institution is peculiar to British society has been disputed (Banton, 1970). Various Scandinavian forces meet with similar approbation. In a Seattle study (Smith and Hawkins, 1973) three-quarters of the respondents, ranked the police highly. J. Q. Wilson has claimed that in the U.S.A. there is general support for the police irrespective of ethnic grouping (Wilson, 1972). There is almost identical opinion poll evidence from that country. The relative popularity of the British police is exaggerated.

But a more central critique of the opinion poll evidence relates to its failure to relate the question of consent to the variables of age, of ethnicity, and of social class. This is peculiar, given that police forces are structured, organizationally and ideologically, to act against the marginal strata. Several North American studies have documented the effects of that orientation on attitudes to the police (Albrecht, 1977; Sarat, 1977; Thornton, 1975). In Britain, however, the evidence has been limited largely to the age factor, with some evidence and much supposition on the question of ethnicity and the police, and an almost negligible amount on the effects of social class, in relation to the question of consent.

Several British studies document the importance of age as a variable in consent. The ethnographic studies of Gill (1977), and Parker (1974), demonstrate the significance of street encounters between police and adolescents on Mersey-side for the resultant hostile attitudes of the latter. Corrigan (1979) details the different interpretation of "doing nothing" by young adolescents and by police officers, and the level of antagonism between the two. A number of broader studies show antagonism to the police by young working-class groups (Armstrong and Wilson, 1973; Doyle, 1972; West and Farrington, 1977). To Shaw and Williamson, in their important re-examination of evidence to the Willink Commission: ". . . the young tend to be more critical and respect the police less . . . this is as important as class" (Shaw and Williamson, 1972, p.30).

There is also some minor support in the few surveys that attempt to distinguish consent on the age dimension. In the Willink Commission survey, the only group (apart from motorists) who were critical of the police were young people. In Belson's eulogistic survey for the Metropolitan Police (a survey which conceals in its presentation a considerable residue of dissent), the general trend of oppositional views relate to age (Belson, 1975). Two Marplan (1977) surveys on attitudes to the police, also identified the age contribution to dissent. In the two surveys of views on police pay-rises, young people were less ready than their elders to regard the police case as exceptional. One of those polls also reported that young people were only two-thirds as likely as their elders to regard police evidence in courts as "true and accurate", and half as likely to describe the police as "very honest".[3]

A major MORI poll (1980) recounted the effects of reported encounters with police officers on younger people. For example, in the inner city Moss-Side district of Manchester, 40% of the respondents under 45 years believed that the police took bribes as contrasted with only 13% of the older respondents. The poll produced similar results on perceptions of the use of excessive violence by the police—53 and 20%. A related poll to that of MORI, O.R.C. 1980, drew attention to the racial dimension of consent. That account reinforced several Home Office and Parliamentary Reports[4] and Demuth's (1978) study for the Runnymede Trust. Apart from those accounts of the attitudes that were evident in the Bristol and Brixton riots, only Lambert's (1970) Handsworth study documented the hostility of young blacks to the police.

If race is largely ignored in the poll depictions of consent, the factor of social class is notable almost entirely by its absence. In the one case (Marplan, 1977) where a stratification dimension is introduced, the lack of any qualitative element in the survey largely disqualifies the evidence.

That fault is partly remedied in the work of Shaw and Williamson (1972). In their comparative study of four city areas (selected on the basis of social class), they found varying degrees of support for the police. The lower the social class, the lower the level of consent (although outright oppositon never encompassed more than a minute proportion of the respondents).

But for those writers, the key factor was not simply the level of consent, rather the qualitative element lies in the differing definitions of police function. Irrespective of feelings about individual police officers, the residents of the marginal areas still had a policing problem. Property in the inner city, or on the decaying housing estates is more susceptible to attack, personal violence more probable.

However, support by them for the ascribed goal of police work, crime prevention, is not necessarily the same as support for particular styles or objects of police work (or for the autonomy of the chief officer as the manager of law enforcement resources). In the inner city, residents wanted police activities to be more crime-related and less directed towards public order. The police's most visible concern with public-house brawls, with maintaining their authority on the street, was seen as a side-track from "real" police work—the maintenance of personal and household security.

Conversely, in suburbia, public order police work was given priority by residents. Interest in personal security was second to the support for the containment and control features of police work—the traditionally-formed parameters of police action.

In other words, consent to policing does not of itself necessarily imply support for what police institutions actually do. Inner city residents believe that police-work is crime-work and support policing in general, because their conception of ideal police function stems from media accounts, from the rhetoric of police institutional statements, and from their immediate requirements. Public order police-work is conceived of as a kind of accidental by-product of the primary duties of police officers, engaged in the "war against crime". They would support a call for more police manpower and resources, in order to provide for more "front-line" troops in that battle. The inability of the police to affect the crime figures is not readily apparent.

But suburban residents recognize the objective function of police-work—maintaining social and public order. The concentration of police officers in the inner city, on public order duties, and on the prevention of incursions into suburbia, are functions which fit that conception. Police expansion enables the police to be more efficient in those duties. Support for the police is support for a public-order police, and particularly for the symbolism of police presence.

Marplan's 1978 survey offers some additional evidence—two-fifths of the inner city residents considered that the police were ineffective compared with only one-fifth of suburbanities. Both views may have some justification. Where the police are assessed according to crime-fighting indices, they are highly ineffective. Where their work is evaluated according to a public-order criterion, they may be considered generally efficient at that work. Finally, most of the published surveys fail to draw out the interpretations from their own data, that reflect some of the real contradictions in the consent thesis.

An alternative reading of Belson's data, for example, might highlight his finding that half the total respondents considered that the Metropolitan police were occasionally bullying, corrupt, and dishonest. In that production, Belson followed the Willink Commission precedent in ignoring the less attractive conclusions (Whitaker, 1966; National Council for Civil Liberties, 1966). These reservations lie under the surface of most superficial demonstrations of the popularity of the police institution in Britain. While consent to policing is widespread, as a phenomena, it is much more complex than is normally acknowledged by chief officers in search of an accountability placebo.

There are divisions between support for the institution in principle, and the degree of underlying distrust of police practice. There are differences over what constitutes the police function—public order versus crime control. The qualitative level of consent varies from city area to city area, and according to age, to race, and to social class. Lower-class and minority groups in the inner city the recipients of primary police experiences, give only a tenuous approval to policing. There is, moreover, some indication that they make least use of police services. For example, in a London victimization study: ". . . respondents in Kensington were more likely to have contacted the police about a non-criminal matter . . . than respondents in either Brixton or Hackney . . ." (Sparks et al., p.172). Rock makes the same point (quoted in Scull, 1979). Calls for assistance comes predominantly from those areas and social classes which recognize an identity of purpose with the police institution. Consent therefore oscillates according to an ecological structure of the city. Consent to policing is tentative and subject to rapid withdrawal, given the appropriate ignition. The 1980 MORI poll made the point: ". . . when particular city areas do become hostile to the police, that hostility is not confined to age, race or class . . . but the whole community swings against the police" (*The Sunday Times*, 6th March, 1980). Young people may be the first to express dissent but they are soon followed by other residents of the inner city, and of the deteriorating housing estate.

The problems for the police chiefs, in the physical expression of hostility (as in the Brixton disturbance), and in the ground-swell of working-class distrust, (as reflected in Merseyside after the 1979 "death in custody" case) is not simply that it makes police work more difficult. Instead, the problem is one of police autonomy. Where the chiefs have carved out (as facilitated by the legal relation) a position of relative independence within the state, that situation can only be legitimized as long as community support is demonstrable. The principle of accountability to the community rests on the expression of that notional community's solidarity with the police institution. Autonomy and consent are different sides of the same coin. The more substantial police independence, the more that consent must be demonstrated. Consequently, in the last two decades, significant police effort has been placed upon constructing and re-constructing consent through the major institutional tool—the practice of service work.

## The Construction of Consent

Crucial to the expansion of police service work is the fact that the founding legislation was an enabling measure, which prescribed no plan of organization nor specification of duties. As elsewhere in police work, the legal relation was permissive. Contemporary chief officers have inherited the powers to define as a police responsibility any social context which has a legal relation. Local initiatives, from the organization of diversionary football leagues to school lectures on civics, have minimal formal constraints.

There is little new about the varied service functions of the police institution. Victorian police forces were the repository for all manner of undesirable tasks within the local states. Responsibilities such as the provision of winter relief, the pursuit of smallpox suspects, the inspection of common lodging-houses, the opening of flood drains, and even the duty of ensuring that the streets were cleaned of night-soil, all fell to the lot of the early police. But there are two novel elements in the post-war practice of that general service role. It has largely been incorporated into specialized departments within local forces. Service work now merits the application of professional expertise.

More significantly, its occupational status has been elevated. No longer subsidiary to direct crime control work, and no longer paid lip-service in the furtherance of preventive policing, it has moved from police rhetoric to concrete practice.

Its instalment in the heights of the professional tree owes something to three separate sources—the input of professional managerialism into the police institution, the particular conjunction of crises within the local state, as well as the search for an ideological rationale for the new police autonomy. Service work, above all else, reinstates police officers within the community. Changes in police training at higher levels, from the Trenchard scheme onwards, broadened police managerialism beyond the traditional grounding in legal theory. Managerial credentialism entailed (in the sixties and seventies), the acceptance of some of the language and modes of explanation from functionalist social science. From Durkeimian and Parsonian sociology, concepts of community, role, and social integration, followed ecological theories of crime to intermesh with a professional search for a managerialist identity outside the framework of the political accountability process. Ideology, the demonstration of an alternative focus of allegiance to that of the political representatives of the social classes, intermeshed, and was sustained, by a conceptual framework that legitimized in academic parlance, the police relation with the legal construct of the community of citizens.[5]

This ideological conjunction with the paraphernalia of managerialist professionalism, was consummated in the crisis of the local state, from the midsixties onwards. In that moment, the economic pressures on the local state (with the added complication of the race issue), combined with police managerialism to reconstruct the preventive creed. The social impact of the crisis threatened the tentative consent to the police institution (and hence to the autonomy of the police institution) by the lower strata. Whereas in the past, the consent or dissent of the marginal groups could be ignored, at the time that consent was increasingly required in the service of autonomy its viability was least likely. Service work, in its various forms, was the most effective way of "selling" the police institution. The up-grading of service policing was the organizational solution to the structural question. The community constable was recalled from Reithian oblivion. (The Reithian resurrection had a further function for the police chiefs. It legitimized as valid police work what some in the Police Federation in particular, saw as extraneous duties.)

Three forms of police service work can be distinguished in the re-construction of consent—the general service function of the patrol officer, the specialized concerns of youth, juvenile, and school liaison; and the various schemes that shelter under the amorphous heading of community policing. In practice, all the categories of police work may intermesh in the role of the community constable. The latter carries out both general service and law enforcement functions, in the course of his working days, is involved in youth work, and participates with local residents in wider affairs. However, in most forces, these functions have developed sequentially.

## The broad service aspects of police work

The legal relation[6] of the police institution permits wide-ranging social duties within civil society. A general catch-all function has been assumed. Whenever a ill-defined emergency arises, from the transportation of medical supplies to initial support for a spouse bereaved in a traffic accident, the local police station is often the first to respond. Similarly, the police act as an agency of last resort — the state institution which handles the "hot potato" cases rejected by other agencies (for example, the mentally-ill individual causing a disturbance outside the day-time schedule of the social service officer). Police officers may also play a broker role, sorting-out the raw material of deviance for allocation to the appropriate institutional slot. The police institution is in the front-line of allocation decisions. According to Superintendent Dow: "We are the sole agency available twenty-four hours a day, seven days a week to enter into any situation, garbed with the cloak of authority, to sift and assess the gravity of any occurrence" (Dow, 1976, p.133).

These duties provide concrete rewards for members of all social classes. They survive and expand as police work, because they confer significant benefits on their recipients. Service heterogeneity and breadth have reached the status of a truism in the sociological accounts of police work. However, the reciprocal benefits conferred on the police institution — the degree of consent bred through those multifarious activities — is subject to a number of qualifications and caveats, only some of which are recognized in the same studies.

There is, for example, some recent limited evidence (Brogden and Wright, 1979) that in one context, the extent of the service work may be exaggerated. Some of the service work undertaken by police officers has not been institutionally appropriated by other state agencies. But other duties — coping with the mentally ill, re-housing homeless families, advising parents on delinquent children — have become the statutory responsibility of the Social Service Department of the local state.

During the 1978-1979 Social Workers' strike in Britain, a study was conducted of its effects on established clients of the social services, and of the substitute agencies used by the established clients and by new referrals (clients appearing on the Social Services register, immediately post-strike). If the police institution is the agency of last resort, it would have been reasonable to expect that in the absence of the Social Workers, that police officers would have become responsible for dealing with a large proportion of those cases.

In fact, in Liverpool, in the absence of all Social Workers for the six months duration of the strike, only six of the sample of 110 established clients had approached police officers for assistance, in any way, and of those six, only one spoke approvingly of that assistance.

Indeed, three of the cases involved statutory factors such as court appearance, which made police involvement inevitable. In other words, in those situations where a particular social need had already been established (in cases ranging from alcoholism to mental disorder and Non-Accidental Injury), less than five per cent of the clients had recognized police officers as alternatives to Social Workers. The hot-potato characteristics of these clients, with no obvious welfare home, did not make them land on the doorstep of last resort-the local police station.

Secondly, of the sample of 50 new clients emerging during the strike, only three were caught by the police safety net. In the social workers' own accounts of the way such clients were dealt with during the strike, the police rarely figure. Potential social service clients in the city did not see the police as in any way relevant to their needs, even when the local authority social worker was absent.

Such a critique is limited in extent and in kind. But within its narrow scope and in the unique context of the overnight disappearance of a major social service, it tempers the notion that the police institution is perceived by all social strata as the ultimate safety net. Police officers obviously do play a broad service role. But that role like other forms of police action is affected by the stratified context of urban policing.

General service functions underpin the constitution of support for the police institution but service calls, like that support is not randomly distributed across social classes. Social service clients are not a recognizable local lobby, whose grievances or problems can be readily articulated to the police institution. For the most part, they belong to that historically formed residuum from which both welfare clients and small-scale offenders are selected. Often isolated from familial and neighbourhood networks, they are concentrated in the inner city, and on the council housing estate. In those well-demarcated "problem" areas, they possess no political muscle to demand a different qualitative level of service from the police. Neither expecting nor receiving that service, for the most part, they are left outside the consent equation. Approval of policing through the receipt of police service is limited by the structural context.

Organizational limitations similarly compound the problem of consent mobilization through general service work.

Few police officers reside in the area where social and domestic crises are most common. They have (in the jargon of the Merseyside Police) little sympathy with the "bucks" and "buckesses". The lack of status of service work within the occupational culture of policing needs little repetition.

The ideology of law enforcement officers is shaped around the rare moments of excitement and unambiguity. Crime is clear-cut, the problem crystallized, the moral distinction between "right" and "wrong" easily made, definitive action possible, and the result statistically measurable. Service actions are rarely other than confused on all dimensions and have few immediate cues to resolution. The service duties are low-key and rarely attract publicity—of which the stuff of promotion is made. "Community bobbies" do not have spectacular successes. The skill of the service craftsman diminishes the publicity value of events whereas that of the C.I.D. officer has a potential for court and media amplification. In his study of one division of the Merseyside force, Jones (1980) argued that the general beat duties of the constable (from which most service tasks are conducted) simply acts as a staff reservoir to supply the various specialist squads. The main escape route from that reservoir of "lumpen" policing is via a good arrest rate, not by successful and awkward intervention in a domestic dispute. In the main, the beat constable recognizes that his function is not one of service but of looking-out for suspects (Lambert, 1969).

But the primary handicap of the police institution intervening in civil society in a service role is, paradoxically that same legal relation that facilitates entry. Crisis interventions by police officers are interpreted by the recipient within the "relations of force" (Bittner, 1974). The unique feature of police authority is not its emergency availability but rather its access to legally sanctioned force in those actions. "The benign bobby, polished at handling domestics, still brings to the situation, a uniform, a truncheon, and a battery of resource charges" (Punch, 1979, p.116). Legal powers (and its physical product, the discretionary use of force) provides the parameters of social intervention.

The potential clients of police general service functions assess the contribution of the police institution by the criteria of force and authority, within the law. Police officers, in turn interpret the situation not in terms of a particular skill but according to the degree of legal authority to be exerted (Hough, 1979).

Consent to policing rests, in part, on the general service function. Co-operation between the police institution and social classes depend upon the quality of the police role in service work. However, that role, and the mobilization of consent, is limited by the complexity of police organization and by the legal relation of the police to the state, and to civil society. Even the history of service work is subject to class relations. As Walker says of policing in America in the nineteenth century (in a comment echoing police practice in Victorian Liverpool), the police ". . . dispensed social welfare in the same arbitrary manner that they meted out 'curb-side' justice; the 'undeserving poor' were simply turned away and often threatened with arrest if they did not promise to leave town" (Walker, 1977, p.55).

## Specialization in service work

Specialized service units have proliferated in England and Wales over the last fifteen years, with the larger forces taking the lead. By 1981, the majority of forces possessed units with similar functions (if varied titles) in the service area.

The Annual Reports are liberally sprinkled with references to Juvenile Liaison, Social Liaison, Youth, Community Relations, Community Involvement, and Public Relations Branches. (In some forces, Press and Public Relations Units are a synonym for Youth and Community Branches.)

The growth of these new units has considerably affected force profiles, shifting manpower into contexts less crime-oriented, and requiring more direct contact with the public. Police forces in the 1980s have a substantially different image from the pre-amalgamation forces of the early 1960s. However, these alterations in force structure were not so much new developments as a revival of older, less formalized, practices. Police intrusion into narrow areas of social work (such as youth work) and the progressive alteration of juvenile liaison to school liaison, (with the concomitant pressure for increased police presence in the school-room) suggests a police advance into domains already colonized by other bodies of functionaries. But these ventures were not the appropriation of new territory, or an attempt to re-colonize lost ground. In the 1890s for example, the Liverpool Police had unilaterally introduced a system of clothing and licensing juvenile street-pedlars. Involvement in juvenile welfare had long been regarded as a police duty. Prior to the emergence of juvenile and youth branches, specialized selling of the police institution, was limited to displays by dogs and horses sections, by the police band and (in one Welsh force) by the male voice choir. But in the post-war period (beginning with the oft-cited Liverpool Juvenile Liaison Scheme in 1949), a new consent offensive commenced via unit construction. The original juvenile schemes were born out of the traditional commitment to the social containment of the residents of the inner city, and to the patrolling of street activities. Backed by early quasi-sociological and psychological theories of criminogenic environment and homes, juvenile liaison strategies permitted police officers to intervene at an early stage in the assumed development of criminal careers. They involved preventive home visits, informal (and later formal) cautions, and consultation with other local state apparatus concerned with youth.

Over time, the units acquired some reputation as a progressive form of policing. The Liverpool scheme for example was much admired by some writers (Whitaker, 1979) and cited favourably by more critical commentators (Moodie, 1972). Juvenile Liaison Units were the police spearhead in the realm of social welfare. But gradually, their limited impact, together with a recognition of the contribution of school experiences to the aetiology of delinquency, encourage some local police forces to move from individual preventive cautioning tasks, to generalize prevention within the educational milieu. Time-consuming individual re-active policing was to be supplemented by a preventive policing, aimed at cultivating in the school territory, attitudes and values inimical to delinquency. Over time, the instillation of anti-delinquency tendencies became equated with (given the recognition of the ambivalence to the police institution amongst young people) the construction of "pro-police" attitudes—the mobilization of youthful consent. At first, school interventions were low-key in the service of ". . . a newer philosophy of policing . . . in which policing is seen not only as a matter of controlling the bad but also activating the good" (Alderson, 1980, p.38). In practice this entailed, in the Metropolitan Juvenile Bureau ". . . terms of reference . . . to identify and combat areas of delinquency, and to this end a very comprehensive school programme is undertaken with a view to aiding young people to become better citizens" (Oliver, 1973, p.504).

As the city forces gradually transformed their Juvenile Liaison Units in to School Liaison Units in the seventies, the drift of function continued. Character re-construction became merged with ideological accounts of the "police role in society". Instrumental functions of crime and accident prevention were combined with direct attempts at mobilizing consent to a particular image of policing. In the Greater Manchester police for example, a large part of the school curriculum and syllabus structure was catered for in the synthesis of these two functions "Art classes study accident posters, French classes study French police systems, English classes study the role of the police" (Community Contact brochure, 1978).

A later Metropolitan scheme described in detail the attempt to influence the school territory. That scheme ranged from play school "where the tots blow the policeman's whistle and play with the truncheon" (May, 1978, p.155) via discussion of police work in each school year to lectures on "the history of the Met." in the final year. Direct service functions—accident prevention, warning against "going with strangers" slowly gravitated via admonitions against involvement in crime to the delineation of the centrality of the police institution in society and to the construction of Reithian man.

While forces vary in their commitment to the penetration of the educational domain, most large local police forces have moved towards the arrangement reported in the Avon and Somerset Annual Report (1978) where full-time officers are permanently attached to large comprehensive schools. The extent of educational entrepreneurship through the medium of the legal relation varies from force to force. But the joint A.C.P.O./Association of Municipal Authorities Conference (1979) showed remarkable enthusiasm for police initiatives in the teaching of citizenship and of General Studies (one Chief Constable claiming that all such teaching should fall within the police prerogative). Local elites and the police apparatus combine to legitimize the educational intrusion.

Although many school liaison schemes look better on paper than in practice, they represent an attempt to socially construct an image of society built around the Reithian ethic. Social order via the medium of School Liaison is a society centred on the police institution. Crime and accident-prevention, school visits have exploited the educational precinct as a major forum for the mobilization of consent to policing, and to particular notions of society and of a social order.

Coupled with the penetration of the educational domain, is a similar incision into the leisure and recreative time of young people. The corollary of the penetration of the home territory via juvenile liaison, and educational space via school liaison, is the colonization of the recreational sphere. Under the banner of preventive policing, liaison and community units combine in an attempt to re-structure the leisure context. With crude assumptions that "idle hands make evil work" and the moral character is a product of team spirit and sporting relations the city forces organize a variety of diversionary schemes. Young people are reaped from the city streets to participate in a range of morally up-lifting exercises—from angling and football competitions to venture weekends in the mountains under the aegis of the Duke of Edinburgh Award scheme. Black youths from the inner city combine with short-haired police cadets to demonstrate the "Boys' Own Paper" virtues of inter-dependence and healthy exercise, in establishing clean minds, community spirit, and consent to policing. The Staffordshire description of one football diversionary scheme, summarizes the intent: ". . . a very beneficial scheme, which has done much to channel young people away to a more responsible and fruitful way of life, and in particular, to give them an insight into the police role in society" (Staffordshire Annual Report 1978, p.19).

In the endeavour to construct consent in the three territories of youth, there are of course, organizational as well as structural obstacles that the police institution must overcome.

The early studies of the effectiveness of J.L.O. schemes in terms of their professed aims of crime-prevention do not rate them very highly. Mack's account of the Liverpool programme in the 1960s did not depict it as the safe foundation for substantial resource investment (Mack, 1963). The practice of juvenile liaison work is essentially that of collating other agencies' views of the presumed offender—accounts which are then sieved through the law enforcement mesh. Like other service duties, it conflicts with the dominant occupational cultural of the police institution (Cain, 1968). Training for police officers in liaison duties is minimal. In-service lectures, general policing experience, common-sense, and familiarity with home visits, are apparently sufficient (Oliver, 1973). The legal relation not merely permits the intervention but also defines its objects. Experience as a police officer *per se*, is the central quality for liaison duties.

Several forces use juvenile and school liaison as a repository for the substantial increase in women police officers (as resulting from the Sex Discrimination Act, which had significant effects on the employment of women). In the Cheshire, and Avon and Somerset forces, juvenile work was deemed preeminently suitable for W.P.C's (Annual Reports, 1978). The Northamptonshire Chief Constable curiously found the legal power to sustain a Women's Specialist Section to undertake duties in relation to women and children (Annual Report, 1978).

This three-pronged drive into the social context where consent is most tentative

—the life-space of the young—has a fundamental political function, irrespective of the material benefits to civil society resulting from crime-prevention advice. It is designed to construct a conception of social order which hinges on the centrality of the police institution. In Reithian style, the police officer is signified as the symbol of social unity. Consent to social order includes consent to the politically unhampered police role at the centre of social affairs. Police work with young people is a kind of cultural imperialism. The Bristol Chief Constable summarizes the view from within the police institution:

> ... many officers devote duty and leisure time to their local schools, involving themselves in the academic curriculum, sporting, culture and social projects. The maintenance of this traditional role of the British police officer is important if we wish to make any impact upon society now and in the future. (Avon and Somerset Annual Report, 1978)

## Community policing—
## "Let the Power of the Force be with You"[7]

The service role of the best officer (sometimes, euphemistically re-titled "Home Beat Officer" and the specialized function of the liaison units have been increasingly synthesized within the framework of community policing.[7] While the latter, with its diverse origins, appears in several guises, it has developed sequentially out of service work.

Add juvenile to school liaison, organize a youth club or tenant's association, throw into the brew a dash of the Reithian leadership ethic, and the result is community policing. Within the broad rubric of that title, two general forums of police work can be distinguished—race relations work, and community involvement schemes.

Ethnic relations were the catalyst for police community work in England and Wales. Exacerbated by the developing economic crises, the race question provided the defining feature and problematic of the initial impetus into community schemes. Community work was race work. The first Home Office Circular on the subject determined both the nature of the problem and the parameters of the police reaction:

> There seems little doubt that the most likely source of friction between police and immigrants is lack of knowledge and misunderstanding about each other. It is sometimes that the immigrants think that the powers of a police officer in this country are more extensive than they are ... because the immigrant comes from a country where the police have wider powers ... Other difficulties can arise from a lack of common language ... (7th July, 1967)

Problems between the police and ethnic minorities were due to distorted communications, and the lack of familiarity with British police powers and duties. The police institution was given the mandate to engage in missionary work to explain its own, legitimate, version of those powers. Consent required pro-active policing. Within many Annual Reports, in the late seventies, community policing remained reduced to that mission—legitimating the police institution amongst coloured minorities. The function of the Community Relations Officer (C.R.O.) or Race Relations Officer (Sussex chose that more accurate title) was, variously, to be aware of the danger from "... organizations causing community problems . . ." (Sussex Annual Report, 1978, p.51) and to ". . . provide a true account of police work . . ." (N. Yorks Annual Report, 1978, p.15). Fortunately, the police representatives on the Community Relations Councils have been able to ". . . resolve specific difficulties. There is some doubt however, whether the ethnic representations truly reflects the views of the coloured population" (W.Yorks Annual Report, p.70). The apparent lack of consent to policing by ethnic minorities was due to misunderstandings and to bad communications, and many committed police C.R.O.'s spend their time arranging cricket matches between West Indians and the local police (West Midlands, and West Yorkshire) or taking 50 junior officers to eat curry in the local mosque (Greater Manchester), a task which is often made more difficult by "politically motivated factions . . ." (West Yorkshire). Amongst other forces, the Durham, Cheshire, and Hampshire forces, equated that year's (1978) community problems with race problems. Community policing models derived from these community relations practices.

In the short-term, the wider community policing models were conceived of as instant palliative to immediate issues. In the West Yorkshire police area, for example, community constables were initially appointed to districts where there was a high incidence of vandalism and social deprivation (indeed, in Halifax, the community constable was supported by a bluntly-named "damage-squad"). Police officers lost their transport and were returned to foot patrolling, assumed omnibus service duties and were re-styled "community constable".

But the long-term (or community involvement) schemes, extended the ethnic practices more seriously. Banton phrases the intent blandly: ". . . these branches exist to see that the territorial divisions understand the need to prevent crime by planning for the long-term" (Banton, 1975). The community involvement units extend the boundaries of police work significantly beyond traditional practice, with the goal of social re-construction as the foundation for crime prevention and consent production.

The 1950s Scottish police entrepreneurship by Grey, in Greenock, had imitated a number of American precedents in aiming to co-ordinate action amongst the various agencies of the local state, and in civil society, to produce a different social environment for young people. Material promise was held out, irrespective of the later consent problematic. By 1975 however, one of the three major functions of a Community Involvement Unit was said by its organizer to be: ". . . to project a favourable image of the Police Service . . ." (Butcher, 1975, p.488). By 1978, a third of the police chiefs in England and Wales had developed their own versions of community involvement schemes. In the Northumbria police area, for example, the Community Involvement Officer performed a range of functions — organized publicity visits to police stations and to schools, ran youth diversionary schemes, participated in Victim Support programmes, ran a police cadet force at a local public school and liaised with inner city re-development projects. (In practice, Community Involvement plans rarely matched Grey's early Utopianism.) Partly because of internal criticisms, community involvement was accompanied by a degree of de-specialization. Some forces (for example, Lancashire and Leicestershire) attempted to elevate the status of the uniformed patrol constable by giving him wider community functions. Added to the normal beat responsibilities, are a variety of specific service tasks. In Skelmersdale, for example, the new community constable visited schools, participated in Neighbourhood Councils, and sometimes organized "discos". Community involvement schemes have now progressed beyond the specialization stage towards a general re-casting of general police work as civil intervention.

As preventive policing, the programmes aimed to eradicate the perceived root of the disease, crime, with weed-killer (from supplying information to C.I.D. on suspects, to the boarding-up of vandal-tempting property) and with fertilizer for the potential healthy plants (through plans for urban renewal, through youth diversionary schemes, and through the development of police-sponsored neighbourhood councils). The "positive" elements in social behaviour were to be activated and the physical fabric repaired.

This intervention is fostered by a blend of the Reithian and institutionalist historical conceptions of the police contribution to social order. From the institutionalists, Alderson draws the theme "We have to get used to the idea that the housing manager, the city manager, the youth and community worker, the social worker, the probation officer, and the numerous voluntary bodies have more influence on the prevention of crime than the entire police force" (Alderson, *Daily Telegraph*, 4th April, 1979). The various agencies are interdependent. In normal times, the only function for the police is to assist those other institutions by detecting and removing offenders from the community.

But where there is an increase in crime, that too is attributable to the other agencies which are patently failing to fulfil the required social tasks. In such circumstances, it is for the police institution (in a re-assertion of the Reithian theme) to step in via community involvement ". . . to encourage and foster the social groups and forms of interaction which produce normative integration . . ." (K. McDonald, 1977, p.3). The police institution is the only one that has not suffered from decay and is able to intervene according to its intuition (as the body of citizens-in-uniform) of the real interest of the community. Freedom of action for the police institution is the price that the community must pay, if it wishes to have its agencies of informal socialization restored to full health.

In this strategy for social re-construction, the proponents of community involvement, and of community policing more generally, are concerned to re-assert fundamental principles. The police institution is the supreme custodian of the core value of British society. When all else fails, the police institution is the final safeguard. But it must retain its freedom to act without political restraint to restore the social order. Otherwise, the legal relation which determines its neutrality (and consequently the values that it upholds) will be tarnished. In the final analysis, therefore, consent to policing is inextricably linked to the retention of the police institution as the final bulwark against anarchy and against moral decay. Community future ultimately depends upon consent to the initiatives of the police institution.

## Community Policing and the Re-construction of Consent

Community policing represents the zenith of police intervention in civil society, through the medium of the legal relation. Succeeding the prior incursion via general service work and through the specialized juvenile and educational units, the new commitment to social re-construction as manifest in some of the major police forces in Britain, represents a significant extension of the managerialist creed of the chiefs.

No longer simply concerned with negotiating truces with the social classes, community involvement schemes, in particular, are intended as large-scale extension of the consent problematic. They reinforce the institution's autonomy at the same time that they legitimize civil intervention. Community policing has particular attractions to the chief officers as an ideological premise, and the way that, as a creed, it satisfies the representative of social classes, and of political lobbies. Tactically, it allows consent to be constructed at a political level. Community policing reinforces the traditional common law version of the source of the constable's powers. As Laugharne portrayed the relation at the A.C.P.O./ A.M.A. conference (1980), in an account of a Lancashire community policing scheme ". . . locked inside most of our young policemen and women today . . . is a Tythingman, trying to get out . . .". The community police officer restores the police institution to its natural location at the centre of social affairs. The accountability placebo operates by practical demonstration of the symbiotic connection between the police institution and local community.[8]

Secondly, it satisfies some of the internal critics of civil intervention that it is real police-work. The colonization of home, of school and of leisure territories, the allocation of police officers ". . . to indulge their fantasies of being glorified social workers, child minders, and even school teachers . . ." (Fucso, 1980, p.1449) is construed by the chief officers as the logical extension of preventive policing as constructed by Rowan and Mayne. There is no internal inconsistency in that work.

Thirdly, the commitment to community policing is a panacea at the political level. The local political elite's expressions of dissatisfaction with the rise in the recorded crime rate, meet with an acceptable reply. "When deficiencies can be made up, the policeman most closely identified with the community will re-appear, much to the delight of everyone" (West Yorkshire Annual Report, 1978, p.4). To the chorus of "Put the Bobby back on the beat", the chief officer submits the community policeman (and justifies further expansion).

Community policing also ensured a degree of consent in more critical quarters. When it was first given expression, it fitted with the:

> . . . political culmination of the romantic back-to-nature and peace movements of the 1960's. These involved . . . . both voluntarism and an idealisation of community and thus the theory that a pristine condition of sharing could be achieved by act of will, in despite of structural differentiation. In such a world, there would be no problem of choosing policemen to serve and represent the people . . . (Cain, 1977, p.158)

But as a policing strategy, these community incursions were not just image manufacturing exercises. Despite the various commentators on community policing schemes in the United States (Cooper, 1975; Norris, 1972) and in Britain, (Whitaker, 1979) who have emphasized the programmes contribution to police–public relations, there is as Cain (1977) suggested a more insidious aspect with regard to the legal relation of the police.

In Blackstone's Commentaries, the outline of police functions assumes a Gemeinschaft—a stable, integrated, consensual community. The moral order is well-regulated and passively accepted. Reith too, mirrors this conception of the social order. From Durkheim, and from structural-functional sociology, a similar picture of contemporary society is assimilated by those police officers who attend the Derbyshire force's bi-annual Community Relations training sessions. With a missionary commitment, the exponents of community policing seek to reconstruct social classes in that image. With the social anthropologists' zeal for the discovery of the natural focii of the urban habitat, local forces map out the territory encompassed by the local state, according to models of the organic community. Existing relations between classes are sundered as communities are legitimized or delegitimized according to the crime rate indices. Relationships between members of the same class are individuated according to police perception of the pathological characteristics of social malaise.

Having broken down those features—bad housing, unemployment, and truancy—as manifestations of individual failure, they are then subsumed under a general notion of the loss of legal rights. The symptoms of individual breakdown are important because together they equate the depredatory terrain for crime and vandalism, which in turn deprives the new citizens of their legal due. Only through a process of re-constitution into an approved community can the assumed pathological failings and handicaps of the individuals (Balbus, 1978) be overcome as they adopt a legal identity in a community war against crime. When Superintendent Chapple, in Kirkby, (the 1950s Liverpool overspill area) assembled his new community committee from the professional strata in a campaign against local vandalism and crime (Chapple, 1975) he was attempting to construct the type of community structure to which the police institution could relate. Consent was (unsuccessfully) to be contrived by social re-construction, according to the Reithian model. Service work by the police institution reached its zenith with the attempt to re-align social relations through the up-lifting of the "positive elements" in the practice of consent.

# Notes

1. Quoted in Moylan (1934).
2. See, for example, Mark's (1977) attempt to demonstrate the support for the police, and the centrality of the police institution in Britain, by reference to opinion polls.
3. This age is even more apparent in the N.O.P. survey carried out four months after the anti-police riots of the summer of 1981. Apart from noting specific evidence of the decline in general support for the police institution, it demonstrated that on a number of important issues, that the young were twice as critical as their elders.
4. Select Committee on Race Relations and Immigration (Report on Police-Immigrant Relations) 1972; Home Office Working Party on Vagrancy and Street Offences, 1976; Select Committee on Race Relations and Immigration (Report on West Indian Community) 1977.
5. See, for example, Banton (1964) and that author's later police training manual.
6. The general legal power for the expansion of service work lies in the Town Police Clauses Act, 1847—see on this, McCabe and Sutcliffe (1978).
7. The "Star Wars" title of a Devon and Cornwall Constabulary Project in 1978.
8. The development of community policing schemes in the Devon and Cornwall force in particular, under the supervision of John Alderson, represents a particular ideological and considered commitment and one quite different from those of other forces (the Handsworth scheme of the West Midlands Police has some similarities). One recent and peculiar consequence of that conception of police work was Alderson's refusal to remove squatters from the site of a nuclear power plant, because he believed such action would undermine the local community's support for the police (see *The Times*, 21st October, 1981).

# 9 Police Work, Negotiation, Autonomy and Consent

> This work . . . does not examine empirically the work of senior officers and the pressures to which they are subject. Thus decisions about how police should be deployed and trained, about promotion schemes, and about changes in organisation, are treated as if they were not matters of sociological interest, although lip-service may be paid to their importance. (Cain, 1979, p.152)

Maureen Cain's auto-critique, in practice, applies to the majority of contributions to the sociology of the police, in Britain. The attraction of situationally-framed approaches to policing has ensured that the structural pressures on police organization have been left largely unexamined. That obsession, in an increasingly rich and varied selection of accounts, has correctly pointed to the major gulf between ". . . officers who work on the street and those who work behind a desk" (Fielding, 1981, p.93). It is little more than a platitude to repeat that "The chief makes the decisions, and then the locker room makes the decisions" (Banton, 1970, p.48).

But that commitment has been a blind one. Irrespective of the particular conflicts between the chiefs and their junior officers, of the way the rank-and-file "ease" their way through the hierarchical restrictions, of the way command orders are mediated by interpretation on the street, it is self-evidently absurd to suggest, by omission, that there is no general identity of interest and practice between the force commanders and their troops. The P.C. Joys are notable because they are exceptions, not the rule. Organization rules and demands may cause gripes but there is no structural disjunction between the police manager and his subordinates.

The primary concern of this text has been to demonstrate that the chiefs have developed, historically, considerable freedom of action in their determination of the practice of police work. But it is the freedom of a managerial negotiator, not that of an autocrat. It is the power to have a major say in the legitimization of demands on the police institution. The latitude enjoyed by the chiefs is that of a broker between those structural pressures from the social classes, and the internal audience which converts the chief's decisions into police work. Police managerialism is the application of legal discretion, professional expertise, experience as a practitioner, and judicial knowledge, in that adjudication process. To the extent that the Chief Constable or police Commissioner can produce an acceptable compromise—and one that reflects his own perception of the legitimacy of the actions—between those two sources of restraint, he will enjoy a relative freedom of action. As a manager, he applies his expertise to the production of an equilibrium according to what is feasible, and according to what demands he regards as legitimate.

In this final chapter, the various historically structured demands and constraints on the chiefs (as discussed Chapters 2, 3, 4, and 5) are summarized. To that fraction of the negotiation equation is added a resumé of the various internal sifting mechanisms of which the police managers must take account, in attempting to determine the practice of policing. Those several organizational levels affect the form of policing policies decreed by the chiefs but do not, it is contended, challenge his authority in the assignation of the label legitimate to particular structural pressures.

In compiling that equation, however, there is a major caveat. The dominance, within those latter accounts, of the intra-organizational variables of police work of a-historical and a-structural perspectives has resulted in little other than de-contextualized insights into the everyday world of the police officer.

This common-sense view of the problem gives specificity to 'concrete knowledge of policing as is available' but in the process, it makes it theoretically impossible to link such analysis, however critical with the material base which informs the way the police are organized. (Okojie and Noble, 1980, p.10)

Interactionist and situational accounts of the internal practices of police work cannot simply be added to a view of police command which is structurally informed. Water and oil do not mix.

A more complete equation in the analysis of police work requires a sociology that is structurally and historically contextualized at each level. The use of police discretion, for example, cannot be simply explicated in terms of stereotypes, reflected imagery, and the pressures of the police working-day, but must be located, within the legal form which provides the discretion parameters, and historically, according to the specificity of police–civil society relations. Accounts of the negotiation by chief police officers of the practice of policing in advanced capitalist society, require contributions, structurally and historically grounded, that seek to explicate both extra-organizational and intra-organizational factors. The present account is therefore qualified by its inevitable reliance on qualitatively different material in the recitation of the internal constraints. In considering this composition of the managerial equation, it must be recognized that the outcome of that process is a compromise between the differing elements, and according to the predispositions of the chief. As the negotiator, his task is to construct the common denominator—the allocation and practice of law enforcement resources which can be agreed in the no-man's land of the command position. His autonomy, within the state, rests ultimately on his skill as mediator in producing a result which satisfies all "legitimate" parties. Successful negotiation of "realistic policing" is the way to mobilize consent from social classes, and from the internal audience.

That compromise, police work, has two elements. It contains an ideological relation—an affirmation of the function of the organization for the society. The goals as perceived by rank-and-file police officers must necessarily be ones that also connect with dominant social values, and at the same time can be positively deciphered within the adaptive value system of the working-class. Police work must be portrayed as serving *general* societal interests.

Secondly, the chief surmounts the negotiative divide, in practice, as well as in image. A material relation is constructed which relates police actions to the external demands. Whereas the ideological relation is constructed through the medium of rhetoric, the material relation is conveyed by its expression in police operations. Successful police management is the art of ensuring that police officers display in their deeds, as well as in his words, the representation of the agreed version of police function.

## The Constraints on the Police Manager

### Within the organization

As negotiators, chief police officers are involved in a continuing "balancing-act". External demands are weighed against internally feasible solutions. Policing policy (the ideological statement) and policing practice (the material format) is the outcome. The implementation of external demand is mediated at several levels within the police institution to produce those results.

The chiefs possess a number of devices for influencing the actions of their officers. They allocate resources—deciding between Panda cars and foot patrols. They control force training schemes—giving priority either to re-active C.I.D. instruction or to preventive community guidance. They initiate (with Home Office guidance) special units from Fraud Squads to Vice. They direct by technology—the command-and-control system extends the chiefs authority via

the personal radio. They have an unchallenged prerogative over the organizational rewards system — governing commendations, promotions, demotions,
and expulsions. They can determine the social recognition of particular officers'
by manipulating press relations. They permit or frustrate the career-promising
secondments. In a myriad ways, the managerial authority of the chiefs', by
manipulation of the organizational variables, influences at the general level, the
effectuation of their own institutionally-derived policies. But they cannot
conclusively define the practice.

Policies are screened through formal and informal organizational barriers. Peer
group loyalties sift out unpopular orders. Styles of performance and priorities are
subject to group interpretation. The length of the chain of command in the post-
amalgamation forces interposes physical barriers between the command office
and the peripheral section house. There are varying obligations by police officers
to communal as opposed to organizational norms. The legal autonomy of the
constable may frustrate any directive.

The primary fealty of police officers in the urban forces is to their peer, and to
the "job" not to the organization and its notables. "The most profound source of
control in police work, other than the social audiences to which they play, is the
patrol officers themselves" (Manning, 1979, p.64). Or, as Cohen graphically
describes the conjunction between structure and peer-group loyalties on police
patrols of some housing estates:

> The result has been to narrow the scenario of law and order to a battle
> between two rival gangs, both composed of young, single working-class
> males, each seeking territorial control over the class habitat — but this
> difference, that one mob has the full weight of the state behind them, the
> other, only themselves and their mates to fall back on. (Cohen, 1979, p.135.
> See Parker, 1974, p.163, for a Liverpool example of this phenomenon)

The law acts as a weapon to arm the solidaristic aggression of the patrol
hunting party. The content and style of policing relates, in part, to the cohesion
of the rank-and-file peer group, in the mediation of policing policy. Further,
there are skill peculiarities in police work which endow the patrol officers with a
degree of autonomy. As a craft, it has no prescriptive manual. There are no
detailed specifications to meet every situation. The peers define the "job", its
forms, feasibilities, and frustrations. The only textbook on the constituent
practice of police work lies in the approval of fellow officers. The chief officer, in
issuing directives, has to allow for the way they will be interpreted according to
station, and group conventions and traditions. Organizational ideology will
impinge especially where the required tasks vary from approved conceptions of
the "police role". ". . . the police are more interested in fighting crime than in
either maintaining order or performing social service; their primary interest is to
strive to fulfil the image of successful crime fighters" (Weis and Milakovich,

1974, p.30). The constitution of a "working personality" concerned with "authority" and "danger" (Skolnick, 1966) at the core of the occupational ideology, ensures a back-seat for those roles requiring less crime-related activities. Stereotyped images of the public (Black and Reiss, 1970; Piliavin and Briar, 1964) frustrate consensual instructions on police-minority group relations. Symbolic assailants are essential to the practice of police work.

The spasmodic, episodic, arbitrary nature of the work-life of the patrolling officer is not easily susceptible to formal controls. Ordinary, everyday police work is largely invisible to senior officers (Bittner, 1974; Punch, 1979). Although personal radios may provide more effective communication between the organizational levels, most force tasks occur beyond the visage of superior officers. Similarly, police work is generally inaccessible to control because of the way demands on the police service are constructed:

> Although the police are formally organised as a bureaucratic hierarchy, a high proportion of their work is not delegated to them by management . . . but is police initiated or pro-active work. There is therefore no way in which police management can check on whether a man has done everything he might have done . . . Senior officers have no other source of information. (Cain, 1979, p.147)

The length of the chain of command in the Metropolitan and large combined provincial forces (which include widely spread police districts and station tradition) affects the transmission of directives. The peripheral housing estate is not easily controlled from the centre, irrespective of improvements in communications and in technological controls (Jones, 1980).

Some police work can be "eased" (Cain, 1971) through strategies of independence. While the assignation of officers to Vice Squad duty in the public toilets may not lead to open rebellion, the officers will endeavour to find their own reliefs from that task. Fast cars provide thrills for the beat officer (Holdaway, 1977). Bicycles may give a good image to the community policeman. But there is more comfort in a saloon car seat.

Command instructions may be countermanded by the effect of the relation between officers and the wider public. Where the major role-definer lies outside the force police work will be more resistant to the force commands on those occasions when directives flout informal community codes (Cain, 1973). Social relations with the policed, and obligations to the policed, may affect the transmission of orders.

Finally, the authority of the chief may be circumvented by the discretionary legal powers of the constable. Both sides — rank-and-file and command officers — avoid situations where that legal relation could be tested. Some directives are not issued because they appear to confront the legal prerogative of the constable.

The chief officer, as an organizational manager, in negotiating the external demands on the police organization, must take these varied hazards into account. He cannot predict their specific strength but must allow for the possibility of policy modifications in policing practice. In interpreting and legitimating the pressures for police action, as an effective manager, he is constantly aware of the internal audience.

Consequently, to avoid a manifest conflict between what is conceived as politically and legally desirable, and what is organizationally possible, the police manager plans strategically. From an historically derived location within the state, he attempts to construct a bridge between internal and external audiences, emphasizing the continuity of police function and police target.

## Outside the organization

The chief officer is subject to various external pressures. His balancing act on the tight-rope between intra-organizational constraints, and extra-organizational demands, requires considerable skill at mediation. He is confronted with demands, articulated through local and especially the central state, to represent class interest, albeit masquerading as the national interest, in police practice. The resource-providers of local police authority, and of Parliament and the Home Office have some right to call the police tune. On a number of occasions, he is faced with specific sectional or single-interest demands. But fundamentally, in so far as his authority derives from the law, from the legal form, the paramount extra-organization influence is the requirement for law enforcement.

> Sociologists of the police have tended to treat the notion of legality as unproblematic, not because they assume the police operate according to those principles, but because they assume the opposite, that they are largely irrelevant in practice. (McBarnet, 1979, pp.24–25)

Legal powers constrain and generally determine police work. Police officers are law enforcement officers according to the powers vested in traditional common law, in statute, and in Police Regulations. Their authority to act stems from that legal status. But the legal relation is determining only at the extremities. Chief officers are generally constrained by the legal form and are required to organize and deploy their forces to conduct law enforcement. Illegal actions are proscribed and positive action prescribed, in the face of violation by others. But these extra-organizational pressures are non-specific and only influence policing at the general level. As the primary source of the chief's autonomy, obedience to the permissive structure of law is the foremost tribute to the extra-organizational pressure stipulated from the chief police officer.

Secondly, the chief faces overt and direct class pressure, as well as the demands from the dominant political class that are articulated through the political organs of local and central state.

Working-class requests are commonly fragmented—relating to specific localized concerns such as football hooliganism, racial attacks, or the victimization of the old. They can be resisted (denied legitimacy) or incorporated in a manner that leaves policing practices and objectives largely unaffected. In the past, dictates from the local middle-class had been directed to the Watch Committee, which itself filtered-out and counterpoised the fractional demands. Within the local state of the 1980s, such requests now go direct to the local chief (or sometimes to his community relations officers), thus adding to his authority while diminishing that of the civil elite on the police committee. Through the sieve of the legal autonomy principle, he offsets their sectional demands.

Apart from at the general level—the imperative to maintain public order—the pressures on the police institution rarely embody cohesive class interests. The conflicts between elites over specific policing practices in nineteenth-century Liverpool, are mirrored in contemporary schisms between class fractions over calls for police action. For example, police pressure on industrial pickets may be sponsored by small-scale employers, who require low wage costs in order to survive, and opposed by large monopoly employers, concerned with the twin objectives of the institutionalization of industrial conflict, and with raising the costs of their smaller competitors. The more divided the demands, the more the chiefs negotiate from a position of strength. The chiefs cannot flout the requirements of the dominant political elites—their resources remain dependent upon that final submission. But except where the demands are constructed through the state into a notional public interest, direct pressures can be resisted. Observable subordination to class pressures undermines—de-legitimizes—the chief's managerial autonomy.

For those social classes without access to the state machinery, the demands remain at the formal, political level. Only working-class demands on policing, when they reflect concrete differences, survive as political pressures. They are restricted to a residual political realm, which serves as the repository for those appeals which represent a substantive challenge to the constructed impartiality of the chiefs, and are consequently denied legitimacy. (For example, calls by the Lambeth Labour council leader for a lower police profile, during the Brixton disturbances, were denounced by the police commander as emanating from an "extremist".)

Within the provincial towns and cities, direct pressures from local elites had largely and spasmodically withered away by the end of the nineteenth-century. Changes in the composition of capital; fractional clashes within the local dominant class; the later rise of police managerialism (in its various manifestations); the increase in central state intervention; the organizational changes in police work (amalgamations, expansion and the rise of the police institution); and the fiscal crisis of the 1960s and 1970s; had all contributed to the inconse-quentiality of local police authorities.

As the authority over the police of the local elites disintegrated, as police work became routinized and its intrusions into civil society institutionalized the new centralized economic and political interests did not inherit the authority mediated through the local state. In the post-war period the police institution became more autonomous within the complexity of the various state apparatus. The simultaneous development of the police institution, buttressed by the ideological creed of the traditional common law tradition, effectively outflanked new forms of central political direction. The chiefs achieved an authority beyond any immediate political claims from their paymasters.

But residually both local and central constraints on the chiefs remained intact. The police managers were still required to negotiate policing definitions within boundaries determined by the residual powers of those bodies. Finite financial resources and the explanatory accountability principle, ensured a modicum of reserve power. Police action must proceed along paths generally approved of by the dominant external interests. The dis-use of those residual powers is a recognition not of their absence but rather of the success of the chiefs in negotiating a satisfactory compromise between internal constraints and external pressure over the ideological and material form of police work.

Finally, there are, of course, pressures (mainly at a local level) which have affinities with pluralistic analyses. The chiefs are regularly bombarded by campaigners on specific issues. The Automobile Association opposes random breath-testing of motorists. The Festival of Light demands a clamp-down on sales of pornographic literature. Community Relations Council oppose the use of "stop-and-search" powers. Residents outside football grounds require actions against Saturday invasions of their streets.

All these matters fall within the local chief's prerogative. Their adjudication depends upon the extent to which they will pass unscathed through the intra-organizational barriers. But their acceptance for consideration primarily, depends upon whether they are viewed by the chief as legitimate pressures. That label legitimate is dependent upon the source, the style, and the breadth, of common ground between the pressure group, on one side, and the police institution, on the other, and the extent to which the demands challenge existing police definitions and interpretations of the problematic.

The Automobile Association is legitimate in that its leadership is drawn from the dominant class; its demands are couched in the approved form — via evidence to Parliamentary Committees and in correspondence with local chief police officers; and it has a membership with divergent interests who would find no other bones of contention with the chief. Finally, there is a shared problematic with the police organization — safe driving is an agreed concern. In such a case, the acceptance of the demand depends upon the strength of the intra-organizational barriers.

Conversely, Community Relations Councils are liable to be labelled as a source of "illegitimate" pressure. Their members are drawn from either a racially suspect and lower class strata, or from middle-class radicals (who would be liable to challenge the police institution on other matters). Some of the forms of pressure take a disapproved form—street demonstrations rather than via the "correct" channels. They challenge the police definition of the problem, and its extent, and consequently, confront both the chiefs' negative definition, and also the organizational resistance.

In conferring these labels, of legitimacy and illegitimacy on the outside pressures, chief police officers are attentive to their most sympathetic social audience—their male peers within A.C.P.O. The primary definers of the applications of police managerial expertise in acceptance or denial of external demands are fellow chief officers. They constitute a major source of extra-organizational pressure. In general, chief officers do not negotiate external demands as individuals but as part of the larger collective. The practical conservatism of the negotiators outlined in Chapter 6, is marked by a reliance on precedent and on advice (both formally from A.C.P.O. committees) and informally (from fellow commanding officers). The demands on policing are weighed, proposals for police action and development evaluated, in the context of a collective decision-making structure. In practice, the role of the chief officer, in the face of these extra-organizational pressures is rarely a controversial one. Historical precedents have modified both demands and their solutions. For the most part, from the legitimate pressure groups, and from the dominant political and economic interests, only "reasonable", "realistic" demands are made on the brokers of law enforcement resources. The predispositions of the chief, as the organization manager, to interpret and modify requests for police services, have been learnt. Demands are framed in a constitutionally acceptable form.

The contemporary authority of the chief police officers in Britain relates to the historical construction of a negotiating position between organization, social classes, and local pressure groups. Chief officers, conscious of the intra-organizational constraints upon the implementation of policing policy, seek to develop at both ideological and material levels a conjunction between organization and the legitimate external interests. Police management is the art of achieving that conjunction. The outcome of the negotiating process, which is continuing and historically formed, depends upon the strength and the source of the external pressures, the relative independence and authority of the chief officers as referees and mediators, and the degree of resistance within the organization.

The major practical problem facing the chief is analogous to that of the marketing director of a large business. Police work must be sold like a commercial product. But the prospective consumers of that product vary in their purchasing power. All must be satisfied but some more than others. The chief police officer's problem is to convince the major social classes that he holds and implements an approved conception of that product—police work—and that police organization is committed (so far as is operationally feasible) to the maintenance of the present social relations. He has to phrase the organizational reality in terms that are socially acceptable—how to manage consent.

## The Conjunction Between Police Organization and the Major Social Classes

### Consent and ideological inversion

The priority is to keep "the public" content. As the source of negotiative independence, as the arbiters of police resources, and as an accountability placebo, the legitimate community clients of the police institution, the citizenry, must be persuaded that the institution is seeking to effectuate their legal rights. Crime-talk, the rhetoric of the chiefs, is the major technique by which this problem is resolved. Consent changes from a simple ideological prop of police autonomy, to being both contributor to, and consequence of, the complex result of the negotiation process.

The police manager's task is to construct a relation between the organizational value system, the professional culture of the police institution, and the dominant norms and values in the society. Consent is manufactured through this process. The punditry of chief officers, the content of the Reports required under the explanatory accountability principle, are the techniques by which the organizational values—the institution's interpretation of its problematic—is articulated with the social problematic.

The predicament for the police managers is to portray the approaches to crime prevention and to social control, within the law, of the police institution as fitting directly with social priorities. Resources will be forthcoming, and consent reliable, only when crime prevention and the police institution's interpretation of that function, are given precedence on the social agenda. Quinney, in the U.S.A. makes the case:

> It is not to be doubted that public concern about crime is widespread and has increased sharply in recent years . . . a majority of people are greatly concerned about their personal safety and private property. Moreover, the fear of crime has affected people's lives and has prompted the public to alter their behaviour and activities. More important from the official ideological standpoint, however, are the attitudes people share in the control of crime. It is here that officials would like the public to agree that action is needed and that the policies made and the actions taken deserve support . . . (that)

> public opinion must be shaped, if necessary, to rationalise official policies of
> crime control. (Quinney, 1974, p.151)

Crime-talk, the rhetoric of the chiefs, aims to connect with that focal concern
(which is spread across social classes) and to re-shape it into support for the
particular practices of the police institution.

Hall *et al.* (1978) relate that crime-talk of the police institution to the specificity of the primary assumptions within the dominant and subordinate value
systems of the middle- and working-classes. Crime-talk connects with existing
focal concerns, re-shapes them, and incorporates those re-shaped beliefs within
the official, institutional account of the problem. They distinguish seven of these
focal concerns—respectability, social discipline, the family, the city, England,
the law, and the police. Each of these conceptions, enjoys a specific meaning in
each social class but can be connected and incorporated, through the medium of
crime-talk within the institutional ideology of policing. Partly subsumed under
the concern with law, stands a particular conception of the police—that Reithian
figure, the English bobby. Crime-talk allows for an interpretation of police work
that connects varying class conceptions of policing within an acceptable
institutional interpretation. As Chapter 8 demonstrated, there is some special
strength in that final construction for the major social classes.

For the middle-classes, the British constable epitomizes the traditional virtues,
of civilization, of the thin blue line thwarting social anarchy, of social stability, and of
"English" character—the triumph of reason and forbearance over the barbaric
elements that continually lie in wait. To the urban elites, the police provide
the symbol of legal and civic status in the allegorical war against crime.

Within the working-class, the ambivalence of the subordinate culture,
regarding the police, makes the connections required through crime-talk more
tenuous (Brogden, 1981). The image contains both residual commendatory and
antagonistic elements. But the former links with the conception of *England,* in a
demonstration of native superiority in relation to "foreigners", who require
armed police to maintain social order.

Through the declamations of senior police officers in law-and-order, these
varying conceptions of policing are linked and incorporated within the organizational ideology, as extolled in the Reithian histories. Supporting the police
function, valuing police work, means in practice legitimizing the model of the
police officer as re-constructed through the organizational mesh.

The rhetoric of the chief police officers, concerned with resource production,
with the sustenance of consent, and with negotiating a relation between police
institution and civil society, is aimed at making these connections. Crime-talk
links with key elements within the cultural systems. It elucidates, makes sense
of, via the existing meaning systems, the police institutional problematic
and definitions.

Through the focal concerns, an ideological relation is mediated between the intra-organizational constraints and the external pressures.

> Each of these themes . . . organises crime within it. Each one connects with and identifies crime—and inserts it into a discourse about normality, rightness, and their inverse . . . This complex centrality of 'crime' as a public issue, a powerful mobilising force—support can be rallied to a campaign against it, not by presenting it as an abstract issue but as a tangible force which threatens the complexly balanced stabilities which represent the "English way of life". (Hall *et al.*, 1978, pp.149-150)

By constructing the relation between the police problematic, the institution's raison d'être, and the domain assumptions, the chiefs situate the police institution at the centre of social affairs. The contrived identity between institution and social classes, through ideology, re-locates the police institution from the periphery to the centre of social relations. The police function becomes the crucial societal problematic.

A process of ideological inversion occurs (Young, 1979). The police protect citizens against crime. Crime is the major threat to the legal order, on which social order hinges. Without the police institution, enjoying a relative independence from partisan political constraints, crime would be rampant, and the key citadels, the domain assumptions, would fall. Crime control, the protection of people, property, and cultural values, become the defining goal. "People are . . . protected against crime and the control of crime is presented as a major raison d'être of the system" (ibid p.27).

Citizens survive, work, play and enjoy legal rights only because the police institution is there to safeguard them. The institution is fetished, and its commanders assume the right to make Delphic pronouncements on the social order. As Balbus says of the legal order, the police institution comes to function:

> . . . autonomously of, or independently from the power, or will of the subjects, who originally set it in motion but do not know, or have forgotten, that they have done so. The police institution comes to have a "life of its own" . . . (Balbus, 1978, pp.84-85)

## Consent and the material relation—the policing of the marginal strata

The conjunction between the police institution and the social classes is not simply negotiated rhetorically, restricted to the declamations of the chief officers. Consent to policing, relates to police practice as well as to crime-talk.

The compromise between external pressures and organizational constraints is constructed dramatically, and symbolically, through the negotiative device of a common enemy, a legitimate police target — the marginal groups on the streets of the city. Police work has been historically constructed to contain and occasionally cull the residual social strata whose social activities and economic pursuits are capable of criminalization by the control apparatus, at minimal cost.

> Our enforcement . . . bureaucracies are in large measure organised and geared to detecting, sorting out, and adjudicating the kinds of crime most often and visibly engaged in by the socially marginal strata . . . (Blumberg, 1976, p.48; Manning, 1979, p.162)

The criminalization of the participants in the street economy in the nineteenth and early twentieth centuries; the continuing clamp-down on street leisure amongst the marginal strata and age groups; the foundation of street patrolling (the "beat") as the basis for establishment construction; the continuing police entrepreneurship over new powers for street control; the concentration of manpower and resources on the policing of the inner city — all represent the surface manifestations of the compromise.

The historical process of negotiation, formally initiated in London by Commissioners Rowan and Mayne, with the statutory extension of police powers in 1839, and in policing practices aimed primarily at the marginal groups (Cohen, 1979; Ignatieff, 1979; Miller, 1978) mirrored Liverpool practices in the first century in the concentration of police work on the streets — the public habitat of the lower classes.

In the present day, this practice and focus of police work is equally manifest. Most offenders appearing in the lower courts in Liverpool, for example, have in common their lack of employment in the primary economy (A. Brogden, 1982), and are prosecuted for one of a range of street-related offences. The parade of petty offenders through the Magistrates Courts encompasses the inebriated, car-thieves, prostitutes, handbag snatchers, street-pedlars, street gamblers, and brawlers outside the city centre club. The normality of police work, in its proactive mode, consists of the arrest and subsequent prosecution of the chaff of the street population, reaped mainly from the inner city. (Even much of the work brought before the traffic court relates to the trivia of vehicle maintenance and taxation offences produced in the course of stop-and-search practice in the twilight areas around the city centre.) Discretionary selection of the residuum for criminal process is peculiar. On economic considerations alone, action against the marginal strata squanders scarce resources. Similarly, the policing of the unwaged, of the drifting groups of teenagers, and of the minority ethnic groups, outside the primary economy, is not easily explained by any reductionist argument. The Jimmy Kelly's and the Liddell Tower's do not pose the same threat as industrial workers to the new monopoly capital. Nor could their deaths in police custody be readily construed as in some way related to disruptive effects on the social relations of production, or on the consumption process required by capital. The social groups and strata that are the least threat, that moreover, suffer major depredations from capital, as well as from crime, are the front-line recipients of police practice.

Nevertheless, there is an indirect relation between class structure and policing focus. The negotiation of structural pressures with organizational constraints results in a material compromise over the practice of police work. The lower strata have peculiar attributes which make them a convenient bridge for the interests of the dominant and subordinate classes, and a conjunction between the structural pressures on the police institution and the intra-organizational constraints.

Both major social classes, as well as the solidary peer groups within the police institution, can unite against them. As a target, the marginal groups are central to the mobilizaton of consent.

They are highly visible, their activities transparent, and action against them creates the impression of social unity between the classes themselves, and between social classes and the police institution. They are readily available for organizational processing and transformation, for the manufacture of reported crime rates, and for the inflation of "clear-up" rates. Finally, the marginal groups have particular attributes which dove-tail with the occupational requirements of police officers.

*Social Unity*

The pursuits of the street offenders, where there are indentifiable victims arouses universal, inter-class condemnation. It connects with both dominant and subordinate value systems. It provides a common denominator, in the reaction to it, which strengthens consent to policing.

Police patrols against latter-day garrotters, promote a cathartic unity between social classes in a common statement of revulsion. The violent street offender, in particular functions as a contemporary witch (Erikson, 1966), confirming the con-sensual features of the silent majority, and providing prestige, rewards, and support for the witch-finder—the police. Street crime and the action against it, serves to legitimize the wider functions and relative independence of the police institution.

A democratic police force readily yields to the articulation of external pressure for the prosecution of those forms of crime amongst the marginal strata for which there is universal condemnation. The autonomy of the police manager benefits from his skill at negotiating and satisfying these demands, in the culling of the marginal groups.

*Transparency*

Deviance by the marginal groups is, for the most part, highly visible (Young,

1979). It is largely practised in public territory, the street. Unlike infractions of the Factory Acts, the evasion of taxes, local council corruption, and business fraud, street crime is historically exposed to a wider audience. The proclivities of the street people are subject to the constant surveillance.

This transparency has functions for both police institution and also for the civic elites. For the former, the uniformed beat patrolling of the inner city provides a convincing demonstration of police responsiveness to legitimate external pressures. Preventive measures against street crime especially, are developed in the sight of an appreciative audience. (Reactive painstaking investigatory work rarely induces evocative accolades.)

For the local elites, measures to thwart street crime have a symbolic function. Where their hegemony over the city has long disappeared, dramatic action at their behest against the marginal populations of the inner city, re-affirms their moral authority. It signifies a unity between themselves and the police institution as they bask in the reflected symbolism of the guardians against social disorder.

Finally, for working-class people (participants in an historically uneven and spasmodic truce with the police institution), the deviance may be encountered at first hand. For those communities in the front-line, street, and personal crime may be omnipresent. It is not an anonymous or impersonal activity observed from behind the net curtains of suburbia, or through the banner headlines of the more staid tabloids. Working-class communities complain bitterly over the presence of street prostitutes and especially, over the presence of the parasitic "kerb-crawlers".

For all three parties—the police institution itself, the civic elites as representative of the urban bourgeoisie, the working-class communities on the fringes of the inner city—the transparency and visibility of street crime make it a symbol for the expression of disgust, of personal virtues, and of public unity.

*Organizational processing*
Crime by the marginal groups has two immediate organizational attractions. The reservoir of deviance is readily tapped and transformed into recorded crime. Efficiency in the suppression of some forms of it, is demonstrable. The various forms of lower-class crime together contributes to a pool of deviants accessible for processing. Deviants can be transformed into criminals according to the demands of the police working day. Drugs, vice, and drink problems are susceptible to the ebb and flow of organizational requirements. Moral panics can be satiated, and pressure groups acceded to, by a quick trawl. Prostitutes, street-traders, and unemployed youths are available for culling with minimal expenditure of effort by the police organization. The marginal groups provide a reservoir of deviants for sieving and transforming, to satisfy the external demands on the force.

In that redefinition process, the police have a major advantage. The marginal groups are not organized, cannot fight back (Spitzer, 1975). Unless the general level of harassment (in conjunction with other factors), precipitates a community rebellion, they have not the collective muscle to enable them to resist the process of criminalization.

Lower-class crime has a second organization attribute. Much of it is "victimless". Most illegal transactions in the streets — between prostitute and client; by illegal street traders; or in the course of a game of pitch-and-toss — have no direct effects on an unwilling victim. Its reporting depends upon police initiative. Consequently, there is no inconvenient gap between the reported crime rate and the clear-up rate. Crimes known are, for the most part, crime cleared-up. Street enforcement has its own built-up efficiency factor. Such lower-class crime contributes to the solution of a police management problem.

*Occupational Pay offs*

Similarly, the policing of the marginal groups permits occupational compensations for police officers. There is a cause-and-effect relation between lower-class crime and some of the complexities of the police occupation.

The varied features and indeterminate qualities of the former permits the patrol officer to use the maximum discretion. His or her legal power to define criminality, and to determine appropriate charges, secures, simultaneously, the legal relation of the police institution, and allows the constable to relieve the tedium of patrol work, through the use of independent powers, in the course of encounters with the marginal groups.

The exercise of that authority lies within a fixed relation of domination and subordination. The suspected offender from the lowest stratum has little knowledge of legal rights, considerable fear of asserting any such knowledge, and no ready access to legal expertise. Flight or dexterity is the only defence. The policing of the marginal strata emphasizes the authority inherent in the officer's occupation. As Cain (1973, p.69) pointed out, the police victim is also likely to have no fixed abode and to be lacking in social contacts. However, black people, and perhaps young people, are socially integrated within their own communities, and therefore are in a stronger position to resist police harassment strategies than some of the other target groups are and have been.

*Identification and Interpellation*

Finally, street, and lower-class crime generally, have an identification function for police officers. In the street, the probationers learn to identify the unlawful — the policing target (the stereotypes of race, age, and class, and the cues of dress and demeanour), and to construct colleague loyalties with peers. In that police work, the novitiate develops obligations to, and solidarity with other officers. An identity as a police officer is constituted through the process of encounters with the marginal populations. The patrolling of the inner city or of the dilapidated housing estate gives the police institution, and its functionaries an idiomatic identity.

Each of the features in the policing of the lower-classes—its contribution to social unity between the two main classes; the transparency of criminality of those groups, allowing symbolic police action against them; their accessibility for organizational processing; and the functions of those strata for policing as an occupation—assists in the material conjunction between social classes and intra-organizational constraints. The marginal social elements, the participants in the secondary economy, the social residue outside the primary economy, are the convenient, historically-derived, focus of the compromise over police function.

Through the material relation of police practice against those strata, and through the medium of crime-talk, the chief police officers, are the negotiators of law enforcement resource allocation, construct a bonding relation between the police institution, as a state apparatus, and the key elements of civil society.

## Autonomy and Consent—The "Concrete" Limits

Police management, the practice of the major functionaries of the police institution is a specific art. Following from the example of Head Constables Greig and Dunning in Liverpool at the end of the last century, it has developed into a unique skill. It is the practice of combining judicial knowledge of the requirements of the prosecution process; professional expertise in the handling of resources and in the devising of policing tactics and strategies; of legal autonomy (as the beneficiaries of an unique form of managerial power); and of practical experience as police officers, in the negotiation of a symmetrical relation between police institution and social classes, in the political space between central and local states. Legitimate pressures (as construed by the chiefs) are satisfied by that negotiation. Crime-talk and material practice are the bedrock of the relation. Consent is maintained. Autonomy is safeguarded. The internal audience is re-assured. Consent to policing, institutional freedom from the political representatives, and a surrogate form of accountability, is fashioned on the back of the residual strata.

But that relative political independence is a mirage. It is true, as Chapters 2, 3, and 4 documented that direct intervention by both local and central elites has long since disappeared and only residual powers remain intact. Further, as Chapter 5 demonstrated, the police institution possesses considerable autonomy under its final formal constraint, the permissive structure of law. The new cohesion of the intra-police organizations, and managerial peer-groups, (Chapter 6), has given additional strength to that apparent independence. But total autonomy is impossible. On one hand, the police institution is situated at the crux of the contradictions of the advanced capitalist state, confronting the particular effects of the fiscal crisis in the inner cities. It cannot act independently of those determinants but can only react to them. Secondly, the legitimacy of the police institution, and hence its relative independence, can only be sustained as long as it maintains some "imaginary" relation with the social classes—a relation of consent. But that consent, with all its complexities, and which is interdependent with the economic crisis, is significantly more tenuous than is recognized within the police institution. As I write these words, coincidentally, three miles from here, the second of two nights of serious rioting in the inner city of Toxteth, is drawing to a close. Precipitated by anti-police feeling by unemployed black and white youth, the events have, so far, included major confrontations, between petrol-bomb and concrete brick-throwing youngsters and large numbers of police officers. Some 280 of the latter have been reported injured. A significant number of buildings have been burnt to the ground. Large-scale looting has ensued. C.S. gas has been used for the first time on the British mainland. What commenced as an anti-police riot, has metamorphosed into grand pillage.

The contradictions in consent, and the fragility of police autonomy were never more evident in Britain. The tale is already recounted of well-meaning police officers attempting to stem the early incidents with bags of sweets for local onlooking children. The children took the sweets—and half an hour later were throwing Molotov cocktails. A century and a half after the inception of the Liverpool police, the chickens of the Toxteth merchants have come home to roost.

# Postscript: The Toxteth Riots, 1981

## by A. and M. Brogden

There is a certain irony in the location of the major anti-police riots in Liverpool, in July, 1981. Toxteth (or rather, as it is better known locally, Liverpool 8), in the 1830s had been riven by a *de facto* barrier between the mansions of the city merchants, in Toxteth Park, and the habitations of the participants in the secondary economy, on and immediately adjacent to, the South Docks. As Chapter 2 indicated, the patrolling of this boundary, to prevent incursions from the latter to the former, was a major justification for the creation of the New Police.

That friction and the use of the early Liverpool Police to contain the residual groups of the nineteenth century city, has considerable parallels with the factors that led up to the events of 1981. Both relate to the peculiar economic structure of the city. Similarly, both series of precursors can be understood most coherently through the way the law enforcement machinery developed a partly autonomous link with dominant elements in civil society, in constructing a common target for police work. Liverpool 8 in the 1980s, and North Toxteth in the 1830s, provided the pool of deviants available for processing according to the demands of the organizational day, and according to the moral panics engendered through civil society.

There are, of course, already several accounts of both the riots and the causes embedded in those multifarious scenes. When on July 3rd, 1981, and spasmodically over the succeeding weeks (culminating in a major anti-police march on August 15th), a proportion of the population of Liverpool 8 (distinguished initially only by youth and race), gave vent to a collective frustration aimed primarily at the police institution, explanations were instantly forthcoming.

On one side, that mini-rebellion was caricatured on the conspiratorial left as a revolt of the people against the oppressive arm of the state, and in the phantasmagorical right-wing Press, as a Red plot (complete with masked organizers and Red gold).

While these accounts, and the hybrid ones in between those polarities, vary in wisdom and in depth, they have universally failed to situate the events within material, organizational, and ideological frameworks. The accounts of the riots, and the imputation of their cause, primarily lack an historical dimension. They offer only fragmentary references to the relationship between police organization and the particular events preceeding the riots. They have generally failed to explain the specificity of the anti-police character of the disturbances — the challenge to the legal relation that governs the lives of the residents of the inner city. Finally, only a few commentators have touched upon the connection between the riots and the degree of autonomy achieved by the police institution in the city, and the dependence of that autonomy upon a surrogate form of accountability constructed through the consent principle. The following analysis flows from the preceeding work in making those connections, but like all attempts to account for those events, it necessarily remains partial — it cannot do justice to the complexity of the inter-relationships between unemployment, inferior housing and education, and the major factor of racism, in the construction of the riot scenario.

The following therefore is an attempt to extrapolate one major factor as causal — the police-public relation. The chronology, necessarily selective, which documents some of the major preceeding events, as well as the immediate form of the disturbances, follows:

*1972:* Evidence from various sources (McNabb *et al.*; Kuya; Humphry) of continuing racial harassment in relations between black people in Liverpool 8 and the then Liverpool and Bootle Police.

*1978:* "Death in custody" of elderly African from Liverpool 8 (eventually to have been charged with "extracting electricity illegally").

*1978:* Article in *The Listener* gives orthodox and unquestioned police explanation of crime in the area as the problem of "half-castes".

*1979:* Incident on city market in which young blacks are charged with "causing affray", and counter-claims of racial harassment.

*1979:* Widespread accounts of alleged police violence in a separate part of the police area ("K" Division).

*1980:* March of protest by Liverpool 8 young blacks to local police station (Admiral Street) protesting against racial harassment.

*1980:* Series of incidents result in temporary withdrawal of Community Relations Officers from police-community liaison committee, in protest against the way they claim the Chief Constable is using Community Relations work for Public Relations purposes.

*1980:* Easter anti-police riot in St Paul's, Bristol, involving mainly young blacks.

*1981:* Easter—major anti-police riot in Brixton, London, again involving primarily young blacks.

*1981, 3rd July:* Precipitating chase and arrest of young black motor-cyclists; rescue by friends; small-scale conflict; late-night missile-throwing at police vehicles.

*4th July:* Heavy police presence in Liverpool 8 during day; early evening—several incidents of stone-throwing; late-night barricade across main road (Upper Parliament Street) by mainly black youths; retreat by police after attempt at dispersal; continuing crowd build-up; several individualized conflicts.

*5th July:* Early morning small-scale fires; new barricade by larger group of black (and white) youths; missile-throwing (including fire-bombs) at reinforced anti-riot police until 06.00; car show-room wrecked and some cars driven at police line; minor clear-up during day; 600 police on stand-by; late evening—new barricade; considerable missile-throwing; police assailed from several sides and chased half-mile down Upper Parliament Street, simultaneous and partly independent looting and burning of local shopping area by heterogeneous groups, young and old; 450 police reported injured up until this point.

*6th July:* Early morning conflict continues; burning of several large buildings of symbolic significance; conflict winds down as police use anti-building C.S. gas against individuals; late-night small-scale disorders in surrounding area; massive police presence during following week under mutual aid scheme.

*7th July:* Late-night stoning in relation to pervading police presence; police go on to offensive with fast vehicles driven at demonstrators; youth has back broken by police van—allegedly beaten after arrest.

*8th July:* Late-night stoning, continuing aggressive police patrolling; disabled man killed by police vehicle (police report initial difficulty in tracing driver).

# The Historical Context

As Chapters 2 and 7 documented, the peculiar economy of Liverpool has produced a particular form of class structure. A major feature of that class structure historically, has been the segmentalization of a large minority of the population, compressed into a residual social and economic context outside the primary economy. This factor has significant implications for the outbreak of both the 1981 anti-police riots and its several predecessors.

Whereas in most manufacturing towns, the occupational structure had the form of a flattened diamond, with most workers concentrated in the semi-skilled and skilled strata, in the nineteenth and early twentieth centuries the class structure of Liverpool was better represented through the image of a pyramid. The peculiar mercantile economy—the dependence of the city primarily upon trade, and on small docks-related industries—ensured a high proportion of casual, unskilled work, and a rising level of unemployment as imperial trade went into decline after World War I.

This mercantile economy had four other relevant effects. It concentrated labour in those unskilled occupations most exposed to unemployment. Moreover, it ensured the maintenance of a secondary economy, of varying size, in certain of the inner city and dock-side districts. It permitted a degree of early migration into the city as a port (Irish, Welsh, West African, Chinese, and West Indian communities all existed in the city early in the twentieth century). Finally, the form of the economy hampered the development of an articulate class-based Labour Party (through lack of an industrial base) and substituted instead a working-class political organization wracked with internal conflicts between Protestant and Catholic workers, and simultaneously excluding the residual groups outside the primary economy from participation.

Consequently, a sizeable proportion of the city's population was institutionally segregated on the margins of the city's economic structure, and practically debarred from involvement in formal political relations.

Throughout the century and a half since the inception of the New Police, those excluded strata had found voice only through political articulation on the streets, against the most visible agents of that exclusion. While the focus of the allegiances of the police institution had changed markedly over that period, it retained the forms of deployment, of patrolling, that had developed in the context of the surveillance of the lower-classes in the first half of the nineteenth century. Policing the residual strata, and opposition to that form of control had always been a major manifestation of that continuing exclusion.

In successive forays over two centuries, primary hostility had been turned against the immediate oppressors. In 1776, enraged sailors had swamped the local Watch on the way to the Cotton Exchange. In 1835, Irish Catholics had captured the gates of the Main Bridewell as their hunted enemy, the Day and Night Watch fled inside. in 1855, and again in 1861, the Bread Riots on Scotland Road, had resulted in onslaughts against the most visible form of suppression, the New Police. During the sectarian disturbances of the 1900s, reports to the Liverpool Police Enquiry documented the mutuality of dis-possessed Catholics' and Protestants' antagonism towards Head Constable Dunning's Liverpool Police. During the 1919 Police Strike, there had been bitter confrontations between the Liverpool "mob" and the remaining blacklegs and middle-class Specials. In a series of minor incidents up to the 1970s, there had been occasional outbursts against the police institution.

These manifestations, while possessing varying degrees of political conscious-ness about the class nature of the police, had the primary object of settling old scores arising from the daily individualized conflicts on the streets. They were a reaction to what Pryce (1979) has called the "endless pressure" of survival under surveillance in the inner city, for which there was no legitimate safety-valve.

The composition and objectives of the street combatants of July, 1981 replicates the sentiments of those earlier anti-police demonstrations. Almost entirely young (although with the tacit support of many of their elders), the Liverpool 8 participants had in common their exclusion from the political process, from decisions over resource distribution in the city, from the job market, and in their availability for police-culling exercises on the streets. In the early stages of the riot, their ascribed characteristics of age, race, and location (third and fourth generation Liverpool blacks) reflected their susceptibility to targeting by a police institution seeking to bridge the gap between societal expectations of police function, and the restraints of police organization, as demonstrated in Chapter 9. The riots represented an episodic inchoate reaction to the effects of that conjunction between organization and class.

## The Conjunction Between Police and Society

Historically, successive districts of the city have borne the brunt of police expeditionary forces in a display of the rule of law. The Vauxhall area (near the North Docks), and the part of Toxteth adjacent to the South Docks had been the traditional centres of the secondary economy (the "criminal areas" of ecological scholarship). But with the dispersion of the upper-classes from the Toxteth Park area, and with the advent of council clearance and re-building schemes in the dock-side districts, the residual groups outside the waged economy were increasingly pushed into, and confined within, the very area whose defence had been a primary function of the New Police.

In post-World War II years, the district (now known as Liverpool 8), had become allegorized in the demonic ideology of the local police. It was *the* problem area—the primary location of the "bucks". In 1976, for example, the current Chief Constable had claimed that at some future date an "army of occupation" might be required to control it. In particular, the institutionalized racism reflected in local force orders in much earlier years (see Chapter 7) was still prevalent about one segment of the population of Liverpool 8, in the 1970s. For example, a bland B.B.C. account of the "crime problem" in the city, gave as objective truth without qualification, a senior officer's assessment of the primary cause of that social disorder. It was the "problem of half-castes . . . the product of liaisons between black seamen and white prostitutes in Liverpool 8 . . . they do not grow up with any recognizable home-life . . . the half-caste community is well outside recognized society" (*The Listener*, 2nd February, 1978).

Specifically, Liverpool 8, and the characteristics of its inhabitants, ascribed and achieved, served to provide a bridge between organizational interests and constraints, and social classes. Within local bourgeois society, the district had become accepted as the "red-light" centre, where deviant supplies and services, proscribed by conventional law-abiding society outside, were readily available.

This attitude was especially manifest in the extent of "kerb-crawling" by motorists from elsewhere on Merseyside, seeking the services of prostitution.

Police action through surveillance and control of this assumed location of vice provided for a symbolic assertion of unity between police apparatus and the dominant elements of civil society. Pro-active patrolling of Liverpool 8 was permissible, indeed, desirable, to keep the contagion of vice, crime, and race in its place.

Historically-derived police practices of preventive police action against the street people (technologically-updated through sweeps by police jeeps and Ford Transits in the 1970s), were re-affirmed in the generalized oppression of the participants in the street economy and in street leisure. The personal attributes of the inhabitants, real and imaginary, and the normality of their street presence (in Corrigan's 1979 words "doing nothing"), ensured a high degree of transparency, permitting symbolic police action at the behest of the moral order outside. Readily available for organizational processing, in front of a primary audience (the Merseyside Police Headquarters, at the time, lay literally across the street from Liverpool 8), the culling of offenders from Toxteth required minimum resource input.

The street location of the potential offenders had a further function for police organization. It allowed the maximum use of police discretion—the autonomy of the street patrol group within which the probationers learnt the easy stereotypes and cues for identifying the "suspects", functionally and dialectically contributing to the development of a supportive occupational ideology in confrontation with the "enemy", within a fixed relation of domination and subordination.

The location (the battered streets of Liverpool 8), personal characteristics (race and age), accessibility (the streets of the inner city), of the inhabitants of the district had several functions for the sustenance of the organizational ideology itself, as well as making possible an articulation between police apparatus and civil society which continues to prove functional for both.

## The Legal Relation

In Chapter 5, it was argued that the primary characteristic of police work is law enforcement. But that function is not restrictive. The law does not require mandatory action but rather, in its direction of police work, it embodies a permissive discretionary relation. In the use of legal powers, the resultant enforcement procedure is selective, owing as much to organizational requirements as to external (structural) pressures for the maintenance of social order.

It is in the control of street life that the legal powers of the police institution are at their most permissive and allow the most discretion. Until recent years, in Liverpool a primary part of that armoury had been the "sus" provisions of the 1824 Vagrancy Act. Guilt was established if in the opinion of a patrolling officer, an individual was about to embark on a felony, having previously carried out a similar suspicious act. During the seventies, selective enforcement of such legislation against the street people had been rampant in Liverpool. For example, in 1978 the area had by far the highest rate of proceedings under that police power in the country [358 per million population in Merseyside, 278 in the Metropolitan Police District, and 99 in Greater Manchester. (In contrast, in about a third of the police areas, the rate was no more than 10 per million — *Home Office Evidence to the House of Commons Home Affairs Committee, 1979-80*)]. In his post-riot report to the Police Authority, the Chief Constable argued curiously that such a rate was not unreasonable given that the vast majority of such defendants were white rather than black, and that the rate for a similar offence, "going equipped for stealing", was also high on Merseyside.

But central to police powers in Toxteth has always been not "sus" but the "stops" — the *local* bye-laws (the historical continuity of which was outlined in Chapter 5) which permit a patrolling officer to stop and search an individual, whom he/she regards as suspect. Stops, recorded and unrecorded, are the bedrock of street encounters between police patrols and the residual groups of the inner city. Parker (1974) amongst others, has documented the ritualistic features of the stop experience as part of the everyday life of youths in an area immediately adjacent to Liverpool 8. The routine of the stop and search practice is a central pivot of police-youth interaction in the inner city.

Conventionally and bureaucratically, this peculiar legal power (which like "sus", places the onus upon the suspect to prove his/her innocence) has been defended in terms of its crime-fighting function. That justification is largely a spurious one. The following table documents the relation between the number of *recorded* stops overall and the number of resulting arrests, for the four police stations in the area.

TABLE VII
Recorded stop-and-searches, Toxteth area, January-June 1981.

| Police stations | No. of stops | Arrests | Ratio |
|---|---|---|---|
| St. Anne Street | 1187 | 27 | 43:1 |
| Copperas Street | 1244 | 68 | 18:1 |
| Wavertree Road | 712 | 43 | 17:1 |
| Admiral Street (the central Liverpool 8 station) | 699 | 41 | 17:1 |

Source: adapted from the Chief Constable's *Public Disorder on Merseyside, July-August 1981* (Report to the Police Authority).

While it is impossible to quantify success in the prevention of crime through the stop power, it is self-evidently ineffective as measured by the ratio of stops to arrests. *The vast majority of recorded stops involve the harassment of individuals against whom no charge is eventually laid* (although that procedure may involve, for some, temporary restraint in the local police station). The victims are selected for the stop procedure on the basis of stereotypes inculcated by force tradition, by occupational culture, and according to the guidance of police training manuals of the quality of Powis (1977).

But there are in any case two major caveats about these figures which undermine their crime prevention rationale as well as their surface success rate.

It seems probable, given the practical autonomy (irrespective of the present standing orders to the force), that a large number of stops are never recorded or justified as such. Casual confrontations on the street are rarely exalted by legal definition in terms of stop-and-search powers. The latter are essentially residual powers, available like a battery of resource charges, formally to structure the interaction if the officer's authority is questioned.

Secondly, as Gill (1977) has documented across the Mersey, in Birkenhead, the use of the stop practice may generate its own arrest rate. Many of the prosecutions listed in Table VII relate to nebulous and subjectively assessed charges—causing a disturbance, obstruction, resisting arrest, assault on the police, and so on—incidents which are often socially constructed through interaction between the officer and the suspect, independently of any third party complaint. Take the following example of one youth, reporting an arrest in a 1980 study (A. Brogden, 1981) of stop-and-search practices in Liverpool 8:

> I was stopped at 10.45 pm. I'd been to phone my girl-friend. When they asked to search my bag, I said 'What for?'. I was told to shut my mouth, and when I didn't, I was charged with obstruction. (19-year-old white)

Justifications of the prevalence of the stop practices in terms of crime-related functions have little apparent or demonstrable validity. However, if the power is construed as a technical device to assist in the construction of a symbiotic relation between the police apparatus and elements in civil society by the symbolic targeting of the street population of Liverpool 8, surveillance through stop-and-search is more effectively interpreted.

Given the level of youth unemployment in the district (between 40% and 60%, and inevitably skewed by the race factor), and the consequent visibility of young males, particularly, in the street, stops represent the key mode of policing in Liverpool 8 and its environs. To be out late in the evening, and to have material possessions (bikes, bags, cars, and even chip bags) merits suspicion, and search proceedings.

A youth in the inner city can expect to be stopped two to three times a year. In those stops, (according to respondents in A. Brogden's 1980 study), they are most likely to be accosted by different officers—reputation and identification of "known" criminals does not seem to play major part in the practice. Stereotypes, the cues of dress, demeanour, age, and race, are the organizational base for the stops. Although they may be prefaced with "Don't I know you, haven't I pulled you in before?", "Not you again!", and similar remarks, it is the anonymity of the *apparently* arbitrary features of the encounters that is signified. The random culling of the street population replicates directly, the structured forays of the Victorian Liverpool police into similar territory, on behalf of the merchant class in the last century. It should also be borne in mind that the organization of police work into area based street patrols is based on, and constitutive of, a definition of prevention as "getting to know" the street population, this knowledge being demonstrated organizationally by culls and arrests. A different organization of police work, as well as different legal powers, would yield different results. At the moment law and organization complement each other in producing a situation which the victims at least can only interpret as harassment.

Age rather than race provides the primary cue for stops. Social class becomes almost irrelevant given the relative homogeneity of the groups within Liverpool 8, so that bed-sit students may also be stopped, when not wearing the dress of their class of origin. White and black youths, "the wrong people, wrong age, wrong sex, in the wrong place, at the wrong time" (Cohen, 1979, p.131) in the streets of Liverpool 8, day or night, or the adjacent city centre during shopping hours, are subject to surveillance and suspicion.

> I'd just come out of the city. I was asked whether I'd been in any of the shops. When I said "Yes", I was told that I'd been followed and asked where I'd bought the stuff from. I was searched and then told to beat it. (17 year-old white, cited in A. Brogden, 1981)

But racial imagery compounds the potential for "nicking":

> I was picked up in the market and searched. The day before some coloured lads had been fighting there. Six of us were looking at clothes. I was with my mate, Nicky, a coloured lad. I'd gone to the toilet when the rest were stopped. I came out and stood behind the others. I was called a "fucking hard case" because I wouldn't leave my mates. When I said I lived in Admiral Street, they said 'You must have brains like niggers if you live there'. (18 year-old white, cited in A. Brogden, 1981)

It is not however, just the physical act of being stopped-and-searched that leads to the primary oppositon to police harassment. Rather it is the authoritarian style, the domination-subordination relation, that ignites the eventual mass reaction:

> I'd never been charged with anything official but I've been stopped ten or maybe eleven times on my bike. At night, they said "What are you doing?"

or "Hey you, come here. Whose is that bike? . . . Where did you get it? . . . What's the serial number? . . . I didn't know your kind could afford that sort of thing." Once, when I was standing outside the Rathbone (a black youth centre) a policeman said "What are you doing here?". When I asked why, he replied "When I ask questions, you answer them, you coon" and flicked his paper in my face. The police do it to make you mad so that you'll swear or do something so that they can pull you in. (17 year-old black, cited in A. Brogden, 1981)

Similarly:

I've been stopped three times during the last year. The third time I was coming home from my girl-friend's house along Upper Parliament Street. I'd been to Karate that night and was carrying my bag. Policemen stopped me and one said "What have you got in that bag, son?". I told them my Karate suit. As soon as I said that, four of them jumped me and searched the bag. The same policeman said "What you learning Karate for son — to scare us?". When they finished, they left my things on the floor filthy. (17 year-old black, cited in A. Brogden, 1981)

This use of a particular form of the legal relation in Liverpool is not a deviant practice, the mis-use of police powers, or simply explicable in terms of the lack of experienced officers (as both the Chief Constable and Lord Scarman have separately postulated). Instead, it lies within the mainstream of the historical lineage of the city police. It stems directly from the way police work is constructed, as has been argued in this text, at the nexus between structural demand and organizational constraint. The oppression of a particular segment of the population relates to the requirement to build a bridge at the level of ideology, and of material practice, between what suits the police institution, as a formal organization, and what is required of police work by key elements in civil society, as mediated by the chief officer and force tradition. The legitimacy of this construction of police work in Liverpool 8 relates to the wider questions of autonomy and consent.

## The Riots and Autonomy and Consent in the City

In some radical circles, the primary focus of attention has been on the personality of the Chief Constable of Merseyside rather than on the larger context of the anti-police riots in Toxteth. But while the idiosyncracies of the contemporary chief officer Kenneth Oxford, undoubtedly affected the form of the particular conflict in July 1981, and while they provided a ready target for denunciation, culminating in an "Oxford Must Go" campaign immediately after the first outbreak, these factors have distracted attention from the accountability of the office of chief officer itself, its political autonomy, and the true relation between police and public which is that ambiguous consent by the latter to the practices of the former.

Throughout this text, it has been argued that the problem of the political relations of the police institution, and the relations with civil society, are inter-dependent. Essentially, through the construction of a consenting, supportive, public, the police institution has developed a surrogate form of accountability. Evidence of a wide measure of public support has legitimized police material practice at the expense of the residual populations. A political relation has been constructed, and constantly renewed, at the ideological level through joint manufactured agreement as to the target of police work, within the permissive framework of law. The local police authorities and representatives from the legislative arm of the central state can legitimately be ignored if an accountability placebo has been created.

Within the Merseyside Police Area, this specific relation over the policing of Liverpool 8 was renewed in the late 1970s through three particular issues—an anti-mugging panic, a call for police action against kerb-crawling motorists, and through continuing demonstration of the high recorded crime figures for the district.

Between 1978 and 1980 the local press featured prominently the activities of a law-and-order campaign led by a certain Joan Jonkers. The structured moral panic focussed upon a number of attacks upon old people in the area—ranging from hand-bag snatching to more violent assault in the course of theft. The campaign reached a climax in 1980, with a B.B.C. television programme drawing upon joint contributions from Mrs Jonkers and from the Chief Constable, and featuring a number of cases of old age pensioners, in Liverpool 8 who had suffered from such depredations at the hands of youthful (sometimes black) assailants. As the Chief Constable said (in a Report to a Parliamentary Committee in February, 1981):

> It was with these offences . . . that "Man Alive" made such an impact upon the conscience of the nation with its report of elderly persons being set upon by loitering youths around their houses, shops etc. (quoted in *Public Disorder on Merseyside* p.60)

The effect of the campaign was to reinforce the stereotype of the presumed offenders—adolescents in Liverpool 8 and the surrounding streets—to confirm them as a legitimate target for police action, and to emphasize the primacy of the district as a "criminal area".

Secondly, police intervention in Liverpool 8 was legitimized in a different way and formally, at least, with a different target in mind. During the late 1970s and early 1980s, local community groups campaigned for police action against the large number of motorists who cruised the streets during evening hours, searching for the services of prostitutes. In the course of that continual presence, numerous local women passing through the streets were subjected to unwanted attention by the car-drivers, and occasionally to aggressive language and gestures. In effect, the kerb-crawlers had come to define any lone woman on the streets of Liverpool 8 at night as a potential prostitute, plying for hire. The community groups pressed for police action against the nuisance. The Chief Constable saw fit to regard those demands as legitimate, and increased the number of mobile patrols.

Although the consequences of that police reaction are uncertain with regard to the level of kerb-crawling (it was one of the few issues on which community groups were prepared to relate to the chief officer after the riots), the police reaction together with the initial complaint both amplified the outsider's view of Liverpool 8 as a red-light area, and, critically, legitimized the presence of large numbers of police vehicles on the streets, patrol cars and vans which retained the wider brief of watching-out for suspects.

Finally, the Chief Constable was able to demonstrate on several occasions, when challenged with the pervasiveness of the police presence, that this activity simply reflected the crime-proneness of Liverpool 8. He and his force were simply reacting to the high level of crime as illustrated by the reported crime figures. For example, in his Report to the Police Authority after the riots, he contrasts the recorded crime rate for Toxteth with apparently similar areas elsewhere on Merseyside:

> . . . the area which saw the recent disturbances is also the scene for a high proportion of such crime. It is against this background that one should consider the allegations of police harassment which rank so highly on the list of causes attributed by local community groups to the "Toxteth Riots". (Report, p.26)

Together, these three items, the Jonkers campaign, the demands for action against kerb-crawling, and the references to the reported crime figures, helped to convince the public audience of the chief officer, that police action on the streets of Liverpool 8 merely represented the reaction of the police institution to legitimate public demands. Crime existed as a real problem in Liverpool 8, and there was a demand for action against the perpetrators. The police response signified their essential consensual relation to the majority, law-abiding, citizens. Consent to policing, as to the acknowledged crime-fighters, is therefore reinforced.

It was, however, for the chief officer, as the resident crime-fighting expert, to determine crime priorities and the form of police response. It is in his perception and organizational construction of the demands for action against crime that is reflected the crucial ambivalence to police action by the residents of Liverpool 8, and by the working-class in the city as a whole. Within this ambivalence, this social space, is constructed police autonomy. Irrespective of the hostility to the manifest police style and practice, local people still have a crime problem—of arguable size—that is constructed within the subordinate value system as a policing problem. But (as was argued in Chapter 8), that general support for the principle of police officers as the primary crime-fighters, assumes that police action in and against the public domain of the streets, is an accidental mal-functioning of the policing system. It has been argued here, however, that such street based activity is intrusive and endemic, providing the symbolic conjunction between articulate, dominant, and class originated if not class specific societal demands, and organizational constraints.

Soon after the riots, this confusion was again evidenced. Labour councillors in the area were accused by some residents of that most heinous of all crimes, of being "anti-police". Representatives of the Liverpool 8 Defence Committee were humiliated by members from the same ethnic background on the Merseyside Community Relations Council. There was no united class or ethnic reaction to the police institution either before or after the riots. From this lack of unity has been constructed historically the autonomy of the police institution, its power to demonstrate consent, and its authority to adjudicate the legitimacy of demands made upon itself. Selective harassment of the residual population is the price paid for the choice of a professional and legally accountable police organization rather than a democratic and publicly accountable one. This book has demonstrated that in so far as there was a choice historically, it was made by the class of mercantile capitalists; and that increasingly since that day the police institution itself has made the creative choices about its own development, with the active consent of sections of the middle-classes and the passive consent of the rest—the majority—of us.

# Note

1. A. Brogden interviewed a sample of defendants from Liverpool 8 as part of a wider research project into the system of criminal adjudication in that area. This is reported in Brogden, A., 1981 and 1982.

# Bibliography

Ackroyd, C., Margolis, K., Rosenhead, J. and Shallice, T. (1977). *The Technology of Political Control.* Penguin, Harmondsworth.

Albrecht, S. L. (1977). Attitudes towards the police and the larger attitude complex. *Criminology* **1**, May.

Alderson, J. (1975). People, government and police. In *The Police and the Community* (J. Brown and G. Howse, eds). Teekfield, Farnborough.

Alderson, J. (1976). Police leadership in times of social, economic turbulence. *Police Journal* **XLIX**, 2.

Alderson, J. (1980). *Policing Freedom.* Macdonald and Evans, Plymouth.

Almond, G. A. and Verba, S. (1963). *The Civic Culture.* Princeton University Press, New Jersey.

Althusser, L. (1971). Ideology and ideological state apparatuses. In *Lenin and Philosophy and other Essays* (L. Althusser, ed.). New Left Books, London.

Armstrong, G. and Wilson, M. (1973). City politics and deviancy amplification. In *Politics and Deviance* (I. Taylor and L. Taylor, eds). Penguin, Harmondsworth.

Ascoli, D. (1979). *The Queen's Peace.* H. Hamilton, London.

Baines, T. (1859). *History of the Commerce and Town of Liverpool,* n.p.

Balbus, I. (1978). Commodity form and legal form: an essay on the relative autonomy of law. In *The Sociology of Law* (C. E. Reasons and R. M. Rich, eds). Butterworth, Toronto.

Baldwin, J. and McConville, M. (1979). *Jury Trials.* Clarendon Press, Oxford.

Bankowski, Z. and Mungham, G. (1976). *Images of Law.* Routledge and Kegan Paul, London.

Banton, M. (1964). *The Policeman in the Community.* Tavistock, London.

Banton, M. (1970). Social order and the police. *Advancement of Science,* September.

Banton, M. (1975). The definition of the police role. *New Community* **III**, 4.

Barnard, D. (1974). *The Criminal Court in Action.* Butterworth, London.

Bean, R. (1980). Police unrest, unionisation and the 1919 strike in Liverpool. *Journal of Contemporary History* **15**, 4.

Belson, W. (1975). *The Police and the Public.* Harper and Row, London and New York.

Bittner, E. (1974). Florence Nightingale in pursuit of Willie Sutton: a theory of police. In *The Potential for Reform of the Criminal Justice System* (H. Jacobs, ed.). Sage, Beverley Hills.

Black, D. and Reiss, A. (1970). Police control of juveniles. *American Sociological Review* **35**, February.

Blumberg, A. (1971). Criminal justice in America. In *Crime and Justice in American Society* (J. Douglas, ed.). Bobbs Merill, New York.

Blumberg, A. (1976). The historical setting. In *Ambivalent Justice* (A. Blumberg and A. Niederhoffer, eds). Holt, Rinehart and Winston, New York.

Bowden, T. (1976a). Men in the middle—the U.K. police. *Conflict Studies* **68**, February.

Bowden, T. (1976b). Protest and Violence: the police response. *Conflict Studies* **75**.

Bowden, T. (1978). *Beyond the Limits of the Law.* Penguin, Harmondsworth.

Bowley, A. S. (1975). Prosecution—a matter for the police. *Criminal Law Review*, 442-447.

Breathnach, S. (1974). *The Irish Police.* Anvil Books, Dublin.

Brewer, D. M. (1968). *The Inauguration of the Liverpool Police,* B.A. thesis, Ethel Wormald College of Education, Liverpool.

Brogden, A. (1981). 'Sus' is dead but what about 'Sas'? *New Community* **IX**, I Spring-Summer.

Brogden, A. (1982) Defendants in the penal process. *International Journal of the Sociology of Law* **10**, 49-73.

Brogden, M. (1977). A police authority—the denial of conflict. *Sociological Review* **25**, 2.

Brogden, M. (1981). "All police is conning bastards". In *Law, State and Society* (B. Fine, A. Hunt, D. McBarnet and B. Moorhouse, eds). Croom Helm, London.

Brogden, M. and Wright, M. (1979). Reflections on the Social Work Strikes. *New Society* **53**, 927.

Brooke, R. (1853). *Liverpool as it was During the Last Quarter of the Eighteenth Century.* Mawdesley, Liverpool.

Browne, D. G. (1956). *The Rise of New Scotland Yard.* Harrap, London.

Bunyan, T. (1976). *The Political Police in Britain.* Julian Friedman, London.

Bunyan, T. and Kettle, M. (1980). The police force of the future is now here. *New Society* **53**, 927.

Bunyard, R. S. (1978). *Police: Organisation and Command.* Macdonald and Evans, Plymouth.

Burnham, J. (1960). *The Managerial Revolution.* Indiana University Press, Bloomington.

Butcher, N. M. (1975). Can forces afford not to have a Community Involvement scheme? *Police Review* (18th April).

Byford, L. (1975). Hands off the police authorities. *Police* March, 16.

Cain, M. (1968). Role conflicts amongst police Juvenile Liaison Officers. *British Journal of Criminology* **VIII**, 4.

Cain, M. (1971). On the beat. In *Images of Deviance* (S. Cohen, ed.). Penguin, Harmondsworth.

Cain, M. (1972). Police professionalism: its meaning and consequences. *Anglo-American Law Review* **1**.

Cain, M. (1973). *Society and the Policeman's Role.* Routledge and Kegan Paul, London.

Cain, M. (1977). An ironical departure: the dilemma of contemporary policing. In *Yearbook of Social Policy in Britain* (K. Jones, ed.). Routledge and Kegan Paul, London.

Cain, M. (1979). Trends in the sociology of police work. *International Journal of the Sociology of Law* **7**, 2.

Campbell, D. (1980). Society under surveillance. In *Policing the Police* (P. Hain, ed.). John Calder, London.

Card, R. (1979). Police accountability and the control of the police. *Bramshill Journal* **I**, 1.

Castells, M. (1978). *City, Class and Power.* Macmillan, London.

Chapple, N. L. (1975). Community relations in Kirkby new town. *Police Journal* **XLIX**, 4.

Chatterton, M. (1973). Resource charges and practical decision-making in peacekeeping.

Paper at the Second Bristol Seminar on the Sociology of the Police, University of Bristol.

Chatterton, M. (1976). Police in social control. In *Control Without Custody* (J. Kline, ed.). Cropwood Papers.

Chatterton, M. (1978). The supervision of patrol work under the fixed point system. In *The British Police* (S. Holdaway, ed.). Edward Arnold, London.

Chesney, K. (1968). *The Victorian Underworld.* Penguin, Harmondsworth.

Chibnall, S. (1977). *Law-and-Order News.* Tavistock, London.

Chibnall, S. (1979). The Metropolitan Police and the news media. In *The British Police* (S. Holdaway, ed.). Edward Arnold, London.

Clarke, R. V. G. and Hough, J. M. (1980). *The Effectiveness of Policing.* Gower, London.

Coates, K. (1967). *Tom Mann's Memoirs.* Macgibbon and Kee, London.

Coatman, J. (1959). *Police.* Oxford University Press, London.

Cockburn, C. (1973). *The Devil's Decade.* Sidgwick and Jackson, London.

Cockburn, C. (1977). *The Local State.* Pluto, London.

Cockroft, B. (1969). *The Liverpool Victorian Police.* University College of Bangor, Bangor.

Cockroft, B. (1974). The Liverpool Police Force, 1836-1902. In *Victorian Lancashire* (S. P. Bell, ed.). David and Charles, Newton Abbot.

Cohen, P. (1979). Policing the working-class city. In *Capitalism and the Rule of Law* (B. Fine, R. Kinsey, J. Lea, S. Picciotto and J. Young, eds). Hutchinson, London.

Coleman, T. (1966). *The Railway Navvies.* Hutchinson, London.

Colquhoun, P. (1779 ed.). *A Treatise on the Police of the Metropolis.* Joseph Maurman, London.

Cooper, L. (1975). Controlling the police. In *The Police in Society* (E. Viano and J. Reiman, eds). Lexington, Massachusetts.

Corrigan, P. (1979). *Schooling the Smash Street Kids.* Macmillan, London.

Critchley, T. (1970). *The Conquest of Violence.* Constable, London.

Critchley, T. (1979 ed.). *A History of Police in England and Wales.* Constable, London.

Dahl, R. (1963). *Modern Political Analysis.* Prentice Hall, Englewood Cliffs.

Dearlove, C. (1979). *The Reorganisation of British Local Government: Old Orthodoxies and New Political Perspectives.* Cambridge University Press, Cambridge.

Demuth, C. (1978). *'Sus'—A Report on the Vagrancy Act, 1824.* Runnymede, London.

Devlin, P. (1960). *The Criminal Prosecution in England.* Oxford University Press, London.

Ditchfield, J. (1976). *Police Cautioning in England and Wales.* H.M.S.O., London.

Dixon, A. L. (1966). *The Home Office and the Police Between the Two World Wars.* Home Office, London.

Donajgrodzki, A. P. (1973). *The Home Office, 1822-1848,* Ph.D. thesis, University of London.

Donajgrodzki, A. P. (1977). *Social Control in Nineteenth Century Britain.* Croom Helm, London.

Douglas, J. D. (1971). *American Social Order.* Free Press, New York.

Dow, M. (1976). Police Involvement. In *Violence in the Family* (M. Borland, ed.). Manchester University Press, Manchester.

Doyle, P. (1972). *The Paint House.* Penguin, Harmondsworth.

Dumpleton, J. (1963). *Law and Order.* A. and C. Black, London.

Erikson, K. T. (1966). *Wayward Puritans.* John Wiley, New York.

Evans, P. (1974). *The Police Revolution.* Allen and Unwin, London.

Farman, C. (1974). *The General Strike.* Panther, London.

Fielding, N. (1981). The credibility of accountability. *Poly Law Review* **6**, 2.

Forman, C. (1978). *Industrial Town*. David and Charles, Newton Abbot.
Forward, W. B. (1910). *Recollections of a Busy Life*. Henry Young and Son, Liverpool.
Fosdick, R. B. (1914). *European Police Systems*. Allen and Unwin, London.
Foster, J. (1973). *Class Struggle and the Industrial Revolution*. Oxford University Press, London.
Fowler, N. (1979). *After the Riots*. Davis-Poynter, London.
Fox, I. (1978). Is there a need for a Third Force? *Police Journal*.
Fraser, D. (1976). *Urban Politics in Victorian England*. Leicester University, Leicester.
Fusco, R. (1980). Community police—an alternative view. *Police Review* No. 4563.
Gattrell, V. A. C. (1980). The decline of theft and violence in Victorian and Edwardian England. In *Crime and the Law* (V. A. C. Gattrell, B. Lenman and G. Parker, eds). Europa Publications, London.
Gill, O. (1977). *Luke Street*. Macmillan, London.
Gillance, K. Khan, A. N. (1975). The constitutional independence of a police constable in the exercise of the powers of his office. *Police Journal* **XLVIII**, 1.
Ginsburg, N. (1979). *Class, Capital, and Social Policy*. Macmillan, London.
Glover, E. H. (1934). *The English Police*. Police Chronicle, London.
Gordon, P. (1980). *Policing Scotland*. Scottish Council for Civil Liberties, Glasgow.
Gorer, G. (1955). *Exploring English Character*. Cresset Press, London.
Gough, I. (1979). *The Political Economy of the Welfare State*. Macmillan, London.
Gray, J. C. (1978). Police establishments. *Police College Magazine* **15**, 2.
Griffiths, J. (1978). *The Politics of the Judiciary*. Fontana, London.
Hall, S., Critchley, C., Jefferson, A., Clarke, J. and Roberts, B. (1978). *Policing the Crisis: Mugging, the State, Law and Order*. Macmillan, London.
Harper, T. (1975). Police cautions. *New Society* **31**, 643.
Hart, J. M. (1951). *The British Police*. Allen and Unwin, London.
Hart, J. M. (1955). Reform of the borough police. 1835-1856. *The English Historical Review*, July.
Hart, J. M. (1977). The Police. In *Social Control in Nineteenth Century England* (A. J. Donajgrodski, ed.). Croom Helm, London.
Hart, J. M. (1978). Police. In *Crime and Law* (W. Cornish, ed.). Irish University Press, Dublin.
Hay, D. (1975). Property, authority, and the criminal law. In *Albion's Fatal Tree: Crime and Society in Eighteenth England* (D. Hay, P. Linebaugh and E. P. Thompson, eds). Allen Lane, London.
Hayburn, R. (1972). The police and the hunger marchers. *International Review of Social History* **17**, 624-644.
Hikins, H. (1980). *The Liverpool General Transport Strike, 1911*. Toulouse Press, Liverpool.
Hindess, B. (1971). *The Decline of Working-Class Politics*. Paladin, London.
Hirst, P. (1975). Marx and Engels on law, crime, and morality. In *Critical Criminology* (I. Taylor, P. Walton and J. Young, eds). Routledge and Kegan Paul, London.
Holdaway, S. (1977). Changes in urban policing. *British Journal of Sociology* **28**, 2.
Hough, J. M. (1980). *Uniformed Police Work and Management Technology*. Home Office, London.
Howard, G. (1957). *Guardians of the Queen's Peace*. Odham's Press, London.
Humphry, D. (1972). *Police Power and Black People*. Panther, London.
Hunt, A. (1976). Law, state, and class struggle. *Marxism Today* **20**.
Hurd, G. (1979). The television presentation of the police. In *The British Police* (S. Holdaway, ed.). Edward Arnold, London.
Ignatieff, M. (1978). *A Just Measure of Pain*. Pantheon, London.

Ignatieff, M. (1979). Police and people: the birth of Mr Peel's blue locusts. *New Society* **49**, 882.

Jackson, B. (1968). *Working Class Community*. Penguin, Harmondsworth.

Jacob, I. (1967). The future of the police. *Police Journal*, 309-320.

James, L. (1974). Police and public relations for an open society. *Justice of the Peace and Local Government Review*, 116-135.

Jefferson, A. and Grimshaw, R. (1981). The accountability of the police to law and democracy. Political Studies Association Annual Conference.

Jessop, B. (1977). Recent theories of the capitalist state. *Cambridge Journal of Economics* **1**.

Jessop, B. (1980). The transformation of the state in post-war Britain. In *The State in Western Europe* (R. Scase, ed.). Croom Helm, London.

Jones, J. M. (1980). *Organisational Aspects of Police Behaviour*. Gower, London.

Judge, A. (1972). *A Man Apart*. Arthur Barker, London.

Judge, A. and Reynolds, G. (1968). *The Night the Police Went on Strike*. Weidenfeld, London.

Keeton, G. W. (1975). *Keeping the Peace*. Barry Rose, Chichester.

Keith-Lucas, B. (1960). The independence of Chief Constables. *Journal of Public Administration* **XXXVIII**, Spring.

Kettle, M. (1980a). The politics of policing and the policing of politics. In *Policing the Police II* (P. Hain, M. Kettle, D. Campbell and J. Rollo, eds). John Calder, London.

Kettle, M. (1980b). Looking after the police. *Police Review* **4566**.

Kettle, M. (1980c). The Police take a political road. *New Society* **51**, 980.

Kettle, M. (1980d). Quis custodiet ipsos custodes? *New Society* **53**, 922.

Kuya, D. (1972). *Evidence to the Select Committee on Race Relations and Immigration*. H.M.S.O., London.

Lambert, J. R. (1969). The police can choose. *New Society* **14**, 364.

Lambert, J. R. (1970). *Crime, Police, and Race Relations*. Oxford University Press, London.

Lane, T. (1978). Liverpool: city in crisis. *Marxism Today* **22**.

Leigh, L. H. (1973). Prolegomenon to a study of police powers in England and Wales. *Notre Dame Lawyer* **48**.

Leigh, L. H. (1975). *Police Powers in England and Wales*. Butterworth, London.

Leigh, L. H. (1977). The Police Act, 1976. *British Journal of Law and Society*, **4**, 115-124.

Lewis, R. (1976). *A Force for the Future*. Temple Smith, London.

Lidstone, K. W., Hogg, R. and Sutcliff, F. (1980). Prosecutions by private institutions and non-police-agencies. *Royal Commission on Criminal Procedure*, Research Study 10, H.M.S.O., London.

Lyman, J. L. (1964). The Metropolitan Police Act, 1829. *Journal of Criminal Law, Criminology and Police Science* **55**.

Macdonald, K. M. (1977). The forces of social control. *British Sociological Association*, Annual conferences.

Mack, J. A. (1963). Police Juvenile Liaison schemes. *British Journal of Criminology* **III**, 4.

Mallet, S. (1969). *La Nouvelle Classe Ouvriers*. Seuil, Paris.

Manning, P. (1971). The police: mandate, strategies, and appearances. In *Crime and Justice in American Society* (J. Douglas, ed.). Bobbs Merill, New York.

Manning, P. (1977). *Police Work*. M.I.T. Press, Cambridge, Massachusetts.

Manning, P. (1979). The social control of police work. In *The British Police* (S. Holdaway, ed.). Edward Arnold, London.

Mark, R. (1977). *Policing a Perplexed Society*. Allen and Unwin, London.

Mark, R. (1978). *In the Office of Constable.* Collins, London.

Marshall, G. (1965). *Police and Government: the Status and Accountability of the English Constable.* Methuen, London.

Marshall, G. (1978). Police accountability re-visited. In *Policy and Politics* (D. Butler and H. Halsey, eds). Macmillan, London.

Martin, J. and Wilson, G. (1969). *The Police: a Study in Manpower.* Heinemann, London.

Mather, F. L. (1959). *Public Order in the Age of the Chartists.* Manchester University Press, Manchester.

May, D. (1978). Community relations. *Police Review* (2nd Feb.).

McBarnet, D. J. (1978a). The police and the state: arrest, legality, and the law. In *Power and the State* (G. Littlejohn, B. Smart, J. Wakeford and N. Yuval-Davis, eds). Croom Helm, London.

McBarnet, D. J. (1978b). False dichotomies in criminal justice research. In *Criminal Justice: Selected Readings* (J. Baldwin and A. K. Bottomley, eds). Martin Robertson, London.

McBarnet, D. J. (1979). Arrest: the legal context of policing. In *The British Police* (S. Holdaway, ed.). Edward Arnold, London.

McBarnet, D. J. (1981). *Conviction.* Macmillan, London.

McCabe, S. and Sutcliff, F. (1978). *Defining Crime.* Blackwell, Oxford.

McDonald, I. (1973). The creation of the British police. *Race Today* **V**, December.

McNabb, P., Melish, I. and Ben-Tovim, G. (1972). *Evidence to the Select Committee on Race and Immigration.* H.M.S.O., London.

Melville Lee, W. C. (1901). *A History of Police in England and Wales.* Methuen, London.

Midwinter, E. C. (1971). *Old Liverpool.* David and Charles, Newton Abbot.

Miliband, R. (1969). *The State in Capitalist Society.* Weidenfeld and Nicholson, London.

Miliband, R. (1977). *Marxism and Politics.* Oxford University Press, Oxford.

Miller, W. R. (1977). *Cops and Bobbies.* University of Chicago Press, Chicago and London.

Miller, W. R. (1979). London's police tradition in a changing society. In *The British Police* (S. Holdaway, ed.). Edward Arnold, London.

Minto, G. A. (1965). *Thin Blue Line.* Hodder and Stoughton, London.

Moir, E. (1969). *The Justice of the Peace.* Penguin, Harmondsworth.

Moodie, P. (1972). The use and control of the police. In *Direct Action and Democratic Politics* (R. Benewick and T. Smith, eds). Allen and Unwin, London.

Morris, G. S. (1980). Lawful orders and the police. *Police Review* **4553.**

Morris, M. (1977). *The General Strike.* Penguin, Harmondsworth.

Morris, T. (1980). The top cops. Political Studies Association Annual conference.

Moylan, J. (1934). *Scotland Yard.* Putnam, London.

Muir, R. (1907). *History of Liverpool.* University of Liverpool Press, Liverpool.

Norris, D. F. (1973). *Police-Community Relations.* Lexington Books, Lexington.

Nott Bower, W. (1926). *Fifty-Two Years a Policeman.* Edward Arnold, London.

O'Connor, J. (1973). *The Fiscal Crisis of the State.* St James Press, New York.

Okojie, P. and Noble, M. (1980). Police authorities and democratic control: a re-appraisal. n.p., Manchester Polytechnic.

Oliver, I. T. (1973). The Metropolitan Police Juvenile Liaison scheme. *Criminal Law Review,* 499-506.

Oliver, I. T. (1975). The office of constable, 1975. *Criminal Law Review,* 313-322.

Pahl, R. (1975). *Whose City?* Penguin, Harmondsworth.

Pahl, R. (1977). Managers, technical experts, and the state. In *Captive Cities* (M. Harloe, ed.). John Wiley, New York.

Pain, B. N. (1978). Autonomy and responsibility in England. *Law Enforcement News*, November.

Parker, H. J. (1974). *View from the Boys*. David and Charles, Newton Abbot.

Parkin, F. (1974). *The Social Analysis of Class Structure*. Tavistock, London.

Parris, H. (1961). The Home Office and the provincial police in England and Wales, 1856-1870. *Public Law*, Autumn.

Peet, H. ed. (1915). *Liverpool Vestry Books III*. Liverpool University Press, Liverpool.

Pelling, H. (1968). *Popular Politics and Society in Late Victorian England*. Macmillan, London.

Phillips, D. (1974). *Crime and Authority in Victorian England*. Croom Helm, London.

Phillips, D. (1978). Riots and public order in the Black Country, 1835-60. In *Popular Protest and Public Order* (R. Quinault and J. Stevenson, eds). Allen and Unwin, London.

Phillips, D. (1980). A new engine of power and authority. The institutionalization of law in England, 1780-1830. In *Crime and Law* (V. A. C. Gattrell *et al.*, eds). Europa Publications, London.

Picton Davies, G. (1973). *The Police Service of England and Wales 1918 and 1964*. Ph.D. thesis, University of London.

Piliavin, I. and Briar, S. (1964). Police encounters with juveniles. *American Journal of Sociology* **70**, September.

Plehwe, R. (1974). Police and government: the Commissioners of Police for the Metropolis. *Public Law*, 316-335.

Poulantzas, N. (1973). *Political Power and Social Classes*. New Left Review, London.

Powis, D. (1977). *The Signs of Crime: A Field Manual for Police*. McGraw Hill, London.

Pryce, L. (1979). *Endless Pressure*. Penguin, Harmondsworth.

Punch, M. (1979). The secret social service. In *The British Police* (S. Holdaway, ed.). Edward Arnold, London.

Punch, M. and Naylor, T. (1973). The police: a social service. *New Society* **24**, 554.

Quinney, R. (1974). *Critique of Legal Order*. Little, Brown and Co., Boston.

Radzinowicz, L. (1956). *A History of English Criminal Law IV*. Sweet and Maxwell, London.

Rathbone, E. (1905). *W. Rathbone: A Memoir*, n.p., Liverpool.

Reiner, R. (1978). The police, class and politics. *Marxism Today* **22**, 3.

Reiner, R. (1979). Fuzzy thoughts. British Sociological Association Annual Conference.

Reiner, R. (1980a). The politicisation of the police in Britain, n.p., University of Bristol.

Reiner, R. (1980b). Forces of disorder: how the police control riots. *New Society* **52**, 914.

Reith, C. (1940). *Police Principles and the Problem of War*. Oxford University Press, London.

Reith, C. (1956). *A New Study of Police History*. Oliver and Boyd, London.

Rex, J. and Moore, R. (1967). *Race, Community and Conflict*. Oxford University Press, London.

Roberts, R. (1973). *The Classic Slum*. Penguin, Harmondsworth.

Robinson, C. D. (1978). The deradicalization of the policeman: a historical analysis. *Crime and Delinquency* **24**, 2.

Russell, K. (1976a). *Complaints against the Police*. Milltake, Leicester.

Russell, K. (1976b). Younger chiefs now being appointed. *Police Review* (8th Oct.).

Sarat, A. (1977). Studying American legal cultures: an assessment of survey evidence. *Law and Society Review* **11**, 3.

Saunders, P. (1980). *Urban Politics*. Penguin, Harmondsworth.

Scott, J. M. (1968). *Law and Order in Liverpool 1835-56*. B.A. thesis. Ethel Wormald College of Education, Liverpool.

Scull, A. T. (1979). *Museums of Madness.* Allen Lane, London.

Shaw, M. and Williamson, W. (1972). Public attitudes to the police. *Criminologist,* 18-32.

Simey, M. (1979). More politics for policing. *Rights* **III**, 4.

Skolnick, J. H. (1966). *Justice without Trial.* John Wiley, New York.

Smith, P. E. and Hawkins, R. O. (1973). Victimization, types of citizen-police contracts, and attitudes towards the police. *Law and Society Review* **7**, 2.

Solwyn, A. (1935). *The English Policeman.* Allen and Unwin, London.

Sparks, R. F., Genn, H. R. and Dodd, D. J. (1978). *Surveying Victims.* John Wiley, New York.

Spitzer, S. (1975). Towards a Marxian theory of deviance. *Social Problems* 22 June.

Stead, P. (1977). *Pioneers of Policing.* Patterson Smith, Montclair, New Jersey.

Stedman Jones, G. (1971). *Outcast London.* Clarendon Press, Oxford.

Steer, D. (1970). *Police Cautions: A Study in the Exercise of Police Discretion.* Blackwell, Oxford.

Stevens, P. and Willis, C. F. (1981). *Race, Crime and Arrest.* Home Office Research Study, 58, H.M.S.O., London.

St. Johnston, E. (1978). *One Policeman's Story.* Barry Rose, London.

Storch, R. D. (1975). The plague of the blue locusts: police reform and popular resistance in Northern England, 1840-57. *International Review of Social History* **XX**, I.

Storch, R. D. (1976). The Policeman as domestic missionary: urban discipline and popular resistance in Northern England. *Journal of Social History* **9**, 4.

Taylor, I. (1981). Policing the police. *New Socialist* **2**.

Thompson, E. P. (1963). *Making of the English Working Class,* Gollancz, London.

Thompson, E. P. (1978). *The Poverty of Theory.* Merlin, London.

Thompson, E. P. (1979a). Trial by Jury. *New Society* **50**, 895.

Thompson, E. P. (1979b). The secret state. *Race and Class* **XX**, 3.

Thompson, S. P. (1958). *Maintaining the Queen's Peace.* n.p. Birkenhead.

Thornton, S. M. (1975). People and the police: an analysis of factors associated with police evaluation and support. *Canadian Journal of Sociology* **1**, 3.

Thurston, G. (1972). *The Clerkenwell Riot.* Allen and Unwin, London.

Tobias, J. J. (1967). *Crime and Industry: in the Nineteenth Century.* Batsford, London.

Tobias, J. J. (1974). A statistical study of a nineteenth century criminal area. *British Journal of Criminology* **XIV**, 3.

Tobias, J. J. (1979). *Crime and Police in England, 1700-1900.* Gill and Macmillan, London.

Touraine, A. (1966). *La Conscience Ouvriers.* Sewil, Paris.

Van Maanen, J. (1973). Working the street: a developmental view of police behaviour. In *The Potential for Reform of the Criminal Justice System* (H. Jacob, ed.). Sage, Beverley Hills.

Veblen, T. (1921). *The Engineers and the Price System.* B. W. Huebach, New York.

Walker, S. (1977). *A Critical History of Police Reform.* Lexington Books, New York.

Waller, P. J. (1981). *Democracy and Sectarianism.* Liverpool University Press, Liverpool.

Walmsley, H. M. (1879). *Life of Sir Joshua Walmsley.* Chapman and Hall, London.

Weber, M. (1917). Parliament and government. In *Max Weber on Economy and Society* (G. Roth and C. Wittich, eds). University of California Press, Berkeley.

Weber, M. (1930). *Protestant Ethic and the Spirit of Capitalism.* Allen and Unwin, London.

Weis, K. and Milahovich, M. E. (1974). Political mis-uses of crime rates. *Society,* July-August.

West, D. J. and Farrington, D. P. (1977). *The Delinquent Way of Life.* Heinemann, London.

Whitaker, B. (1964). *The Police.* Eyre Methuen, London.

Whitaker, B. (1979). *The Police in Society.* Eyre Methuen, London.
White, B. D. (1951). *A History of the Corporation of Liverpool.* Liverpool University Press, London.
Wilcox, A. F. (1972). *The Decision to Prosecute.* Butterworth, London.
Wilcox, A. F. (1974). Police 1964-72. *Criminal Law Review*, 144-157.
Williams, D. G. T. (1970). Protest and Public Order. *Criminal Law Journal*, p.115.
Williams, D. G. T. (1974). Prosecution, discretion and the accountability of the police. In *Crime, Criminology and Social Policy* (R. Hood, ed.). Heinemann, London.
Wilson, J. Q. (1975). *Thinking about Crime.* Basic Books, New York.
Wren, P. (1971). Police Inspectorate. *Police Review*, 14th May.
Wright Mills, C. (1956). *The Power Elite.* Oxford University Press, New York.
Young, J. (1979). Left idealism, reformism, and beyond. In *Capitalism and the Rule of Law* (B. Fine *et al.*, eds.). Hutchinson, London.

## Official Reports

Committee on the Police Service of England and Wales (Desborough), H.M.S.O., 29.
Police Post-War Committee, H.M.S.O., 1946, 1947, 21, 53, 40.
Royal Commission on the Police, 1962-3, H.M.S.O. Cmnd. 1728.
A.C.P.O. Committee on Police Establishments, A.C.P.O. Leicester, 1962.
Committee of Inquiry on the Police (Edmund-Davies), Report III, 1979, H.M.S.O. Cmnd. 7633.
Royal Commission on Criminal Procedure:
  (a) The Investigation and Prosecution of Criminal Offences in England and Wales: The Law and Procedure, 1981, H.M.S.O., Cmnd. 8092-1.
  (b) Report, 1981, H.M.S.O. Cmnd. 8092.

## Liverpool Primary Sources

Head Constable/Chief Constable Annual Report, 1839 (Annual Report).
Head Constable Report Book, 1836-1911 (H.C. Report).
Head Constable Order Book, 1856-1862 (H.C. Orders).
Watch Committee/Police Authority Minutes 1836-1945 (W.C. Mins.).
Watch Committee Orders to the Head Constable, 1836-1918 (W.C. Orders).
Council Proceedings 1830-1910.
Liverpool Directory (the "Red Book") 1835-1910.
Liverpool Stock Exchange Minutes 1918-1921.
Trade Council Records 1910-1935.
*Liverpool Albion.*
*Liverpool Chronicle.*
*Liverpool Courier.*
*Liverpool Mail.*
*Liverpool Mercury.*

# Index

Fowler, N., 15, 16
Fox, J., 26-27
Fucso, R., 218

# G

Gattrell, V., 190, 195
General Strike, 183-184, 188-189
Gill, O., 203, 245
Gillance, K., 126
Ginsburg, N., 32
Glover, E., 182
Gordon, P., 21, 91, 97
Gorer, G., 173, 174, 195, 198-199
Gough, I., 13, 85
Grant, Home Office, 112
Gray, J., 104, 108
Grey, H. M. I. C., 112
Griffiths, J., 133

# H

Hall, S., 7, 12, 22, 27, 152, 230-231
Harper, J., 141-142
Hart, J., 41, 47, 56, 90, 99, 101, 171, 178, 179
Hay, D., 46
Hayburn, R., 102
Hikins, H., 186-187
Hindess, B., 7
Holdaway, S., 224
Home Office, 16, 20, 97-120, 140-141, 155
Hough, J., 210
Howard, G., 173, 174, 188
Humphry, D., 239
Hurd, G., 24

# I

Ideological inversion, 229-231
Ignatieff, M., 191, 232
Imbert, Chief Constable, 152
Industrial conflict, 71-72n, 73n, 184-189
Information manipulation, 91
Inspectorate, 39, 97, 99, 110-114

# J

Jackson, B., 202
Jacob, I., 74, 110, 150
James, L., 118
Jefferson, T., 134
Jessop, B., 10, 12, 13, 19
Jones, M., 210, 224
Judicial controls, 130, 132-134
Juvenile Liaison, 211, 213
Keeton, G., 185, 188
Keith-Lucas, B., 78, 112
Kettle, M., 79, 91, 148, 152, 159, 163
Kuya, D., 239

# L

Lambert, J., 204, 210
Laugharne, Chief Constable, 17, 217
Leigh, L., 77, 96n, 115, 136, 141
Lewis, R., 171
Liaison work, 210-214
Lidstone, K., 136
Liverpool, 23, 27, 39-73
  decline of, 81
  police — class relations in, 185-195
  Social Workers' strike in,
  and Toxteth riot, 239-250
Liverpool and Bootle Police Authority, 88-94
Local state, 39-94
  decline of, 80-88
London, accountability in, 117-118
Lyman, J., 50

# M

Macdonald, I., 55
Macdonald, K., 216
Mack, J., 213
Magistrates, 75, 78, 130
Mallet, S., 3
Managerialist police function, 18, 22, 83-84, 207, 220-221
  constraints on, 222-229
Mann, Tom, 187
Manning, P., 47, 91, 112, 195n, 223, 232
Mark, R., 15, 25, 26, 122, 146n, 169, 219n